HOW TO BE AN EFFECTIVE TRAINER

Skills for Managers and New Trainers

Second Edition

Barry J. Smith

Brian L. Delahaye

Queensland Institute of Technology

WILEY PROFESSIONAL DEVELOPMENT PROGRAMS

John Wiley & Sons, Inc.   New York ● Chichester ● Brisbane ● Toronto ● Singapore

To our wives, Cathy and Yvonne,
and our children, and our parents.

Publisher: Stephen Kippur
Editor: David Sobel
Managing Editor: Andrew B. Hoffer
Editing, Design, and Production: Publication Services

Library of Congress Cataloging-in-Publication Data

Smith, Barry J., 1947–
    How to be an effective trainer.

    (Wiley professional development programs)
    "Second edition"—Introd.
    Bibliography: p. 395
    Includes index.
    1. Employees, Training of.   I. Delahaye, Brian L.,
1946–   . II. Title. III. Series.
HF5549.5.T7S642   1987   658.3′1243   86-26774
ISBN 0-471-85239-2

Printed in the United States of America
87 88 10 9 8 7 6 5 4 3 2

INTRODUCTION

SO YOU'RE ABOUT TO DO SOME TRAINING

We can vividly remember how we felt standing in front of a group of trainees for the first time. So many things happening at once! A dozen pairs of expectant eyes watching every move. The anxieties of the night before come crowding back:

"What will I say next?"
"Will I make a fool of myself?"
"Have I got anything useful to say?"
"What if they know more than I know?"
"Have I got everything I need?"
"How much longer to go?"

These anxieties are quite common, and the energy they generate can be channelled into constructive activity. You can make your training session a dynamic learning experience for your audience, as well as minimize your anxieties, by answering the following questions during your session preparations:

"What are my objectives?"
"What do the trainees already know?"
"How can I use this to introduce the unknown?"
"Is my material arranged logically?"
"Have I chosen the right method of presentation?"
"Will my visual aids have sufficient impact?"
"How will I know if my session has been successful?"

This book is about how to find and use the answers to these questions.

WHO IS THIS BOOK FOR?

In the broadest sense, the book is for anyone involved in:

- Formal training sessions.
- On-the-job training.
- Conferences.
- Sales promotion.
- Production meetings.
- Presentations to higher management.
- Coaching subordinates.
- Public relations presentations.
- Interactions with local citizens groups, government, agencies, or concerned action groups.

Managers and Supervisors

If you are interested in *training your own staff* on the job, you will find the following chapters particularly useful:

If you are required to *conduct sessions* in an area of particular expertise, then you will be interested in these chapters:

New Trainers

If you are starting in training, then the entire text is highly relevant. You should study Chapter 1 carefully to give yourself an overview of the training process. This will enable you to integrate the specific skills and knowledge developed in subsequent chapters.

HOW CAN YOU MAKE BEST USE OF THIS BOOK?

We would like to explain our point of view. We believe that it is important to first master one method of handling a situation. When this mastery is established, you can develop variations on the method. We feel that attempts to reverse this order can produce a "jack-of-all-trades-master-of-none" approach in which you properly assimilate no one method.

As a result, we recommend certain courses of action to users of this book in the interests of obtaining that initial mastery. In particular, the first part of our book revolves around the *theory-session model* and the *skill-session model*. We see both of these as useful vehicles for gaining and shaping experience. Because the models incorporate basic principles of learning, you can avoid making the glaring blunders so often seen in unskilled presentations. In other words, the models offer relatively safe vehicles within which you can develop your skills. Once you establish initial mastery, you can experiment and develop a style suited to your preferences and particular situation.

HOW IS THIS BOOK ORGANIZED?

The book has been organized into short chapters. Each chapter focuses on a particular skill or topic. A typical chapter contains:

1. Key concepts that highlight the major points in the chapter.

2. Specific learning objectives.

3. A segment providing basic information needed to achieve the objectives.

4. A checklist to use as a guide in skills development exercises and in evaluating progress. The checklists are also on-the-job guides.

5. Tests and exercises aimed at checking your knowledge of the chapter and developing the skills discussed in the chapter.

The aim of this structure is to make the book suitable for use in a number of ways—as a self-instructional tool, as the focus in group work where several people use the text together, and as a basic textbook in more formal courses.

SHOULD YOU DO THE EXERCISES?

One of the basic principles of training is that you learn by *doing*. This suggests that, to develop the skills described in this book, you will have to practice them. We have included tests and exercises in each chapter to give you the opportunity to do this.

WHAT WILL THIS BOOK DO FOR ME?

This is a "how-to" book. It does more than discuss methods and techniques: it examines the important basic skills necessary for communicating with an audience, and it will show you how to use these skills in practice.

ACKNOWLEDGMENTS

No book develops in a vacuum and ours is no exception. Our ideas have been influenced by a number of people—some identifiable, some not. Our thanks to those who have contributed to our development and to the development of this book.

Some have had such a direct and personal influence on our ideas that we would like to mention them by name:

- John Damm, who initiated and motivated Barry's interest in the area.

- For Brian, his father, who gave him a love of books and reading; Vic Day, who started him off in training; and Paul Chesher, who gave meaning to the phrase "to teach is to learn twice."

There are a number of people who have assisted us with the book. These are:

- Mark Nester and Cathy Smith for detailed critiques and suggestions on earlier drafts of the manuscript.

- Maria Colligan Taylor and David Sobel, our editors at John Wiley & Sons for editorial guidance.

- Irving Hulteen, for his valuable contribution in developing and helping to fine-tune the final manuscript.

Finally, two groups of very important people deserve mention—our students and trainees, who continue to teach us how to be trainers, and our families, who shared the agonies and the ecstasies.

INTRODUCTION TO THE SECOND EDITION

While it is a pleasure to include additional material on advanced training techniques in this second edition, we feel it is *essential* to offer a word of advice and warning to readers regarding these techniques.

Much of the training literature refers to these advanced techniques as "state-of-the-art," "the sharp end," and "major areas of development." While these statements are all true, they have the unfortunate effect of encouraging new and/or part-time trainers to adopt these techniques before they have the necessary skill base to use the techniques effectively. The result is unsuccessful training, directly created by the "run-before-you can-walk" syndrome.

Now, it is a well accepted fact of life that you don't learn to ride a horse by riding in the Kentucky Derby; you don't learn to pilot a plane by flying off in an F18; and you don't learn surgery by beginning with heart transplant operations. In exactly the same way, we recommend that trainers learn the basic skills of setting objectives, and planning and conducting theory, skill, and discussion sessions before beginning on the advanced techniques. If you don't, you are building a house (your reputation as a trainer) on very shaky foundations indeed, and any training storm you encounter is much more likely to damage or topple the structure.

We would also like to point out that after some soul searching, we have dropped the terms andragogy and pedagogy, and adult and child learning. These terms have, quite inappropriately, taken on unmistakable age connotations and tend to confuse many readers. We have substituted the concepts of trainer- and trainee-controlled learning, which we have found are much more readily understood. The principles of learning remain as before, since they are applicable in both trainer- and trainee-controlled learning.

CONTENTS

I. TRAINING OVERVIEW

1
THE TRAINING ENVIRONMENT AND THE TRAINER'S JOB

Key Concepts

- *Change.* Change at all organizational levels affects the training environment and the role of the trainer.

- *The trainer's role.* The trainer is in the middle of change and must anticipate change as well as cope with it.

- *A training model.* An effective trainer needs a training-process model as a working tool.

Learning Objectives

After you have completed this chapter, you should be able to

- Explain why change is an opportunity and why the trainer must anticipate change.

- Describe the value of process models.

- List the steps in a 22-step training model.

WHO IS A TRAINER?

The effectiveness and efficiency of an organization depend on a number of variables. One of these variables is the continued development of the people in the organization. This development can be the responsibility of managers or supervisors or of a separate training department. Whoever carries out this developmental role (whether for an hour, a day, or a career) is a trainer.

CHANGE AND OPPORTUNITY

A trainer is in the middle of that complex (and often strongly resisted) process known as *change*. In fact, training is the result of change and sometimes the cause of it. The change may be as broad and pervasive as a new direction in corporate strategy or as immediate and personal as helping someone to master the skills of a new job. Whatever the magnitude, as a trainer you are a "change agent" helping others into the future.

Change presents you with professional and personal opportunities that you should explore enthusiastically. This does not mean that you should seize opportunities indiscriminately. Rather, you should examine causes and effects in a logical manner and devise training strategies appropriate to the objectives of your organization. To plan strategies and to function effectively in a changing environment, you must evolve a training model. The model is your planning tool.

A TRAINING MODEL

Let's look at a training model. Take a few moments to become familiar with the flow diagram on page 5. This diagram provides the basis for a comprehensive training model. It also provides an overview of the entire training process. Most trainers are not involved in all these steps, but it always helps to see the total picture. So the model also places the training process in the organizational perspective. From *this* perspective, you can view the trainer as an organizational consultant. The organization can include the trainer and the training function in the diagnosis and solution of organizational problems (whether or not training is the solution to these problems). An experienced trainer is uniquely positioned in the organization and has wide contacts, a detailed knowledge of job requirements throughout the organization, and significant information about the capabilities and skills of personnel. Thus the trainer can perform a function that extends considerably beyond session plans and training techniques.

As a trainer, you must contribute to achieving organizational goals. To do this, you must regularly assess organizational needs and measure the outcomes of your training programs in relation to these needs. The planning, managing, and evaluating activities of training are just as important as the "teaching" activities.

Finally, you can see from the model the kind and range of skills that a competent trainer should have. The model also thus suggests the direction for a self-development program for trainers.

Steps 1–7

Planned training in organizations begins when someone becomes aware of an opportunity or a problem that may create a training need (Step 1). Management then engages in a problem-solving process (Steps 2–7). Let's look at this process. In Step 2, we specify the symptoms of the problem (need). In Step 3, we establish the causes. In Step 4, we define the problem and measure the need. We propose alternative solutions in Step 5, and in Step 6, we evaluate these alternatives in terms of their contribution to solving the problem (satisfying the need). Then, in Step 7, we choose the most effective alternative. So far, you can apply the model to all problem solving in a general way. But from Step 7 on, you can apply it specifically to training.

Steps 8–12

If the alternative we have chosen in Step 7 is a training-based solution, we must then analyze training needs in Step 9. (The training function now has some direct responsibility for implementing the solution.)

If the alternative we have chosen in Step 7 is *not* a training-based solution, as a trainer you still have a role to play. Any non-training solution will almost certainly involve some change in the organization's product(s), personnel, work methods, or policies. Such changes may produce a need for training, and you should monitor these changes to predict any such need (Step 8).

Let's return to Step 9. The purpose of analyzing training needs is to specify what training is needed. In Step 10, we define the "terminal behavior" we are aiming at, and we write the specific objectives for our training activities. Terminal behavior here simply means the behavior expected of trainees at the end of the training program. In writing the objectives, we specify the standards of performance that a trainee must achieve and the conditions under which the trainee must perform. In Step 11, we then define methods of measuring performance, since these may affect subsequent decisions about training techniques and materials. Step 12 involves identifying those employees who need training (the target population) and specifying the content that must be covered to move the trainees from their present performance to the desired behavior.

Steps 13–22

Having decided on the content of training and how we will measure performance, in Step 13 we can write tests and performance criteria. When we have completed these, we can go on

The Training Process

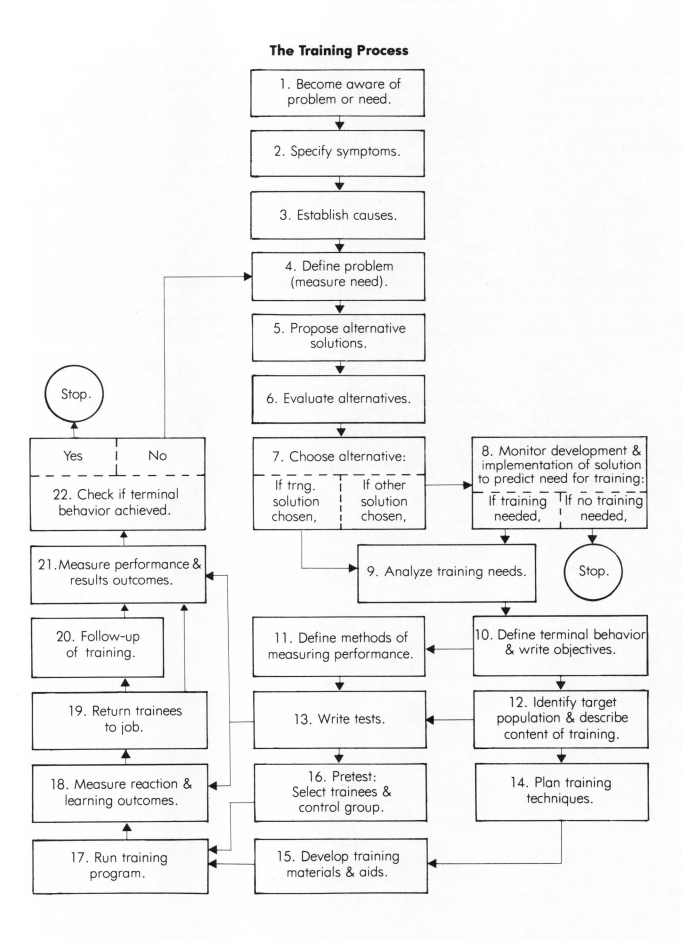

to Step 16 and begin pretesting our target population and selecting trainees and a control group. As we are working with Steps 13 and 16, we can plan training methods in Step 14 and develop training materials and aids in Step 15. (These steps are likely to require a large amount of a new trainer's effort.)

After developing the training materials and selecting our trainees, we can run the training program (Step 17). At this stage, we must apply evaluation skills. In Step 18, we measure reaction and learning outcomes during and immediately after the program. After we return the trainees to their jobs (Step 19), we measure performance to determine if any changes have occurred and if the changes are attributable to training (Step 21). Either as part of the evaluation process or as a separate exercise, we may organize follow-up activities to reinforce what the trainees have learned on the original program (Step 20).

The final step (22) is both a beginning and an ending. Are the trainees now producing the terminal behavior defined in Step 10? If "yes," well done; move on to tackle the next need. If "no," then find the reason. Review each of the steps in the training process. If you establish where errors have occurred, you can use this information to learn from experience. You still have the problem of the desired terminal behavior not being achieved, so return to Step 4, confirm or revise the problem definition, and recycle through the process to find a better solution to the problem or a different solution to the now somewhat modified problem.

SUMMARY

Change is a basic characteristic of the training environment, and the trainer must learn to anticipate and cope with change. The trainer is in the middle of change. This can enhance the scope of the trainer's job. To do the job effectively, a trainer must evolve a training model, and the major contribution and requirement of this model is a sharp focus on the planning, execution, and evaluation phases of training within the organizational context.

Chapter 1 Doublecheck

Fill in the blanks to complete the 22 steps.

1. Become _____ of problem.

2. Specify _____.

3. Establish _____.

4. Define _____.

5. Propose _____ solutions.

6. Evaluate _____.

7. _____ alternative.

8. _____ implementation of solution.

9. _____ training needs.

10. Define _____ behavior.

11. Define methods of measuring _____.

12. Identify _____ population and describe _____ of training.

13. Write _____.

14. _____ training techniques.

15. Develop training _____ and _____.

16. _____.

17. _____ training program.

18. Measure reaction and learning _____.

19. _____ trainees to jobs.

20. _____ training.

21. Measure _____ and _____ outcomes.

22. Check if _____ behavior achieved.

■ Doublecheck Answers

1. aware
2. symptoms
3. causes
4. problem
5. alternative
6. alternatives
7. Choose
8. Monitor
9. Analyze
10. terminal
11. performance
12. target, content
13. tests
14. Plan
15. materials, aids
16. Pretest
17. Run
18. outcomes
19. Return
20. Follow-up of
21. performance, results
22. terminal

2
SOME LEARNING PRINCIPLES

Key Concepts

- *Trainer- vs. trainee-centered learning.* A trainer must understand that trainees differ from one another in maturity, knowledge, motivation, responsibility, and learning skills. The learning experience must be carefully chosen to suit the trainee.

- *Learning principles.* A trainer must apply in practical ways the principles basic to effective learning.

Learning Objectives

After you have completed this chapter, you should be able to

- List and explain the differences between trainer-centered and trainee-centered learning.

- Explain ten basic principles of learning and give examples of each.

Although our discussion favors a practical "how-to" approach, we need to take a little time to look at some very important learning concepts. These are the foundations of any learning experience.

In a learning situation, some learners behave differently from others. Some prefer to be dependent, making no decisions and relying entirely on the trainer. Others become motivated when they perceive that the learning will help them to deal with current problems. Usually, they want to be consulted to some extent about *what* they are going to learn and *how* they are going to learn it as well. However, the degree to which they may wish to accept responsibility for their own learning can vary.

TRAINER- OR TRAINEE-CENTERED LEARNING

In any training program or learning experience there are four major variables. These are

1. the process

2. the content

3. the trainer

4. the trainee

We will examine each of these in turn.

The Process

The method that is used to give the trainees the learning is called the process. In this book we describe a number of models. Some, such as the theory session, the skill session, and the lecture, rely on the trainer to make the decisions on *what* should be learned and *how* it should be learned. These are called trainer-centered learning models. Contract learning, action learning, and the self-teaching action group models are trainee-centered learning approaches as they give the trainee complete decision-making responsibility. Models such as the discussion, the case study, role play, computer-based learning, programmed instruction, and the algorithm are partly trainee- and partly trainer-centered.

The question that needs to be asked, of course, is "when is it appropriate to use each model?" To answer this, we must examine the other three variables.

The Content

The content of the training course is the knowledge and/or skills the trainees are to learn. The content can be viewed on a continuum of simple to complex. Simple knowledge is where there is only one possible correct answer. For example, the equal employment opportunity legislation specifically prohibits discrimination on the grounds of race or sex. There is no other correct way to interpret the law. Similarly, a simple skill is one in which there is only one correct way to carry out the skill. At the other end of the scale we have complex knowledge where there can be many possible correct answers. If we look for the best way to manage staff in an organization, for example, contingency theories indicate that it will depend on the situation. When someone designs a computer program, there may be several possible paths that could be used to achieve the desired result. These problems require complex knowledge and skills as there are multi-answer solutions.

The first variable to examine in deciding whether to use the trainer- or trainee-centered models is the simplicity or complexity of the content of the training course. The more complex the content, the more effective it is to use the trainee-centered models. However, it is more *efficient* to use trainer-centered learning with simple content. Whether it is more *effective* will depend on the other two variables.

The Trainer

The major problem with the trainee-centered models is that the trainer needs to be highly skilled to use them. These higher level skills can only be learned through experience. The basic skills on which the higher level skills are built are incorporated in the trainer-centered learning models and these need to be practiced until they become a natural reaction. The trainer should not move on to the trainee-centered learning approaches until he or she is competent in the basic models of the theory session, the skill session, and the lecture.

The Trainee

The trainee is undoubtedly the most important variable when considering which model to use. To examine this variable we will use a concept called *learner maturity*. Specifically, we need to consider the following characteristics of the trainee:

1. *Content base.* Strong proponents of adult learning would claim that the trainee does not need any knowledge or skill in the subject area to be learned. In theory, this may be true but it certainly makes the learning experience significantly more difficult for the trainee. If the trainee has very high levels of the next element, motivation, then he or she may overcome this difficulty. However, many learners feel that when they have no previous experience in a particular subject, it is better for others to structure the learning steps for them.

2. *Motivation.* The trainee should have an interest in and a certain level of need to acquire the knowledge or skill. The higher this level of need and interest, the more likely it is that the trainee will benefit from trainee-centered learning.

3. *Responsibility.* The trainee has to accept responsibility for his or her own learning before the trainee-centered learning models can be used. The trainee who prefers to rely on someone else to structure the experience and take responsibility for any failure would be happier learning by the trainer-centered learning models.

4. *Learning skills.* The ability to decide what end result needs to be achieved, what should be learned so the end result can be achieved, how it should be learned, and what evidence can be presented to prove learning as a skill. Unfortunately, in most of our educational experiences throughout our life, all these decisions are made for us. This means that, often, we have not been able to acquire these skills that are essential if we are to take responsibility for our own learning.

So, not only does the trainer need higher level skills to be able to manage trainee-centered learning but so does the trainee.

When deciding whether to use more trainer- or more trainee-centered learning processes, we need to examine the variable of the trainee on four levels just discussed—content base, motivation, willingness to take responsibility for his or her own learning, and level of learning skills. The higher these are the more likely the trainee can cope with trainee-centered learning.

THE DECISION

The decision to use trainer- or trainee-centered learning processes depends on three variables:

1. The content—whether it is simple or complex;

2. The trainer—the levels of skill the trainer has;

3. The trainee's level of learner maturity.

Once these variables have been analyzed, the decision can be made on which model on the continuum to use.

Trainer- Centered		Trainee- Centered
• Theory	• Case study	• STAGs
• Skill	• Role Play	• Contract Learning
• Lecture	• Computer-Based Learning	• Action Learning
	• The Algorithm	
	• Programmed Learning	

SOME LEARNING PRINCIPLES

Now that we have described the learning processes that can be used, let's explore some of the learning principles that you use to ensure that the models have maximum effect. The principles are universal and have been shown to be effective when used in both trainer- and trainee-centered models.

1. Whole or part learning

2. Spaced learning

3. Active learning

4. Feedback

5. Overlearning

6. Reinforcement

7. Primacy and recency

8. Meaningful material

9. Multiple-sense learning

10. Transfer of learning

1. Whole or Part Learning

After defining training objectives, you must decide whether to present the knowledge or skill in logical, easily acceptable parts or as a unified whole. Although in making the decision you should take into account the abilities of the trainees, the decision rests largely with the subject matter itself.

You will almost always find that the subject matter can be divided into parts or segments. Frequently, the trainees will prefer to deal with a series of separate segments, rather than a large unified block of material. When dividing the material into segments, you should ensure that:

1. The segments are not too large. Remember, although you are most probably very conversant with the material, this is new ground for the trainee. What you consider to be reasonably small may be perceived as very large by the trainee. So carefully examine the size of each part or segment from the viewpoint of the trainee.

2. The segments have a logical sequence. Present each segment as a part of this sequence. The trainees can then relate one part or segment to the next and so enhance their recall of the total knowledge or skill.

3. Work from the known to the unknown. Cover the first part of the logical sequence until the trainees demonstrate by their behavior that the information or skill has been accepted. Then, and only then, proceed to the next part in the sequence. This is called "known to unknown" and gives the trainer a firm foundation from which to proceed to the new information.

Sometimes, however, we find that the parts or segments are highly dependent on each other. Take, for example, learning how to ride a bicycle. You can divide this learning into at least three parts: balancing, steering, and pedaling. We would find it difficult to learn these parts independently because each part is related to the others. Steering depends on balancing and how hard the pedals are pushed and balancing depends on steering and pedaling. In learning situations such as this, the skill or knowledge would have to be taught as a whole. Such situations are reasonably uncommon, however, and most training models are based on the concept of part learning.

A final word of warning is appropriate. Just as it is possible to demotivate workers by making their jobs on a production line too simple, so it is possible to demotivate learners by making the segments of a session too simple. So when you have divided material into segments based on logic and "known to unknown," check that

1. The segments are not so large that your particular group of trainees cannot handle them.

2. The segments are not so small that your particular group of trainees becomes demotivated.

2. Spaced Learning

Learning that is spaced at reasonable intervals is usually superior to massed (or crammed) learning if you want long-term retention of the material. This principle derives from the phenomenon of "incubation." The brain needs time to assimilate one group of facts before accepting the next group. In addition, spaced learning creates regular review and revision sessions, which slow the rate at which trainees forget the material.

3. Active Learning

If trainees are actively involved in the learning process (instead of listening passively), they will learn more effectively and become self-motivated. Active learning is often described as "learning by doing." Provide ample opportunities, both in the sessions and throughout the program, for the trainees to actively practice the skills and knowledge they are learning.

4. Feedback

This principle has two aspects. First, the trainees need feedback on how they are progressing. Feedback can be simple or not so simple, from explaining why an answer is correct or incorrect to commenting on a trainee's performance of an activity or discussing the results of an examination. No matter how simple or complicated the feedback, provide it as soon as possible. The more immediate the feedback, the greater the value.

Second, you need feedback on your own performance as a trainer:

- Is information being received and understood?

- Do they have any doubts or questions?

- Is any trainee not paying attention?

- Has the session become boring?

- Should I build more active learning into the session?

Therefore, try to use two way communication every session,

like this:

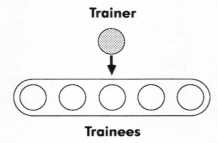

Not like this:

Trainer

Trainees

5. Overlearning

Over time, people gradually forget what they have learned. The following graph illustrates the "forgetting" curve. The time required to forget varies from learner to learner and from topic to topic, but the general form of the curve is always the same.

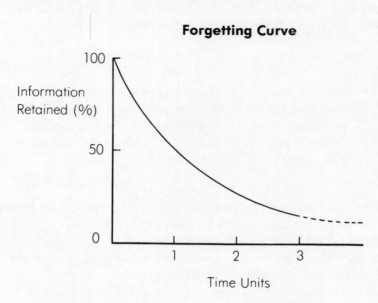

If you apply overlearning, you can alter the curve significantly. Stated simply, overlearning means learning until one has perfect recall—and then learning it some more. The result is a marked decrease in the rate of forgetting.

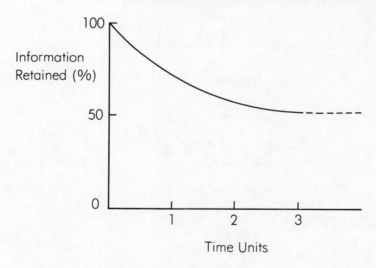

In other words, forgetting is significantly reduced by frequently attempting to recall learned material. Note that repetition by the trainer, while having some value, does not maximize recall. To achieve maximum retention, you must actively involve the trainee in the repetition.

✔ Checkpoint: Five Learning Principles

Indicate true (T) or false (F).

1. The theory session and the skill session are good examples of trainee-centered learning models. _____

2. Where there is only one correct way to perform a relatively simple task, it is better to use trainer-centered learning. _____

3. Content base, learning skills, responsibility, and motivation are all components of learner maturity. _____

4. The decision as to whether or not to break the training topic into parts depends largely upon the subject matter. _____

5. Learning that is spaced at reasonable intervals is usually superior to massed learning. _____

6. A trainee actively involved in the training process tends to become self-motivated. _____

7. Feedback is an essential aspect of two-way communication. _____

8. The more immediate the feedback, the greater the value. _____

9. Applying overlearning increases the slope of the forgetting curve. _____

10. For overlearning to work well, you must actively involve the trainee in repetition. _____

■ **Checkpoint Answers**

1. F   2. T   3. T   4. T   5. T   6. T   7. T   8. T   9. F   10. T

6. Reinforcement

Learning that is rewarded is much more likely to be retained. This is quite evident in every-day life, but it is such a basic idea that many trainers overlook it when conducting a session. A simple "Yes, that's right" or recognition for attempting to contribute can mean a great deal to a trainee.

We would like to emphasize the fact that punishment only teaches the trainee that his or her response was wrong. Punishment gives no guidelines about which responses would have been correct. Reinforcement, on the other hand, specifically confirms the response. (And that's what training is all about!)

7. Primacy and Recency

Given any sequence of facts, trainees will tend to remember what they heard *first* and *last*. What they heard in the middle they often forget. Therefore, emphasize and reinforce facts that are in the middle. Let's try a remembering quiz. Look at the following list for 30 seconds. Then look away and write down every word in it that you can remember.

Soap	Line	Clock	String
Bird	Car	Folder	Hair
Rug	Paper	Mat	Cage
Pocket	Salt	Wire	Glass
Door	Chair	Stove	Boot
Flower	Dog	Pillow	Light
Desk			

You have probably remembered words that appear at the start and end of the list better than you remembered the words that appear in the middle of the list.

One explanation for primacy and recency is that material seen or heard *early* will be remembered better because it does not have to compete with material preceding it. Material seen or heard *late* does not have to compete with material following it. Material in the middle has to compete with both preceding and following material and is therefore remembered less well.

8. Meaningful Material

When presented with new information, we unconsciously ask two questions:

- Is this information valid when I compare it with experiences I've had in the past?

- Will this information be useful to me in the immediate future?

The first question emphasizes the notion of moving from the "known to the unknown" as well as the fact that we tend to remember material related to what we already know. This is why you must assess the trainee's current level of learning when you plan a training program. The second question emphasizes the fact that the trainees want to know that what they are about to learn will be useful to them in the near future.

In this way, meaningful material links the past and the future and promotes two beneficial effects:

- Security when trainees move from the known to the unknown.

- Motivation—because the information will be useful in the near future.

9. Multiple-Sense Learning

Authorities suggest that of the information a person takes in, approximately 80 percent is obtained through sight, 11 percent by hearing, and 9 percent by the other senses combined. Therefore, to achieve maximum input to the trainees, you must use two or more of the senses. Usually you can use sight and hearing, but do not ignore the other senses. Touch may often be the crucial sense. For most learning, however, sight provides most information to trainees, and we consequently emphasize visual aids.

In addition, if the trainees' sense of sight is not used for learning purposes, it isn't just turned off. It frequently becomes an active source of distraction for the trainee.

The Senses Pie Chart

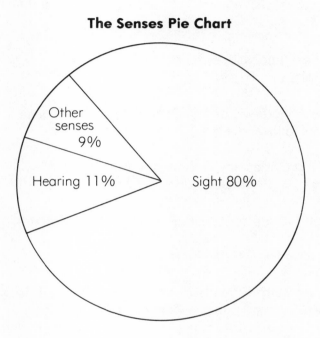

10. Transfer of Learning

The amount of learning that trainees transfer from the training room to the workplace depends, mainly, on two variables:

1. The degree of similarity between what was learned in the training program (and this includes how it was presented) and what occurs at the workplace. (For example, can the trainee apply his or her new knowledge and skills directly to the job without having to modify the training in some way?)

2. How easily the trainees can integrate into the work environment the skills or knowledge gained in the training program. (For example, will the work system or the supervisor allow or encourage the use of new skills?)

The presence of these two variables stresses the importance of referring continually to the workplace when looking for ideas on how to present information or skills and when designing activities and tests for the training session.

✔ Checkpoint: Five More Learning Principles

Indicate true (T) or false (F).

1. Punishment for a wrong response is a less successful motivator partly because it tends to overlook the correct response. _____

2. Reward for a correct response not only confirms the response but also reinforces effective behavior. _____

3. Given any sequence of facts, trainees will tend to forget what they heard first and last. _____

4. Material seen or heard late will be remembered better because it does not have competition from material preceding it. _____

5. Material seen or heard late will be remembered better because it does not have competition from material following it. _____

6. Meaningful material provides new information but can create anxiety if it is not related to previous learning. _____

7. Meaningful material stresses applications in the immediate future. _____

8. Visual aids are not a significant training tool. _____

9. A good transfer of training depends in part on the degree of similarity between what was learned and what occurs at the workplace. _____

10. Place the letter on the correct slice of the pie chart.
    a. Hearing
    b. Sight
    c. Other senses

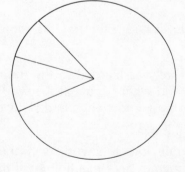

■ **Checkpoint Answers**

1. T   2. T   3. F   4. F   5. T   6. T   7. T   8. F   9. T   10. a. hearing: 11% slice
b. sight: largest slice   c. other: 9% slice

Checklist: Using the Learning Principles

1. Whole or Part Learning

☐ Separate the explanations with activities.

☐ Break the information into parts (with due regard for the topic and the abilities of the trainees). If the steps are *too* small, they will not present sufficient challenge. However, we have found it best for beginning trainers to err on the side of "too small." (Because you already know the information, you can easily overestimate the abilities of the trainees.)

☐ Provide time and activities that will encourage trainees to link the parts into a unified whole.

2. Spaced Learning

☐ Provide regular breaks: For example, conduct your session for 50 minutes and then allow the trainees a 10-minute break.

☐ Don't make training programs last too long. A one-week course is usually ample, allowing the trainees to return to the job to practice new skills and knowledge before embarking on further training.

☐ After presenting an explanation, provide an activity in which the trainees can practice skills before you go on to the next explanation.

3. Active Learning

☐ Don't present the trainees with information; rather, construct questions in such a way that the trainees "discover" the facts.

☐ Assign activities and projects.

☐ Use discussion techniques when appropriate to the objectives of the session.

4. Feedback

☐ Use tests frequently.

☐ Ask questions.

☐ When a trainee gives a correct answer, acknowledge and confirm it.

☐ When a trainee gives an incorrect answer, ensure that the trainee can answer the question correctly by the end of the session.

☐ Look for non-verbal signs of comprehension such as smiles, frowns, and nods.

☐ Provide frequent opportunities for trainees to ask questions.

☐ Return the results of tests as quickly as you can.

5. Overlearning

☐ Ask questions about material presented previously.

☐ Ask trainees to compare/contrast material being presented now with material presented previously.

☐ Include review periods in the timetable.

☐ Give tests that force trainees to recall.

☐ Review the session at its conclusion, actively involving trainees in the review.

☐ At the beginning of the session, review (or ask trainees to review) the previous session.

6. Reinforcement

☐ Compliment correct answers.

☐ Acknowledge initiative, hard work, and answers (even when incorrect).

☐ Provide for early success by initially asking relatively simple questions.

☐ If an answer is not completely wrong, identify the part of the answer that is right and reward it.

7. Primacy and Recency

☐ Cover important materials first or last.

☐ Provide overviews at the beginning and reviews at the end. (These should summarize the important components.)

☐ Emphasize the middle of each session (by means of visuals or an activity).

☐ Provide for summaries throughout the session.

8. Meaningful Material

☐ Recapitulate on a previous (related) session.

☐ Research the background of the trainees before they come to the session.

☐ Ensure that each point is fully understood before going on to the next point.

☐ Visit the workplace to see where the work happens and how it is done.

☐ Provide samples and exhibits. For example, when describing a form, either show an exact replica (especially in shape and color) on the overhead projector or give each trainee a copy.

☐ Use plenty of relevant examples to explain a point.

9. Multiple-Sense Learning

☐ When designing a session, emphasize visuals. (Don't worry about talking; you'll do that naturally!)

☐ Allow trainees to feel tools and materials.

☐ Don't talk about it; show it. (Nothing is harder than trying to describe a form.)

10. Transfer of Learning

☐ Visit the workplace and observe what is acceptable work and what is not.

☐ Visit the workplace to see how the work is done.

☐ Present the situation in the session exactly as it occurs at the work location.

☐ Try to involve the supervisor in the training of his or her subordinates.

SUMMARY

A trainer must understand the special assumptions and attitudes necessary for adult learning—especially for intelligent and motivated adults. A trainer must also apply sound learning principles to the design of the training program and its materials.

Chapter 2 Doublecheck

1. When assessing learner maturity, what variables do you need to consider?

_____

_____

_____

_____

_____

_____

2. You are required to demonstrate to a group of six people the correct method of completing a form. What principles of learning can you use to ensure that the group learns?

_____

_____

_____

_____

_____

_____

Application Exercise

John, a supervisor in an assembly factory, is about to show Hank, a new employee, how to fit a component into an engine. He will show Hank how to fit other components at intervals during the next few weeks. At the moment, John has the engine on the usual assembly bench and has placed the component beside it with the appropriate tools.

With Hank beside him, John picks up the component and briefly explains its function in the engine. He gives the component to Hank to hold for a few seconds. John then takes the component and demonstrates, step by step, how the component is to be fitted into the engine.

He then asks Hank to fit the component. Hank makes several attempts. (John corrects errors as they occur.) Finally Hank succeeds. John congratulates him. John then asks Hank to do it several more times while he watches. Hank successfully fits the component each time.

With a final word of commendation, John then arranges for several engines to be placed on Hank's assembly bench. After ensuring that Hank has the tools and a sufficient supply of components, John leaves Hank to his task.

1. What principles of learning did John use?

   _____

   _____

   _____

   _____

   _____

   _____

2. Could John have used any other principles of learning?

   _____

   _____

   _____

   _____

   _____

   _____

   _____

■ Doublecheck Answers

1. Content base; motivation; accepting responsibility for own learning; learning skills.

2. One principle would be multiple-sense learning. Draw a replica of the form on the chalkboard or use a replica of the form on a transparency on the overhead projector. Give each person several blank forms (transfer of learning).

    Explain how to complete the first section of the form (part learning). Then have each person complete that section (active learning) and continue to do it several times (overlearning) utilizing different details provided by you. Continually check each person's work (feedback). When each has satisfactorily completed the first section, give some expression of approval to each, such as "That's well done" (reinforcement).

    Deal with each section of the form in a similar fashion (part learning and spaced learning). Reinforce and emphasize the middle sections of the form (primacy and recency).

    When trainees have learned all sections satisfactorily, have them complete the whole form again, using different details (whole learning). Ensure that they have a correct completed form to take back to the workplace for reference (transfer of learning).

■ Application Exercise Notes

1. John used the following principles of learning:

    Spaced learning. Showing, at intervals over several weeks, how components fit the engine.

    Active learning. Getting Hank to fit the component.

    Feedback. Correcting errors when first attempting to fit the component. Supervising later practice.

    Overlearning. Asking Hank to fit the component a number of times.

    Reinforcement. Congratulating Hank when he succeeded the first time and giving a final word of commendation before leaving Hank.

    Multiple-sense learning. Demonstrating with the actual components and engine and explaining. Allowing Hank to handle the component.

    Transfer of learning. Training at the work location and using the engine, component, and tools that will be used on the job.

2. John could have first determined Hank's current knowledge of the engine and component. This would have allowed John to link his explanation of the component's function with Hank's current knowledge (meaningful material).

    Hank had to make several attempts before he was successful, which might indicate that the steps (or parts) in the demonstration were too large. These parts could be made smaller (part learning) and separated by activities (active learning). This also takes advantage of spaced learning.

3
THE THEORY-SESSION MODEL

Key Concepts

- *Need for session models.* We need effective models to help us plan and implement training programs.

- *Theory session.* Training session that presents information (facts, knowledge, and principles).

- *Skill session.* Training session that present a physical skill.

- *Theory-session model.* This basic structural unit is composed of three parts: introduction, body (in three-step segments), and conclusion.

Learning Objectives

After you have completed this chapter, you should be able to

- Diagram the structure of the theory-session model.

- List and explain the steps that compose a model segment.

- Plan and schedule a session by using the theory-session model.

TWO BASIC MODELS

Most training sessions have one of two basic purposes:

1. To present information (facts, knowledge, or principles).

2. To present and develop physical skills.

We call the information-oriented session a *theory* session because it stresses ideas and not skills, and (more obviously) we call the skill-related session a *skill* session. We need a model for each session in order to design and manage our training programs. Often the training topic clearly dictates which model to apply, but sometimes the training topic is more ambiguous and suggests the possibility of applying either (or both) models. For example, a session on "how to complete and fill out" an official form may fall into this middle area. To clarify the training approach, look again at the objective of the session. Do the trainees *only* need to learn how to fill out the form, or must they *also* understand the reason for the form or how it relates to work processes or communications?

If the objective is to learn how to fill out the form then use a skill session. If the objective is to fill out the form and also to understand the role of the form, then combine a theory session explaining the role of the form with a skill session showing how to fill it out. As a matter of fact, it is common to precede a skill session with a theory session in which the trainer presents background information for the skill. For this reason, let's first examine the theory-session model.

STRUCTURE OF THE THEORY-SESSION MODEL

You can see the structure of the theory-session model in the simple diagram on the next page.

E = Explanation

A = Activities by trainees

S = Summary

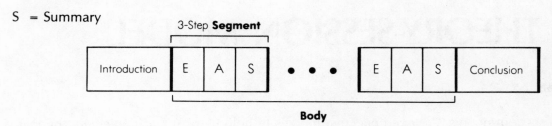

You can divide any subject that you wish to present into a learning-appropriate number of logical segments. The segments may be relatively independent, or they may build sequentially one upon the other. In the theory-session model, each segment is developed in an EAS step. (We will speak more of this later when we discuss the session plan.)

You might find it quite useful to develop an objective for each segment. Thus as you progress through EAS steps, you can test the training objectives, one by one, as the trainees perform an activity that can demonstrate their grasp of the segment. Let's now look more closely at the structure of the model.

1. The Introduction

These are the functions of the introduction.

To gain interest. This is where you "grab" your trainees' attention. How? A joke, a cartoon, a graph on the overhead projector, a controversial statement, a story of common interest, or a startling question. (Needless to say, these should be relevant to the subject.)

To check current knowledge. You must know the quantity and quality of your trainees' knowledge so that you can pitch your presentation at the right level. How do you find out the level of their current knowledge? Ask a few questions or try a written test. (Of course, you should have made basic inquiries about your trainees *before* the session.)

To orient. This is where you set the scene: Explain the session title and relate it to their current relevant knowledge. If there has been a previous relevant session, go over the information presented in that session (preferably by using questioning techniques.)

To preview the session. Some trainers may feel that this is an unsafe step. After all, if you keep secret the knowledge of where you are going to lead them, you will have some power over them. Right? Wrong!!

To motivate. Why should the trainees sit and listen to you? They won't, unless they are motivated to do so. You can motivate them by creating the need to learn. To satisfy that need, they will then listen.

In the introduction, show your trainees that the subject of the session is important. If they acquire this knowledge, they can make a contribution to themselves and to the organization. Show them how this particular learning fits into the total picture. They will want a general idea of where they are going. After all, how would you feel if a taxi pulled up to the curb and the driver shouted, "Jump in, we're going for a ride." You would at least want to know *where* you were going. Also, telling the trainees what ground they will cover in the session provides a target, establishes appropriate expectations about the content of the session, and allows trainees to check progress for themselves.

2. The Body

This is where you transfer the bulk of the information to the trainees. Plan to break this into logical segments. A time or priority order may provide the pattern. For example, perhaps one fact may have to be learned before the second fact can be understood. As we have suggested, the easiest method is to form each segment around an objective.

After you define the number and sequence of segments in the body, you can build them into the EAS pattern.

The E (Explanation) step. In this step, you give the trainee new facts, or lead them to "discover" the new facts. The easiest and most common method is to "tell" the information. Unfortunately, this is also the least efficient method. Research indicates that trainees use only about 11 percent of their learning capacity if you rely entirely on hearing to get the message across. In addition, you will find it difficult to keep their interest long enough. The most satisfactory method is to make use of the trainees' sense of sight, along with visual aids. A more difficult method is to use questioning techniques to elicit the information from the trainees, but it is well worth the effort, for it guarantees trainee interest and motivation.

The A (Activity) step. You have most probably heard of "learning by doing," and this describes the A step. The A step should closely resemble on-the-job behaviors. This resemblance will increase the meaningfulness of the activity and thus reinforce the message in the E step. For example, if your session is on "Written Communication" and you have explained the structure of a paragraph, then the A step could involve writing a paragraph. In a safety course on common hazards, you might follow the E step with an activity such as identifying hazards present in a work situation. In a session on circuit theory for technicians, you could draw various circuits as an activity. In a session on delegation, you could role play from case studies. In a session on the selling features of a new product, you could use activities that incorporate touching and comparing products.

The A step gives four additional benefits. First, it indicates to the trainee how much of the information he or she has retained (and thus points up weaknesses).

Second, the quality of the activity tells you whether your E step was satisfactory. After all, why go on to the next explanation if the preceding explanation has not been understood or cannot be used by the trainees? Observe the trainees very closely during the A step. If they do not demonstrate by their behavior that they have understood the explanation, then repeat the explanation.

Third, the A step separates one explanation from the next explanation and thus stresses structure with continuity.

Finally, if you have made each EAS segment equivalent to one objective, then you have an additional advantage. You may not need a comprehensive test in the conclusion to check your objectives because you have tested each objective in the A step of each EAS segment.

The S (Summary) step. In this step, you bring all the pieces together and tie up loose ends. It also gives you an opportunity to ask for questions from the trainees before you go into the next EAS segment.

3. The Conclusion

Undoubtedly, finishing is the hardest job in any session. Your conclusion should incorporate five basic items:

Review or recapitulate. Briefly go over the main items of your topic. Stress important or key points.

Test to ensure that learning has taken place. Make the test either oral or written, or require some performance activity that will demonstrate to you the level of learning achieved.

Link to subsequent sessions.

Clarify. Allow time for questions to clear up any misunderstandings or problems.

Finish. Leave your trainees in no doubt that you are done. For example, ask the question, "Before I finish, do you have any final questions?"

✔ Checkpoint: The Structure of the Theory-Session Model

Indicate true (T) or false (F), or fill in the blank(s).

1. A theory session is a name for a training session that presents information. _____

2. A skill session is a name for a training session that presents information. _____

3. The three parts of the theory-session model are the introduction, the _____ , and the conclusion.

4. The body of the theory-session model is composed of three-step segments known as the EAS steps. E stands for _____. A stands for _____. S stands for _____ .

5. The functions of the introduction are
   a. To gain interest.
   b. To check knowledge.
   c. To orient.
   d. To _____ the session.
   e. To motivate.

6. You can gain coherence in your training session structure if you form each segment to achieve a learning objective. _____

7. You use the E step to provide practice for the trainees in explaining the topic. _____

8. Behaviors in the A step should resemble behaviors that will be required on the job. _____

9. The functions of the conclusion are
   a. To review.
   b. To test.
   c. To _____ to subsequent sessions.
   d. To allow time for questions.
   e. To indicate that you have finished.

10. Write the labels in the correct place.

Conclusion
Introduction
E Step
S Step
A Step

● ● ●

■ **Checkpoint Answers**

1. T   2. F   3. body   4. explanation, activity, summary   5. preview   6. T   7. F   8. T
9. link   10. Introduction E A S...E A S Conclusion

TIME AND SCHEDULES

Time and schedules are very important considerations for the trainer. Invariably, the training program has a tight schedule and the trainer must define a specific amount of time to present a specific amount of information. As a trainer, you must plan to use time so as to maximize learning per time unit. Looking at the theory-session model, we suggest the following breakdown to help with your planning.

Let the introduction and the conclusion each run to 10 percent of the total time. You can then divide the time left between the EAS segments. Within each EAS segment, let the A step take up 50 percent of the time and the E and S steps the remaining 50 percent. For example, if my session is 40 minutes long, the introduction and the conclusion will take up 4 minutes each (a total of 8 minutes). This leaves 32 minutes for the body. Suppose I have decided to divide my session into four segments; then each EAS segment will run 8 minutes (assuming, of course, that each segment is of equal importance and contains equal amounts of information). With each EAS segment, the A step will take 4 minutes, the E step 3 minutes, and the S step 1 minute.

The time structure would therefore be as follows:

Segment

Introduction 4 min.	E 3	A 4	S 1	E 3	A 4	S 1	E 3	A 4	S 1	E 3	A 4	S 1	Conclusion 4 min.

Having such equal EAS steps will be unusual. Since some segments will be more important than others, some EAS segments will have to be longer than others. Here's a more realistic time structure:

Introduction 4 min.	E 5	A 6	S 1	E 2	A 3	S 1	E 3	A 4	S 1	E 2	A 3	S 1	Conclusion 4 min.

Let the topic, objectives, and needs of the trainees dictate the final timing structure.

In conclusion, we re-emphasize the necessity of time-planning your session in advance. If this virtue is incorporated into your session plan, you can check at a glance the progress of your session while you are actually presenting it.

Checklist: Applying the Theory-Session Model

INTRODUCTION

Did I

☐ Grab the interest of the trainees?

☐ Orient the trainees to the subject in general?

☐ Test the current level of the trainees' knowledge?

☐ Use past experience of the trainees to introduce the session?

☐ Give a preview of what is to come?

☐ Activate the trainees?

☐ State the session objective(s) correctly

☐ Prominently display the session objective(s) throughout the session?

BODY

Explanation Step

☐ Did I help the trainees to "discover" information?

☐ Did visual aids have sufficient impact and imagination?

☐ Did visual aids have sufficient variety?

☐ Did I use visual aids correctly?

☐ Did I use questions effectively?

Activity Step

☐ Were the activities of sufficient duration?

☐ Did the activity steps reinforce the explanation steps?

☐ Were the activities sufficiently imaginative to maintain interest?

☐ Was there sufficient variety in the activities?

☐ Did I use the activity steps to test the session objective(s) progressively?

Summary Step

☐ Were summaries presented at appropriate places in the session?

CONCLUSION

Did I

☐ Summarize the main points of the session?

☐ Ensure that the session objectives had been achieved?

A more extensive checklist in the form of a Theory-Session Feedback Sheet follows. You can use this sheet as it is or modify it to suit your requirements. You can use it as a detailed checklist *before* the session, or an observer can complete it to give you feedback *after* the session.

SUMMARY

We have two basic models that we can apply to designing and planning training programs: the theory-session model and the skill-session model. The structure of the theory-session model is composed of three parts: introduction, body (three-step segments), and conclusion. We can use the model to plan schedules and session content.

THEORY-SESSION FEEDBACK SHEET

Name _____ **Date** _____

Session Title _____

Time Analysis
am / pm

Intro	E1	A1	S1	E2	A2	S2	E3	A3	S3	E4	A4	S4	E5	A5	S5	Concl.	

Directions: Fill in the appropriate squares above with the time each step commences as the session progresses.

Listen carefully to the session, and on completion, place a check mark in the appropriate column to indicate your opinion of the performance.

		No	Partly	Yes
Introduction: Did he/she				
1. Grab the interest of the trainees?	1			
2. Orient the trainees to the subject in general?	2			
3. Test the current level of knowledge in the trainees?	3			
4. Utilize past experience of the trainees to introduce the session?	4			
5. Give a preview of what is to come?	5			
6. Motivate the trainees (specifically)?	6			
7. State the session objectives correctly?	7			
8. Prominently display the session objectives throughout the session?	8			
Explanation Steps:				
1. Did he/she help the trainees ''discover'' rather than give the information to them?	1			
2. Visual Aids				
a. Sufficient impact and imagination?	2a			
b. Sufficient variety?	b			
c. Use visual aids correctly?	c			
3. Questioning Techniques				
a. Use overhead and direct where required?	3a			
b. Use overhead and direct correctly?	b			
c. Use too many yes/no or long, rambling questions?	c			
d. Were the questions directed equally to all the trainees?	d			
Activity Steps:				
1. Were the activities of sufficient duration?	1			
2. Did the activity steps reinforce the explanation steps?	2			
3. Were the activities sufficiently imaginative to maintain interest?	3			
4. Was there sufficient variety in the activities?	4			
5. Did he/she use the activity steps to test the session objectives progressively?	5			

	No	Partly	Yes

Summary Steps:
1. Were summaries presented at appropriate places in the session? 1

Conclusion: Did he/she
1. Summarize the main points of the session? 1
2. Ensure that the session objectives had been achieved? 2

Looking at the session overall:

Presentation:
1. Did he/she appear to have clear objectives?
2. Did he/she appear to have a "plan" for the learning experience? 2
3. Did he/she have all information relevant to the learning experience at his/her disposal? 3
4. Did the session have a logical flow? 4
5. Did he/she explain new terms/words? 5
6. Did he/she present the right amount of material? 6
7. Did he/she make the explanation at the correct pace for understanding? 7
8. Did he/she present the material at the right level for the trainee? 8
9. Did he/she make adequate provision for the trainees to ask questions? 9

General Considerations:
1. Did he/she show enthusiasm and animation? 1
2. Did he/she maintain the interest of the trainees? 2
3. Did he/she maintain eye contact? 3
4. Was the verbal communication satisfactory? 4
     If "Partly" or "No," specify
         Volume   Pace   Pauses
         Clarity   Rhythm   Other_____
5. Were there any distracting mannerisms? 5
     If "Partly" or "Yes," specify

     "Ahs-ers"   Finger or pencil tapping
     Headscratching   Lip wetting or biting
     Ear pulling   Rug Pacing
     Eye rubbing   Cloud gazing
     Toe tapping
     Other_____

Further comments: _____
_____
_____
_____
_____
_____
_____

Chapter 3 Doublecheck

1. Briefly describe the function of the following parts of the theory-session model.

   The introduction. _____

   _____

   _____

   The E (Explanation) step of the body. _____

   _____

   _____

   The A (Activity) step of the body. _____

   _____

   _____

   The S (Summary) step of the body. _____

   _____

   _____

   The conclusion. _____

   _____

   _____

2. Yvonne Dee is an office manager and is required to familiarize her staff with the printed outputs of the new computer system that is to be introduced into the office. To explain the four different types of outputs would take a total of 20 minutes (approximately 5 minutes each).

   Design a theory-session time structure for Yvonne and identify what activities Yvonne could use.

   _____

   _____

   _____

■ Doublecheck Answers

1. The introduction should grab the attention of the trainees and set the scene to orient them. You should check their current knowledge so that you can pitch your presentation at the right level. Preview the session so that the trainees know where they are going. Finally, motivate them by creating the need to learn.

   The E step of the body is where you give the trainees new facts or lead them to "discover" the new facts. The most satisfactory methods of imparting the facts are to use the trainees' sense of sight (multiple-sense learning) and to use questioning techniques.

   The A step of the body is where the trainees "learn by doing." This increases the meaningfulness of the activity and reinforces the message in the E step.

   The S step of the body allows you to bring all the pieces together and tie up loose ends. It also allows you to ask for questions from the trainees before you go into the next E step.

   The conclusion allows you to go over briefly the main items of your topic. You can use a test to ensure that learning has taken place. Provide a link to subsequent sessions and allow time for questions to clear up any misunderstandings. Leave your trainees in no doubt that you have finished.

2. Each E step would take 5 minutes and the S step would take about 1 minute. As the E and S steps together take up about 50 percent of the EAS time, the A step will be 6 minutes. Therefore each EAS step would be 12 minutes. As there are four of them, the body would take 48 minutes. The body is 80 percent of the whole session, which would therefore be of 60 minutes duration.

$$\frac{48}{80} \times \frac{100}{1} = 60$$

The introduction (10 percent) and the conclusion (10 percent) would be 6 minutes each.

The structure of Yvonne's session would therefore be as follows:

Introduction 6 min.	E 5	A 6	S 1	E 5	A 6	S 1	E 5	A 6	S 1	E 5	A 6	S 1	Conclusion 6 min.

The A step should be based on the on-the-job behaviors that Yvonne's staff will be required to perform. Therefore, if they are required to read the printed output, she should provide them with a printed copy of the computer output and then ask each to read a section. If they are required to extract certain information and transpose that information to a form, she should provide them with the printed output and a copy of the form and then have them practice transposing the information.

4
THE SKILL-SESSION MODEL

Key Concepts

- *Skills.* The characteristics or qualities within a person. These skills then enable that person to do a task.

- *Task.* Part of a job; made up of a series of skills.

- *Job.* A purposeful assembly of tasks and their related skills.

- *Skill session.* Training session that presents a physical skill (task).

- *Skill-session model.* This basic structural unit is composed of three parts: introduction, body (in four-step segments), and conclusion.

Learning Objectives

After you have completed this chapter, you should be able to

- Diagram the structure of the skill-session model.

- List and explain the steps that compose a model segment.

- Plan and schedule a session by using the skill-session model.

TYPES OF SKILLS

We would like to mention briefly three types of skills. First, the most basic type of skill involves gathering information (usually by sight) and acting on it (usually with some type of muscle movement). This is sometimes called a *psychomotor* skill. Handwriting is an example. Here the eye sees a line on the page and muscles move the pen along the page. In learning psychomotor skills, the skill is usually broken down into its component parts. For example, when children first learn to print, they learn that *each letter* (a task) is a set of particular strokes of specific shapes that are placed in specific positions on the lines (a task breakdown).

The second type of skill involves procedures, or psychomotor activities linked in a series. The order of the psychomotor activities is crucial. For example, changing a flat tire on a car is a procedural skill because some activities *must* be performed before others. Aspects of driving a car (starting up, turning a corner) are also procedural skills. The main learning aid here is a job breakdown or checklist that specifies the order in which component psychomotor skills must be performed.

The third and most complex type of skill involves diagnosis. All forms of trouble-shooting and problem-definition involve diagnostic skills. Discovering the reason why a car will not start is an example. The main learning aid is a logic chart, or *algorithm*.

Knowing the types of skills included in your session helps you in two important ways: You become more aware of the aspects of the skill that you should emphasize (for example, order in procedures, logic in diagnosis), and you are reminded of the appropriate learning aids that you should prepare while planning your session.

INTRODUCING THE SKILL-SESSION MODEL

When applying the theory-session model, a trainer must sometimes "contrive" an activity that enables the trainer to observe whether or not the trainee has attained the training objective. The situation is a little easier when working with the skill-session model because you can actually *see* the trainee performing the task and applying the content of the session directly. In the skill-session model the physical activity (the behavioral component of the objective) is what the session is all about.

When planning a skill session, break down the task into a series of closely linked steps of physical activity. If the trainee practices this series over and over, he or she will become more proficient at the task (as measured in time and quality). Consequently, the basis of any skill session is a task analysis—a breakdown of a task into skill steps.

TASK BREAKDOWN

The task breakdown is usually written directly from information gathered during a training needs analysis. It is basically a step-by-step definition of the task, arranged so that each skill step is a building block on which to place the subsequent skill steps. Adequate performance of all steps ensures adequate learning of the task. In addition, the breakdown should support each step with *explanatory points*, which answer the "how," "why," "when," and "where" and describe as well the vital "knacks" involved in the task. Explanatory points should also emphasize safety aspects. Let's take a look at a very simple example of a task breakdown.

Task Breakdown: To Light A Match

Steps	Explanatory points
1. Take the matchbox in the left hand.	So that the "striking edge" is accessible.
2. Push the inside container out.	Only half-way.
3. Select a match.	Grasp the match half-way down the shank.
4. Close the inside container.	For safety, so that the remaining matches do not ignite.
5. Scrape the matchhead against the "striking edge."	A sharp action, but not so violent that you break the match.
6. Extinguish the match when its purpose has been fulfilled.	To avoid burns and unwanted fires.
7. Dispose of dead match.	Ensure that it is disposed of safely.

It is quite common to include a drawing or specifications:

How Long Should the Performance of the Task Take?

As a rule of thumb, a trainee should be able to perform the specified task in less than 10 percent of the total length of the session. Thus, if you have a 40-minute session, you will probably have time to present, and the trainees have time to learn, a 4-minute task.

The Training Objective(s)

Having written out the task breakdown, you will find that you have already done the basic work toward preparing the training objective(s). However, you should make the training objective(s) of the session perfectly clear (both to yourself and to anyone else who may see your session plan) by writing out the objective(s).

STRUCTURE OF THE SKILL-SESSION MODEL: SIMPLE TASK

Let's look at the structure of a session for a simple task with an easily attainable objective (such as "to light a match"). Like the theory-session model, the structure of such a skill-session model has three parts:

1. Introduction

2. Body
   Show (S)
   Show and tell (ST)   } Four-Step Segment
   Check of understanding (C)
   Practice (P)

3. Conclusion

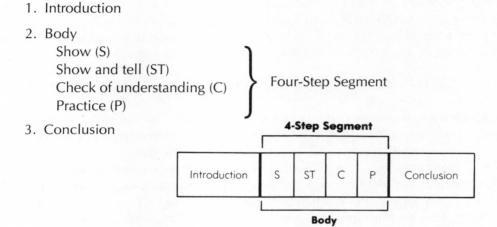

Now let's examine the elements of each part.

1. The Introduction

Orient. Announce the topic of the skill session, and then show trainees how this particular task fits in the whole system. Don't make the explanation too detailed. (A "bird's-eye" view is sufficient.) If the skill session is a follow-up to a theory session (as is often the case), recapitulate the knowledge gained in the theory session, preferably by using questioning techniques.

Motivate. Why is this session so important? Why should the trainees perform the task in the manner you have specified? Your answers to these questions must be logical, and not just "because the instruction manual says so"! Show the trainees that the acquisition of the skill to do this task is important to them. If they do well, the system will operate more successfully and their jobs will be easier.

Measure current knowledge. This is most important. How do you know that your trainees can use a screwdriver correctly? Do they have basic keyboard or typing skills? (For example, a lack of these becomes a problem if you are training new VDU operators.) At times, you may have to find out whether there are any left-handed trainees in the class. (This usually occurs when certain physical/directional manipulation is necessary.)

State complete training objective(s). State the objective(s) clearly and precisely. Always try to include a time standard within which the trainees must complete the task. This gives the trainee something concrete to aim at and makes it easier for you to judge whether or not your instruction has been successful. Further, the trainee thus has an easily remembered standard that he or she can take back to the job. If the end-of-training standard differs from the standard required after subsequent practice on the job, point this out to trainees and specify both standards.

Display the objective(s) before your trainees for the entire session. (We will cover training objectives in more detail in a later chapter.)

2. The Body

When trainees are learning a simple task, the body is a single element with four complete and separate steps, each with its own function.

Show. In short, you do the task as set out in the task breakdown within the time limit set in your objective. This gives your trainees an easy introduction to the task and also gives them a mental picture and a standard to work to. ("No talking" by you or the trainees while demonstrating, but you can draw attention to particularly important point on safety.)

How long should the Show step last? Only as long as the task being taught. (If the task should last only as long as 10 percent of the session, then the Show step will last only 10 percent of the session.)

When you have finished this step, quickly tidy up the work area in preparation to start the task again.

Show and tell. Show and tell each skill step as set out in the task breakdown. Emphasize safety factors and particularly difficult or tricky parts. Stress each skill step, and pause between each so that the trainees know that every skill step has a separate identity.

Make sure that every trainee can see clearly. This is the time when you may encounter the problem of left-handed versus right-handed trainees. If this happens, stand the right-handed trainees behind you and place the left-handed trainees in front (assuming you are right handed!). Make adequate provision for the students to ask questions, and constantly check that they *all* understand each skill step or explanatory point as you progress.

Remember, you are also a model. Throughout the session, *you* must follow all the correct methods and maintain good housekeeping and safety standards.

Check of understanding. This is the initial feedback (for both you and your trainees). A useful technique here is to ask the trainee to name each skill step. You can actually perform the task to the trainees' instructions. But remember two points:

1. Don't let one trainee name *all* the steps. Give others a chance. You must be certain at the end of this stage that all the trainees know the steps and key points.

2. Make sure the trainees stress the importance of all the safety features you have mentioned.

When you are sure that the trainees know all the skill steps, they are ready for the final stage.

Practice. Trainees should practice at least 50 percent of the total time allocated for the body of the session. Thus if your skill session body is 20 minutes, then the Practice step alone must last at least 10 minutes. Before the trainees begin the Practice step, you should have provided them with three basic items:

1. A task breakdown sheet. This should show each step and the explanatory points for each step. Include drawings if they will make your points clearer.

2. The correct tools and equipment to complete the skill. Check that these operate within the safety requirements.

3. Sufficient material. The trainees will most probably need three or four attempts before they become proficient within the standards given in your objective. Therefore provide sufficient material for the task to be carried out at least three or four times.

Be sure to supervise the trainees continually throughout the practice period. Be on the lookout for unsafe practices, untidy "housekeeping," and incorrect methods. Correct errors in a constructive manner. Watch for a trainee who is confused or lost, and spend more time with a slow learner.

The Practice step is your opportunity to give individual instruction, so make the most of it. The previous three steps (Show, Show and Tell, and Check of Understanding) are group oriented, and you have to aim at the average trainee. You will be lucky to have one average trainee in your group, so you can use the Practice step to help slow learners and to give fast learners additional challenging tasks to maintain their interest.

3. The Conclusion

Briefly review the steps and key points (using questions). You can write these on the board for emphasis. Encourage trainee participation throughout the conclusion. In particular, check

- Whether they have found any of the skill steps particularly difficult. (This will reinforce these steps for the trainees and let you know which steps to emphasize next time.)

- Whether they have discovered any new or different techniques. (This is a fertile field for ideas for next time and also gives the trainees a sense of having contributed.) If they create a realistic alternative technique, they will leave the session with that particular skill greatly reinforced. In addition, this quick check can prevent major problems with trainees who identify possible shortcut techniques during training, and decide to do it "their way" back on the job. Frequently, you can point out to the trainee why the shortcut is not acceptable, and prevent negative outcomes ranging from increased costs for the organization right up to permanent injury or death for the employee.

Review briefly the standards of time and workmanship, and emphasize the more important safety factors. Check if there are any questions. Provide a definite finish to the session.

✔ Checkpoint: Structure—Simple Task

Indicate true (T) or false (F), or fill in the blank(s).

1. Skills are the characteristics or qualities within a person. These skills then enable that person to do a task. _____

2. A job is a purposeful assembly of skills. _____

3. The three parts of the skill-session model are the _____, body, and _____ .

4. The body of the skill-session model is composed of a four-step segment. These steps are known as the S, ST, C, and P steps.
   S stands for _____.
   ST stands for _____.
   C stands for _____.
   P stands for _____.

5. The task breakdown is a step-by-step definition of the task, arranged so that each skill step is a building block on which to place the subsequent skill step. _____

6. The functions of the introduction are
   a. To orient.
   b. To _____.
   c. To measure current knowledge.
   d. To announce complete training objectives.

7. The S step should last twice as long as the task being taught. _____

8. The P step should take at least 50 percent of the total time allocated for the body of the session. _____

9. You should not use the conclusion to check difficult steps and new techniques. _____

10. Write the labels in the correct place.

   Conclusion
   Introduction
   P Step
   ST Step
   S Step
   C Step

■ **Checkpoint Answers**

1. T   2. F   3. introduction, conclusion   4. Show, Show and Tell, Check of Understanding, Practice
5. T   6. motivate   7. F 8. T   9. F   10. Introduction S ST C P Conclusion

STRUCTURE OF THE SKILL-SESSION MODEL: COMPLEX TASK

If you must present a more complex task with an objective that covers more than one simple physical activity, then you must expand the model in order to work with it. Take, for example, this objective: "Given a standard tool kit, change a flat tire on a car in 15 minutes." This statement includes a number of sub-objectives:

1. Set out the tools.

2. Take out the spare wheel.

3. Ensure that the car is safe to jack up.

4. Jack up the car.

5. Take off the wheel with the flat tire.

6. Replace with the spare wheel.

7. Jack down the car.

8. Replace all tools and the problem wheel.

Obviously, if you presented all this in a single segment, you would violate at least two of the principles of learning: whole versus part learning and meaningful material (in that trainees would have little chance to master early skill steps, with the consequence that later skills steps may become meaningless). Therefore, present each of the *sub-objectives* using the four-step segment:

1. Show

2. Show and tell

3. Check of understanding

4. Practice

However, to give the trainees some concept of the total task and to show the standard of performance expected by the end of the session, *demonstrate* the total skill immediately after the introduction and before commencing the learning of the sub-tasks. You would structure the plan for presenting the skill of changing a flat tire on a car in this way:

Demonstrate total task to standard:

1. Set out the tools.

   Show
   Show and Tell
   Check of understanding
   Practice

2. Take out the spare tire.

   Show
   Show and Tell
   Check of understanding
   Practice

3. Ensure that the car is safe to jack up.

   Show
   Show and Tell
   Check of understanding
   Practice

And so on, until you reach the final sub-objective, "Replace all tools."

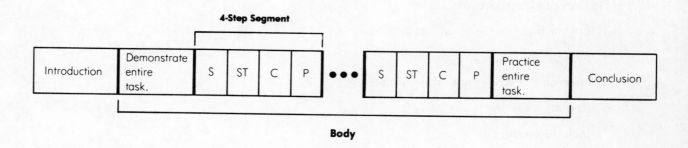

Note that in the expanded model, we have included a Show step for every sub-objective. In many instances, we feel that this is a useful tactic, but we also recognize that with relatively simple sub-objectives or with experienced trainees, this pattern may become pedantic and counterproductive. If that occurs, omit or combine Show steps for some sub-objectives and start with Show and Tell.

In the expanded structure, you cannot go straight into the conclusion after practicing the last sub-objective. Although you know each trainee can do each sub-task, you cannot really be certain that the trainee can do the whole job. Therefore, in the expanded structure, you must include a Practice step for the entire complex task.

The net effect of this model is that the trainee is first asked to practice the skills *within each sub-objective* until those skills and the links between them become a habit. When this is achieved for each sub-objective, the trainee can practice the whole task until the links between the sub-objectives become a habit. This adheres strongly to the principle of meaningful material because the trainee moves securely and consistently from the known to the unknown.

TIME AND SCHEDULES

As with a theory session, time and schedules are very important to maximize learning. In the skill session, 5 percent of the total time can be allocated to the introduction and 5 percent to the conclusion. This is less than the 10 percent allocated in the theory session because the relevance and importance of the skill is usually more obvious to the trainee. For a relatively simple skill, this leaves 90 percent of the time available for the body. Of this time available, one half (i.e., 45 percent) is allocated to the Practice (P) step and the other half (i.e., 45 percent) to the Show (S), Show and Tell (ST), and Check of Understanding (C) steps. As a guide to the amount of material that can be covered in a given time, the Show step should take no more than 10 percent of the total session.

For a complex skill, the introduction and conclusion remain at 5 percent. Additional stages of demonstrating the entire task and practicing the entire task can each use up to 10 percent of the total time. This leaves 70 percent of the session for the body, which is divided into as many S, ST, C, P segments as is necessary. Once again, one half of the body time should be allocated to the P segments.

Checklist: The Skill-Session Model

INTRODUCTION

Did I

- [ ] Clearly and precisely state the session objective(s)?
- [ ] Include time/quality standards in objective(s)?
- [ ] Utilize past experiences to introduce the session?
- [ ] Check current knowledge?
- [ ] Motivate the group?

BODY

Show: Did I

- [ ] Do the job in a competent manner?
- [ ] Observe the time factors, good methods, safety, and housekeeping?

Show and Tell: Did I

- [ ] Show and tell one skill step at a time?
- [ ] Stress key points (pause between skill steps)?
- [ ] Ensure that all trainees could see clearly?
- [ ] Follow the breakdown (no backtracking)?
- [ ] Observe correct methods, good housekeeping, and safety?
- [ ] Make adequate provision for trainees to ask questions?

Check of Understanding: Did I

- [ ] Ask trainees to describe skill steps and key points?
- [ ] Perform the task to trainees' instructions?
- [ ] Ensure that all trainees know how to do the task?

Practice: Did I

- [ ] Have everything ready and properly arranged?
- [ ] Correct errors as they occurred with *constructive* criticism?
- [ ] Ensure correct methods, good housekeeping, and safety factors?
- [ ] Structure adequate trainee practice (50 percent +)?

CONCLUSION

Did I

- [ ] Briefly revise critical steps and key points?

☐ Ensure trainees were aware of the standards expected?

☐ Ask for new ways to perform the task?

SUMMARY

A more extensive checklist in the form of a Skill-Session Feedback Sheet is on pages 46 and 47. You can use this sheet as it is or modify it to suit your requirements. You can use it as a detailed checklist *before* the session, or an observer can complete it to give you feedback *after* the session.

In addition, the block diagrams which follow highlight the similarities and differences of the theory and skill session models.

Theory Session

Introduction	Body							Conclusion
	E	A	S		E	A	S		
Interest									Review
Check Knowledge				Explanation					Test
Orient				Activity					Link
Preview				Summary					Questions
Motivate									Finish
10% of total time	80% of total time (40% to A, 40% to E & S)							10% of total time

NOTE: Each A is 50% of the time spent on its EAS segment.

Skill Session

Intro.	Full Demo.	Body									Practice Full Task	Conclusion
		S	ST	C	P		S	ST	C	P		
Orient Motivate Check knowledge State objective(s)	Whole task done to standard	Show Show and Tell Check of Understanding Practice										Practice to standard	Review Difficult steps New techniques Emphasize -safety -standards Questions Finish
5% of total	10% of total (MAX)	70% of total time (35% to S&ST&C, 35% to P)									up to 10% of total	5% of total

NOTE 1: Each P is 50% of the time spent on its S, ST, C, P segment.
NOTE 2: For a simple skill, the full demonstration and full practice can be deleted.

SKILL-SESSION FEEDBACK SHEET

Name _____ **Date** _____

Session Title _____

Directions: Listen carefully to the session and place a check mark in the column to indicate your opinion.

		No	Partly	Yes
Introduction: Did he/she				
1. Clearly and precisely state the session objectives?	1			
2. Include time/quality standards in objectives?	2			
3. Utilize past experiences to introduce the session?	3			
4. Check current knowledge?	4			
5. Motivate the group?	5			
Show (Demonstrate): Did he/she				
1. Do the job in a professional manner?	1			
2. Observe the time factors—good methods—safety— housekeeping?	2			
Show and Tell: Did he/she				
1. Tell—Show—Illustrate one stage at a time?	1			
2. Stress key points—pause between stages?	2			
3. Ensure that all trainees could clearly see?	3			
4. Follow the breakdown—no backtracking, etc.?	4			
5. Observe correct methods—good housekeeping—safety?	5			
6. Make adequate provision for trainees to ask questions?	6			
Check of Understanding: Did he/she				
1. Ask trainees to nominate stages and key points?	1			
2. Perform the task to trainees' instructions?	2			
3. Ensure that all trainees knew how to do the job?	3			
Practice: Did he/she				
1. Have everything ready and properly arranged?	1			
2. Correct errors as they occurred by <u>constructive</u> criticism?	2			
3. Ensure correct methods—good housekeeping—safety factors?	3			
4. Structure adequate trainee practice (50% +)?	4			
Conclusion: Did he/she				
1. Briefly revise critical stages and key points?	1			
2. Ensure that trainees were aware of the standards expected?	2			
3. Ask for new ways or difficult parts?	3			
Job Breakdown:				
1. Did he/she provide each trainee with a job breakdown?	1			
2. Did the breakdown have sufficient steps?	2			
3. Did the explanatory points cover ''how,'' ''why,'' ''when,'' and ''where''?	3			
4. Was safety emphasized?	4			

Looking at the session overall:

	No	Partly	Yes

Presentation:

1. Did he/she appear to have clear objectives? — 1
2. Did he/she appear to have a "plan" for the learning experience? — 2
3. Did he/she have all information relevant to the learning experience at his/her disposal? — 3
4. Did he/she develop the session with a logical flow? — 4
5. Did he/she explain new terms/words? — 5
6. Did he/she present the right amount of material? — 6
7. Did he/she make the explanation at the correct pace for understanding? — 7
8. Did he/she present the material at the right level for the trainees? — 8
9. Did he/she make adequate provision for the trainees to ask questions? — 9
10. Visual Aids
    a. Sufficient impact and imagination? — 10a
    b. Sufficient variety? — b
    c. Use visual aids correctly? — c
11. Questioning Techniques
    a. Use overhead and direct where required? — 11a
    b. Use overhead and direct correctly? — b
    c. Use too many yes/no or long, rambling questions? — c
    d. Were the questions directed equally to all the trainees? — d

General Considerations:

1. Did he/she show enthusiasm and animation? — 1
2. Did he/she maintain the interest of the trainees? — 2
3. Did he/she maintain eye contact? — 3
4. Was the verbal communication satisfactory? — 4
   If "Partly" or "No," specify

   Volume   Pace   Pauses

   Clarity   Rhythm   Other _____
5. Were there any distracting mannerisms? — 5
   If "Partly" or "Yes," specify

   "Ahs-ers"   Finger or pencil tapping
   Headscratching   Lip wetting or biting
   Ear pulling   Rug pacing
   Eye rubbing   Cloud gazing
   Toe tapping
   Other_____

Further comments: _____

_____

_____

_____

_____

_____

_____

Chapter 4 Doublecheck

1. Your trainees are required to learn a 6-minute task. How long would your session last? Why?

    _____

    _____

    _____

    _____

    _____

2. Briefly describe the functions of the following parts of the skill-session model.

    The introduction. _____

    _____

    _____

    The S (Show) step of the body. _____

    _____

    _____

    The ST (Show and Tell) step of the body. _____

    _____

    _____

    The C (Check of Understanding) step of the body. ___

    _____

    _____

    The P (Practice) step of the body. _____

    _____

    _____

    _____

The conclusion. _____

_____

_____

3. Write a task breakdown for the task of placing a call on the telephone.

Task Breakdown

Steps	**Explanatory points**
_____	_____
_____	_____
_____	_____
_____	_____
_____	_____
_____	_____
_____	_____

4. Indicate true (T) or false (F). In the expanded structure of the skill-session model used for a complex task:

a. Each sub-objective is presented by using a separate four-step segment. _____

b. The entire complex task is demonstrated immediately after the introduction and before commencing learning of the sub-tasks. _____

c. There is no need for the trainees to practice the entire complex task when you know that they can do each sub-task. _____

■ Doublecheck Answers

1. Your session would last 60 minutes. The task the trainees are required to learn takes 6 minutes, and this should be approximately 10 percent of the total time.

2. In the introduction, you orient the trainees by announcing the topic of the skill session and then showing them how this particular task fits into the whole system. Show the trainees that the acquisition of this task is important to them, and also identify their current knowledge of the task. State the objectives clearly and precisely, and display them before your trainees for the entire session.

   In the S step, you do the task to give the trainees a mental picture and standard to work to.

   In the ST step, you show and tell one skill step at a time. Stress each skill step as set out in the task breakdown, and pause between each so that the trainees know that every skill step has a separate identity. You are acting as a model, so follow all the current standards.

   The C step is the initial feedback stage. Ask the trainees to name each skill step while you perform the task to the trainees' instructions. If they know all the skill steps, they are ready for the final topic.

   The P step takes up at least 50 percent of the total time allocated for the body of the session. You should provide the trainees with (1) a task breakdown sheet, (2) the correct tools and equipment, (3) sufficient materials for the task to be carried out three or four times, and (4) continual supervision and constructive criticism.

   Briefly review the skill steps and key points in the conclusion, encouraging trainee participation throughout. Check for difficult steps or new methods. Emphasize standards and safety.

3. Objective: To place a call on a telephone.

Steps	Explanatory Points
1. Obtain desired telephone number.	From the telephone company directory, personal telephone number directory, or other appropriate source.
2. Make a note of the number or keep the directory open in front of you.	So that you do not forget the number.
3. Lift handset.	Using less dextrous hand.
4. Place the earpiece against ear.	
5. Listen for dial tone.	To ensure the telephone is operational.
6. Dial the required number.	Use more dextrous hand.
7. Listen for ring tone.	To ensure that the dialed number is being called.
8. When called person answers, identify self and announce purpose of call.	

4. a. T   b. T   c. F

5
THE TRAINEES

Key Concepts

- *Trainee differences.* Trainees will vary in levels of ability and in their disposition to learn.

- *Consultation.* Early discussion with potential trainees benefits needs analysis and helps to establish good motivation.

- *Selection.* Selecting trainees requires a careful assessment of records and background as well as motivation and on-the-job circumstances.

- *Interaction with trainees.* Each trainer must develop a style that fits the trainees and the training objectives.

- *Cliques and pressure groups.* Informal groups will emerge from the formal group. The trainer must evolve techniques for coping with these groups.

- *Follow-up.* Training is not complete until it is successfully applied on the job. The trainer must help in the on-the-job application of training.

Learning Objectives

After you have completed this chapter, you should be able to

- Outline the benefits of early consultation with potential trainees.

- List five factors that are crucial in selecting trainees.

- Describe factors that may be important in deciding the appropriate style of interaction between trainer and trainees.

- List methods for coping with differences in levels of ability.

- List methods for coping with cliques and pressure groups.

- Explain how to cope with trainees who are thrust upon you.

THE GOOD, THE BAD, AND THE UGLY

Bad and ugly! Well, no trainee is all bad and ugly, and yet the possibility of a "hard-to-handle" trainee creates much anxiety among new trainers.

Trainees vary in their ability and disposition to learn. Some are motivated and have the ability to easily acquire new knowledge or skills (the "good"). Some are motivated but do not have the ability and are thus inappropriate for the training program (the "bad"). And some are distinctly uninterested or may even be actively antagonistic to training (the "ugly"). The last are the "hard cases" whose presence creates stress before and during training.

In our experience, we have encountered very few hard-core "uglies." The majority of trainees fall into the "good" category, although trainee anxiety at the beginning of a training program may temporarily camouflage this. In addition, there are ways to handle the "bads" and the "uglies" in a positive manner, so that with practice, you can become confident of your ability to constructively deal with all manner of trainees. Let's examine how the trainee and his or her characteristics are likely to affect the learning process, the trainer, and the training program.

BEFORE THE TRAINING PROGRAM

Consulting

Trainers normally consult potential trainees very early in the development of a training program. The information derived from this consultation does a lot to ensure that the training program is aimed at real needs. This attention can also positively motivate the employee, both immediately ("they thought it worthwhile to ask my opinion about…!") and in later training ("Ah, this is what they asked me about three months ago!").

Selecting

The characteristics of the trainees can have a strong influence on the success or failure of a program as well as the quality of the benefits to the trainee and the organization. So what should you *look* for if you want to select employees who need training and have a high probability of success in a program? The following five factors are crucial.

1. *The supervisor's attitude.* Is the supervisor aware of a performance deficiency in an individual? Is the supervisor committed to assisting the individual to improve in an area of deficiency? If training is chosen as the method of developing an individual, will the supervisor encourage him or her to apply new learning to the job after training? Will the supervisor give feedback on the modified job performance and act as a coach while new skills and behavior are applied to the job?

2. *The employee's ability.* Does the employee have the ability to handle the intellectual (conceptual) or skill aspects of the program? Will he or she fail to benefit from training because he or she cannot understand the content of the training course?

3. *The employee's level of motivation.* Is the employee motivated? If so, is he or she motivated enough to learn during a training program and then do his or her job even better?

4. *The employee's need for the training.* Is the employee's job performance lower than one would expect on the basis of his or her ability and motivation because he or she lacks knowledge/skills/behavior that would improve performance?

5. *The employee's opportunity to apply the learning.* At the conclusion of the program, will the trainee's job allow him or her to immediately apply new knowledge/skills/behavior? If not, will the trainee be assigned to a job in which he or she can apply the learning in the near future?

If the answers to the questions in 2, 3, or 4 are negative, then the employee will not learn, and no purpose is served by including the individual in a training program. If the answers to 1 or 5 are negative, then the organization will harvest no immediate benefit from any learning that occurs during the program. In this instance, you must balance the immediate costs against possible (and often dubious) long-term benefits.

Now, how can you assess these factors? You need information. Let's look at the following chart. It suggests several sources of useful information and also suggests which factors you can learn about from those sources.

Personal contact with personnel in the organization can provide you with information about an employee's motivation, his or her opportunity to apply new learning, and the supervisor's attitude. Personal contact can also provide you with information about the employee's ability and need for training, but assessing ability and need from more objective sources (if available) is preferable.

Job knowledge will allow you to determine the employee's opportunity to apply new learning in his or her current job.

Performance records will reflect not only an employee's ability and motivation in relation to his or her current job, but also his or her need for further training.

Training records can tell you about an employee's ability and motivation as displayed in previous training programs.

Work sample tests or standardized ability tests may give you a sound indication of an employee's ability and need for training. Use these mainly where job performance measures are not available.

Source of Information About Trainees

Factor \ Source	Personal contact	Job knowledge	Performance records	Training records	Tests
Supervisor's attitude	✔				
Employee's ability			✔	✔	✔
Employee's motivation	✔		✔	✔	
Employee's need			✔		✔
Opportunity to apply learning	✔	✔			

A Decision!

You have two important but contradictory guidelines for selecting trainees. One we already referred to: You select trainees who have a high probability of success in the program. Thus you can demonstrate the worth of the program in a difficult economic or political climate. The second guideline requires you to select trainees according to scientific evaluation procedures. (See Chapter 26.)

To decide which of these guidelines to use is one of your more difficult tasks. A decision must be made for each situation. We prefer the second guideline because the first guarantees that you will "preach to the converted," and this may cast doubt on the validity of training outcomes.

Preprogram Contact

Contact with a potential trainee before the program begins will influence that person. Remember, the first impression of a program is usually formed on the basis of little information;

and this impression, once formed, can be difficult to change. Therefore, take great care in initial contacts with potential trainees, especially in relation to invitations to attend, administrative details, and preprogram study requirements. (See Chapter 25.)

Further, try to develop a track record of creating training programs that are enjoyable and practical and that contain an element of challenge. This combination should produce a positive reaction in trainees and, in time, will create a positive attitude toward training throughout the organization. Then any new program is likely to be regarded positively, even before it has started. If you pay attention to these kinds of details, your chances of motivating trainees are greatly enhanced.

✔ Checkpoint: Before the Training Program

Indicate true (T) or false (F).

1. Trainees tend to have the same level of ability. _____

2. Trainees tend to have the same level of motivation. _____

3. Early consultation with a potential trainee is a good motivator. _____

4. When evaluating a potential trainee, you can afford to ignore his or her supervisor's attitude toward training. _____

5. When selecting trainees, an employee's need for training is more important than his or her ability. _____

6. When selecting trainees, whether or not an employee will have an opportunity to apply the training is unimportant. _____

7. Selecting trainees that you know will succeed is a tactic that may cast doubt upon the training results. _____

8. Select only those trainees who have a high probability of success in the program. _____

9. The first impression of a program is usually formed on the basis of little information. _____

10. Interesting and effective program activities will create a positive attitude toward training on all levels of the organization. _____

■ **Checkpoint Answers**

1. F   2. F   3. T   4. F   5. F   6. F   7. T   8. F   9. T   10. T

DURING THE TRAINING PROGRAM

Problem: Interacting With Trainees

Your best approach to interacting with trainees depends on the situation. Adult trainees usually react negatively to any attempt at force-feeding. If the trainee will accept it, use a person-to-person approach, without reference to status or power. This is probably most productive of learning. If the trainee is uncomfortable with this approach, adopt whatever style of interaction suits the trainee best. If required, be the representative of "the boss," or the technical expert, or the traditional teacher (providing you can undertake these roles without becoming artificial) until the trainee achieves the behavior you want.

However, if you are interacting with a group of trainees, you must modify these approaches to suit the audience. Still try to suggest that you are engaged in a person-to-person dialogue. For example, establish eye contact with individuals and use illustrations that all individuals can relate to. You can also vary your tone of voice and sentence structure to suit a question or comment to a specific individual. For example, a mild comment to a trainee sensitive to criticism will have the same effect as a tongue-lashing to a trainee with a thick skin. In short, know your trainees and, where possible, adapt your interaction to suit them.

Problem: Different Levels of Ability

Let's first examine ways to avoid this problem. One way is to carefully select trainees of approximately equal ability each time you run the program. However, such a procedure can lead to a sameness, a uniformity, that may have negative consequences on your motivation and that of the trainees. It also limits the pool of experience available for sharing in the group.

The second and much more effective way to avoid this problem is to provide training in an individualized format. Programmed instruction courses are examples of this. Here trainees work individually and at a pace that fits their ability and motivation.

In practice, however, you are usually faced with a group that has different levels of ability, so that you are forced to angle your message to the level of an "average" member of the group. You must hope that above-average trainees will not become bored and that below-average trainees will not get lost. You can adjust this "average" level by assigning projects or giving tutorials. Give above-average trainees advanced or difficult projects to keep them interested, and give below-average trainees extra individualized assistance.

Another strategy you can use is to form teams composed of trainees of varied ability levels and to encourage above-average trainees to assist below-average trainees.

Problem: Coping with Cliques and Pressure Groups

Group dynamics. Let's first look at the basic principles of group dynamics. Individuals form a group when they share similar goals. These goals become the goals of the group. One common goal is mutual support in anxiety-producing situations (for example, the beginning of training). To achieve its goals, the group will try to impose certain behaviors (called *norms*) that will be expected of group members. To remain a member of the group, an individual must conform to these norms. When an individual deviates from the norms, other group members apply progressively stronger pressures (or "sanctions") until the deviating member conforms or is expelled from the group.

For example, consider a group of motivated trainees whose goal is to learn. The group will expect its members to listen attentively and to participate actively in discussions. (These behaviors are norms.) If one trainee does not do this (deviates), he or she will be invited to participate in discussions and others will direct questions at him or her. If a trainee interrupts other speakers or will not listen, the group will disapprove, ask him or her to be quiet, and finally ignore this trainee (pressures for conformity to norms).

Group members also play various roles within the group. Two important leadership roles are the task role (or "getting things done") and the group maintenance role (or "keeping the group together"). If these roles are not filled, the group will not achieve its goals and will disintegrate. These roles may be filled by one person or may be shared by many (for example, different "experts" become group leaders according to which goal the group is concentrating on at the moment).

Coping with groups. Groups with the characteristics we have described are often formed during training, particularly with longer programs. Thus one of your early tasks is to attempt to arrange matters so that the group goals and norms will assist the learning process. A useful technique is to try to achieve a "psychological contract" with the trainees by stating and discussing the expectations that you and the trainees have for the program and each other. You can discuss learning goals, work loads, and ways of interaction during training. Then you can discuss differences and reach agreements. These revised expectations then become the group goals, and the group will require behavior that conforms to the agreed-upon expectations.

If this approach fails, however, and the group imposes norms that interfere with learning (for example, consistently arriving late for sessions), what can you do? First, evaluate the degree of interference that is likely. Your attempt to change the norms may also interfere with learning, so weigh the cost of interfering against the cost of *not* interfering. If you decide to act, first discuss the matter privately with the trainee who takes the leadership role in the group. He or she can influence the others. If you can persuade the leader to alter his or her behavior, then the others may follow the lead. If this approach fails, you might try a group problem-solving session to discover more acceptable ways for the group to achieve its objectives. If all else fails, you can use threats of organizational punishment. These will usually drive the problem underground (at least temporarily), but they will also probably make the learning climate worse. Consequently, use this alternative with extreme caution.

Problem: What to Do With Trainees "Thrust" Upon You

The problem. Unfortunately, it is not at all uncommon for a supervisor to decide that a problem subordinate "needs training" and then to send that subordinate to the first available program, without any needs analysis or consideration of alternative solutions. Even if training is a reasonable solution, the strategies required for remedial training are often different from those used in standard developmental training programs, and the presence of such an individual will create problems.

A different problem is created when, with the best of intentions, a supervisor wants to train an employee who either already knows the content or knows that he or she will not be able to use it on the job. This kind of trainee is demotivated from the very beginning, and may demotivate the other trainees.

Solutions. The best solution to the problem of inappropriate trainees is to maintain close contact with supervisors so that you can advise them concerning which subordinates they should nominate for which programs. If it is necessary to reinforce this primary advisory role, try to establish an organizational policy in which the trainer has the right to reject (with explanation) nominations for programs.

If you find yourself with a trainee who requires remedial attention, your best option may be to transfer that trainee to an individualized activity appropriate to his or her need (if you have that degree of freedom of action). If you can't, try regular counseling during the program with the emphasis on motivation.

If you find yourself with a trainee who has already mastered the content of the program, don't panic. This trainee may be perfectly happy to act as a second trainer, passing on practical tips and techniques to the benefit of the other trainees. If the trainee is demotivated because he or she cannot apply the program to his or her job, try counseling with an emphasis on career planning.

✔ Checkpoint: During the Training Program

Indicate true (T) or false (F).

1. Being friendly with trainees is always the best approach. _____

2. When speaking to an audience, avoid eye contact with individuals. _____

3. There are advantages in having a group of trainees with different levels of ability. _____

4. A group will discipline a member who does not conform. _____

5. There is only one leader in a group. _____

6. A psychological contract is formed by discussing expectations. _____

7. Threats of punishment often interfere with learning. _____

8. Supervisors should be allowed to select for training whichever employees they want. _____

9. Individual counseling may help demotivated trainees. _____

10. Since you know the material thoroughly, you do not need to use the knowledge and skills available in the group. _____

■ **Checkpoint Answers**

1. F   2. F   3. T   4. T   5. F   6. T   7. T   8. F   9. T   10. F

AFTER THE TRAINING PROGRAM

After training, the trainee attempts to apply the new learning on the job. This task is often difficult, and you should give all the assistance and support you can by choosing follow-up activities that best suit the trainees and the situations in which they are working.

In conclusion, you can very easily become absorbed in the details of session planning and presentation and thus forget that the single most important factor in the whole learning process is the learner. Try to remember the importance of the learner at all times, but particularly when the learner is an adult who is expected to change his or her on-the-job behavior after the learning experience is over.

Checklist: Coping with Trainees

Selecting

☐ Will the employee's supervisor encourage and support the employee's attempts to apply the new knowledge/skill/behavior?

☐ Does the employee have the ability necessary to undertake this course? Will he or she learn from it?

☐ Is the employee motivated to perform well on the job? Is he or she motivated to learn from this program?

☐ Does the employee need this knowledge/skill/behavior?

☐ Will the employee's job allow him or her to apply the new knowledge/skill/behavior immediately?

Interacting

☐ Do the trainees have a preferred style of interaction?

☐ Is this style conducive to learning?

☐ Are you personally comfortable with this style?

☐ Do you attempt to relate to trainees on a person-to-person basis?

☐ Do you vary your interaction style to suit individual trainees?

Coping With Different Levels of Ability

☐ Do your trainees have differing ability levels?

☐ Can you run the course in an individualized format?

☐ Do you plan sessions so that above-average trainees can work on advanced material while below-average trainees are given individualized assistance?

☐ Do you use the knowledge and experience of above-average trainees to promote learning in all trainees?

Coping With Groups

☐ Have the trainees formed a group or groups?

☐ What are the goals and norms of these groups?

☐ Will these goals and norms promote or detract from learning?

☐ If they detract, do they detract enough to make change necessary?
If change is necessary, can you best achieve it by

☐ a. Group discussions of expectations?

☐ b. Interpersonal influence on the group leader?

☐ c. Group problem-solving sessions?

☐ d. External pressure and/or punishment?

Coping With Trainees Who Are Thrust Upon You

☐ Have you maintained adequate contact with supervisors in relation to nominations for training?

☐ Do you have the right to accept or reject trainees?

☐ Can you assist a demotivated trainee through counseling?

☐ Can you use an "overskilled" trainee (who doesn't need this program) as a trainer's assistant?

SUMMARY

Trainees vary in their ability and disposition to learn. Before the training program begins, the trainer should consult with potential trainees in order to establish rapport and gather information. Selection tactics require good information, which you can develop from various sources. The trainer must also develop a style of interaction that fits the trainees as well as the training objective.

Informal groups will emerge from the training group. The trainer must learn how to cope with these groups and how to work with them to advance the training goals.

Chapter 5 Doublecheck

Fill in the blank(s).

1. The supervisor's attitude partly determines how material learned in training will be _____ on the job.

2. First impressions of a training program are usually formed on the basis of little _____.

3. A history of enjoyable, practical, and challenging training should create a _____ attitude to training throughout the organization.

4. Adjust your style of interaction with trainees to suit the _____.

5. _____ are the behaviors expected of group members.

6. Group members who do not conform to norms will have _____ applied to them.

7. The most important factor in the whole learning process is the _____.

Give brief answers.

8. Why should a trainer consult regularly with supervisors and potential trainees?

_____

_____

_____

_____

_____

9. When trainees in a group have varied ability levels, how can you cope with this?

_____

_____

_____

_____

_____

10. How do you establish a psychological contract?

_____

_____

_____

_____

_____

_____

_____

■ Doublecheck Answers

1. applied

2. information

3. positive

4. situation

5. Norms

6. pressure (or sanctions)

7. learner

8. Increases trainee motivation. Aids in selecting trainees, by giving information about the supervisor's attitudes, the employee's motivation, the employee's need for training, the employee's opportunity to apply learning. Increases the trainer's knowledge of the organization and jobs.

9. Use individualized program (for example, programmed instruction). Aim at the average ability level and then give advanced projects to high-ability trainees and individual assistance to low-ability trainees. Form teams of mixed abilities and have higher-ability trainees help lower-ability trainees.

10. Trainer and trainees state their expectations of the program and of each other. Differences in expectations are identified. Differences are discussed. Agreement on mutually acceptable expectations is obtained.

II. PLANNING THE LEARNING EXPERIENCE

6
WHAT IS TRAINING NEEDS ANALYSIS?

Key Concepts

- *Training needs analysis (TNA)*. Used to uncover gaps between adequate and inadequate job performance. Thus provides a basis for defining organizational needs and training objectives derived from them.

- *Surveillance*. Initial TNA stage: monitoring information in order to compile a broad picture of the organization's performance.

- *Investigation*. Middle TNA stage: probing areas that show symptoms of training needs.

- *Analysis*. Final TNA stage: sorting and classifying data from TNA investigation, and then preparing a report.

Learning Objectives

After you have completed this chapter, you should be able to

- Describe TNA and explain why it is critical to organizational efficiency.

- Explain the stages in TNA.

- Describe some of the problems that accompany the TNA concept.

AN OVERVIEW

Some people may claim that training needs analysis (TNA) is the most important step in the training process. We disagree! Each step is equally important! We do agree, however, that TNA is *critical*. Its position near the beginning of the training process means that errors at this stage put all subsequent stages off target, with an accompanying waste of resources. Conversely, an accurate TNA reduces the possibility of errors at later stages.

The objective of a TNA is to collect and evaluate information in order to find out:

1. What is being done now.

2. What should be done (either now or in the future).

If we find a gap between the two, we can decide whether training is likely to close it. If training can close the gap, then our collected data become the basis for deciding:

- The content and method of training.

- Which people need the training (target population).

- The time constraints that apply at two levels. (For example, the training must be completed within three months, and the trainees must perform Task X in two minutes.)

- How we can measure the training outcomes.

HOW TO DO A TNA

Unfortunately, you have no easy procedure for doing a TNA. Each situation requires its own mixture of observing, probing, analyzing, and deducing. In many ways, TNA is like detective work, with the next step depending on what has gone immediately before. When you do a TNA, follow up every lead and check every piece of information (where possible). Examine every alternative answer before making conclusions. Only then can you be sure you have the evidence on which to base a training strategy.

We have found it useful to describe TNA as a three-stage procedure of

1. Surveillance

2. Investigation

3. Analysis

Let's assume that you have decided to attempt a TNA in your organization.

1. Surveillance

In this stage, you should regularly review the vital data of your organization. See that summary documents with a state-of-the-organization theme are automatically circulated to you. Thus you will have an up-to-date and broad picture of what is happening to the total organization, and you can begin to look for areas of performance problems and training opportunities.

In addition, make an effort to maintain informal contacts with individuals throughout the organization. Regularly assess the attitudes and feelings of members of the organization, even if your assessment is subjective.

Finally, keep informed about all current policies, targets, and standards relating to work performance.

Here are some areas in which you should compile specific data for your surveillance file. You might find the worksheet on page 69 useful in summarizing data. Feel free to modify or expand the areas listed to suit the reporting and accounting procedures of your organization.

2. Investigation

Undertake an investigation if you suspect that you have discovered a performance gap or if management requests training or if management seems to think that a training need may be present. The purpose of your investigation is to gather more specific and detailed data in the pertinent area.

Now you can see the importance of routine surveillance. Without the overall picture, you could overemphasize one training need at the expense of other needs that you don't even know exist. The result would be a less-than-optimum use of resources and a loss of credibility for you.

There are many data-gathering techniques that you could use in a TNA investigation. Here's a list of some common techniques:

1. Observation: personal, filmed.

2. Interviews: individual, group.

3. Questionnaires: checklists, rating scales.

4. Diaries (records of activities).

5. Work samples.

Areas	What's happening now?	What should be happening?
Organizational objectives & policies		
Performance standards		
Budget targets		
Job descriptions		
Production quality & quantity		
Organization & method studies		
Performance appraisals		
Rates of:		
Labor turnover		
Absenteeism		
Accidents		
Disciplinary actions		
Suggestions		
Costs:		
Labor		
Materials		
Equipment		
Distribution		
Waste		
Maintenance		
Overtime		
Economic predictions		
Technical developments		
Legal requirements		

6. Performance appraisals.

7. Organization and methods studies: work studies.

8. Psychological tests.

To examine these techniques in detail is beyond the scope of our discussion, but we suggest that you develop data-gathering skills as part of an ongoing professional development program.

3. Analysis

Analysis, because it is an intellectual skill, is difficult to describe. At a minimum, however, we can say that it involves the rigorous examination of incoming data in order to eliminate invalid information, the grouping and summarizing of the remaining data, the drawing of logical conclusions, and the preparation of a communication (report). These skills can be sharpened by practice and may be assisted by modern techniques of statistical analysis and electronic data processing.

In their influential *Training in Business and Industry*, authors McGehee and Thayer suggest an approach to analysis that we have found useful in grouping and summarizing data and in preparing reports. We analyze data under three major headings.

1. Organization analysis. This includes a statement of objectives and policies at organization, department, and section levels, as well as analyses of the human resources available and of the organization climate. This kind of analysis can include a detailed interpretation of indexes of efficiency so as to focus on performance gaps at the total organization level.

2. Operations (job) analysis. This analysis specifies standards of job performance first. It then provides a breakdown of the job into component tasks and investigates ways of performing those tasks (with a view to improving efficiency). From this, we can specify the skills, knowledge, and attitudes that a person requires in order to do the job to standard.

3. Person analysis. We now look at the occupant of the job investigated in the operations analysis. We measure current level of performance and diagnose requirements (if any) to bring performance to standard.

We have thus defined the training need, the training objectives, the training content, and the target population, which puts us well on the way to developing training activities appropriate to the need.

More details on methods of gathering various types of data are available in "Some Observations On TNA" by B.J. Smith, B.L. Delahaye, and P. Gates in the *Training and Development Journal*, August, 1986.

The Relationships of the TNA Stages

The relationships of the stages in the TNA model can be described via a diagram.

Surveillance is a continuous activity, necessitating a certain level of continual analysis. This is illustrated on the diagram for the period A through F. Surveillance and analysis in the period A to B leads you to suspect a training need at time B. You increase your analysis efforts in the period B to C to provide the basic data you need to begin an investigation at time C. The investigation occupies the period C to D, with the level of analysis building up during that period to process the data generated by the investigation. Analysis of investigation continues beyond the conclusion of the investigation itself, occupying the period D to E. From time E onwards, the continuous surveillance and analysis again represent ongoing TNA activity.

The surveillance, investigation, and analysis model of TNA is systematic, structured, and insists on examining the whole organization. It provides data to define the training needs, the

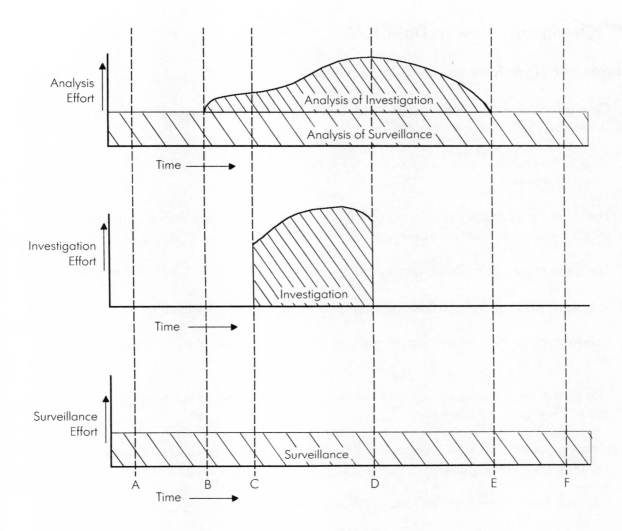

training objectives, the target population, and the training content. This enhances the chances of developing training activities which are effective learning experiences *and* are effective uses of scarce organizational resources.

✔ Checkpoint: How to Do a TNA

Indicate true (T) or false (F), or fill in the blank.

1. One advantage of a TNA is that it reduces the possibility of errors that emerge in later stages but derive from early decisions. _____

2. TNA is interested in how a task should be performed as well as the way it is currently being performed. _____ .

3. The difference between adequate and inadequate performance provides the area from which a trainer can derive training objectives. _____

4. The three stages of a TNA procedure are surveillance, _____, and analysis.

5. In a sense, TNA in the surveillance stage is like _____ work.

6. Informal contacts are not significant sources of information during the surveillance stage. _____

7. In a sense, the investigation stage is a continuance of the surveillance stage, conducted in a more sharply focused area. _____

8. Observations, interviews, and questionnaires are good data-gathering techniques to use during an investigation. _____

9. The final event in the analysis stage of a successful TNA is a _____.

10. An effective TNA report has a threefold analysis: an _____ analysis, an operations analysis, and a person analysis.

■ **Checkpoint Answers**

1. T   2. T   3. T   4. investigation   5. detective   6. F   7. T   8. T   9. report
10. organization

PROBLEMS OF TNA

1. Rewards

In some organizations, the trainer is not rewarded for doing TNAs. If management thinks that a trainer should train (stand and deliver in front of a class), then it will probably regard TNA activities as wasteful. (Fortunately, professional management does not share this viewpoint.)

2. Time

TNA uses a lot of the trainer's time. It also uses other employees' time—time they would usually prefer to spend in different ways. There are always more immediate problems than a TNA, which may (or may not) affect a person's job in three months (or three years).

3. Selling TNA

Because of the time investment required, the trainer is usually in the position of having to "sell" a TNA to the participants in order to gain their cooperation and commitment. In addition, because training may not show immediate results, the trainer often has to "sell" the recommendations derived from a TNA before management will accept a training strategy.

4. Timeliness

Often, a TNA will have a sharply drawn time constraint. For example, "The new equipment arrives on Monday, so I want everyone to have a training course on the mock-up this Friday." You will have to do the best TNA you can in the time available.

5. Cause and Effect

A perennial problem in TNA has to do with a proper analysis of cause and effect. If events A and B occur in sequence, we are tempted to assume that A *causes* B and therefore that training in relation to A will solve a problem in B. But beware! What if C is causing A is causing B? In this case, training in relation to A will have limited effect. Even worse, if C is independently causing both A and B (for example, poor supervision causing low productivity and high labor turnover), then training in relation to A will make no difference whatsoever. A prime aim of TNA, therefore, is to separate the root cause from the effects (or symptoms) so that training may be directed at the cause.

Comment

We conclude this brief overview by emphasizing the desirability of conducting accurate TNAs before designing or running training programs. Developing a program without completing a TNA is like shooting an arrow at a target hidden in a fog. The philosophy—"all we can do is hope"—underlying such an approach is just not good enough for professional decision makers.

SUMMARY

Training needs analysis is a critical part of the training process. The TNA objective is twofold: to collect and evaluate information in order to find out what is being done *now* and what should be done *now and later*. We have no set procedure for performing a TNA, but the activities fall into three stages (surveillance, investigation, analysis) and end with a report. The TNA concept provokes some problems within the organization, and the person sponsoring a TNA must cope with these.

Chapter 6 Doublecheck

1. Why is TNA important?

_____

_____

_____

_____

_____

_____

2. What is the function of the surveillance stage of TNA?

_____

_____

_____

_____

_____

3. Outline the contents of a TNA report.

_____

_____

_____

_____

_____

Application Exercise

John Leonardi is the trainer at Video Supplies, Inc., a manufacturer of specialty components for professional video applications. The workforce consists mainly of technicians/representatives who work almost entirely at customer locations and operators who assemble the equipment in a production line in a factory building in an industrial suburb. Before being promoted to his present job, John was a successful technician. He has received a message that Vince de Souza, the production superintendent, would like to talk to him.

John: Hey, Vince, I got your message. What can I do for you?

Vince: It's these lousy operators! They're not working. Production is down, and we're getting further and further behind in orders. The reps are screaming!

John: I'm sorry to hear that, Vince. You say production is down. Can you give me some idea how much?

Vince: Oh, it's not a sudden thing. The trend has been downwards for about six months now. And we're now about 20 percent below the figures for this time last year.

John: (looking surprised) Yeah, that's bad. We'll have to do something about that. You're the man closest to the scene. What do you suggest?

Vince: Well, they just don't sound too interested to me. It's as if they aren't motivated any more.

John: Say, I have an idea. I just read a review of a new motivational film that's supposed to be terrific. I'll hire it in and we'll try showing it to your people. How's that?

Vince: (looking relieved) You're the expert. I'll leave it to you.

John: Good. Glad I could help. See you around, Vince.

Comment on this incident. Refer specifically to the stages of a TNA.

_____

_____

_____

_____

_____

_____

_____

_____

■ Doublecheck Answers

1. A TNA specifies what is being done now and what should be being done. It gives accurate information on which to base subsequent decisions about the content and method of training, the target population, time constraints, and measuring the outcomes.

2. Surveillance gives you a broad picture of organizational performance and enables you to identify areas of performance problems and training opportunities.

3. A TNA contains three analytical parts: organization, operations, and person analysis.

   Organization analysis states objectives and policies, analyzes human resources, and analyzes efficiency indexes.

   Operations analysis states standards of job performance, breaks down the job into tasks, analyzes the efficiency with which these tasks are performed, and specifies skills/knowledge/attitudes required to do the job.

   Person analysis measures the current performance level of the job holder and diagnoses training requirements.

■ Application Exercise Notes

1. *Surveillance.* John has not kept up-to-date on organizational performance. He did not know about the downward trend in production, or how much production was down.

2. *Investigation.* John did a little investigating by questioning Vince. But he did not question Vince in detail, did not examine organizational records, and did not consult with anyone else.

3. *Analysis.* No analysis was evident. There was no attempt to establish cause and effect, no attempt to examine other factors that might affect production (for example, changes in work methods), and no attempt to analyze the production records of individual workers. John simply latched onto a word he heard Vince say (*motivation*) and tried to apply a solution off the top of his head.

7
WRITING TRAINING OBJECTIVES

Key Concepts

- *Derivation of objectives.* Objectives derive from the observation of performance and are based on information obtained from a training needs analysis.

- *Terminal statement.* A description of the behavior that forms a task and the outcomes of that behavior. These descriptions becomes sources for writing training objectives.

- *Training objective.* Has three components: statement of terminal behavior, standards, and conditions.

Learning Objectives

After you have completed this chapter, you should be able to

- Describe the components of a training objective.

- Write a training objective for a theory session or a skill session.

WHERE DO TRAINING OBJECTIVES COME FROM?

We cannot emphasize enough the necessity for defining training objectives *first* and defining them *exactly.* Training objectives come directly from the training needs analysis. As discussed in the previous chapter, the TNA is performed at the workplace and identifies those tasks that either are not being carried out effectively or are about to change.

Any task is really made up of a series of behaviors. By describing these behaviors, you begin to arrive at *terminal* behavior statements. A terminal behavior statement is the basis for a training objective.

Doesn't Terminal Mean the End?

Yes, it does. By specifying terminal behavior(s) as the end result (or goal) of the training session, you create a specific and real target at which to aim. Setting a target also indicates that you must continue the training until the trainee can perform the behavior(s) satisfactorily. So, the first step in preparing training objectives is to start at the end.

THE COMPONENTS OF A TRAINING OBJECTIVE

Simply describing a terminal behavior is not definitive enough to serve as the basis for the design of a training session. To make the training target more specific, you must write a training objective. A training objective has three components:

1. A statement of the *terminal* behavior.

2. A statement of the *standards* that the trainee is expected to attain.

3. A statement of the *conditions* under which the trainee is expected to perform the terminal behavior.

The Terminal Behavior Statement

A behavior gives you, the trainer, a readily observable basis on which to assess learning. You can see the trainee doing an activity. So as a general rule, an effective statement of terminal behavior will use an *action* verb:

To **type** a paragraph.

An ill-defined statement (with a concept-related verb) such as

To **understand** how to type.

presents a number of problems. How do you observe or judge "understanding"? If you test it, how can you ensure that each trainee is tested in the same way and in the same manner? Exactly what information needs to be given to the trainee to ensure that he or she can achieve the training objective? Of course, typing is a physical activity and is thus expressed in an action verb. What happens, however, when you are planning a theory session (which imparts ideas or facts) and you cannot observe a physical activity? Well, you must "force" the trainee into an activity that demonstrates that he or she has grasped the ideas. For example, if the session was on the safety rules to be observed when using a grinding machine, you might write the following terminal behavior statement:

To **list** and **explain** the safety rules that apply when using a grinding machine.

Here the activity is listing and explaining. In general, when writing the terminal behavior statement, avoid the abstract and use an action verb.

Use the action verb	Avoid the abstract
To write	To know
To demonstrate	To understand
To define	To be familiar with
To solve	To perceive
To explain	To be aware of
To select	To think about

A well-defined behavioral statement gives the trainees a clear goal. Trainees will feel that they know where they are going and what they have to achieve.

The Standards

Both you and the trainees can now visualize the terminal behavior. But how *well* must the trainees perform this behavior?

Take the example of a training objective "To type a paragraph." What constitutes satisfactory performance? Must a trainee type the paragraph without errors? How long can the trainee take to type it? How long is a paragraph?

To avoid these ambiguities, include standards of excellence in the training objective. These standards can generally be divided into three types:

1. Quantity

2. Quality

3. Time

Consider this example:

To type a five-line paragraph without error and in two minutes.

This gives a quantity standard ("five lines"), a quality standard ("without error"), and a time standard ("in two minutes").

Note that setting the degree of difficulty automatically helps to define the amount of time needed to achieve that standard. The typing objective

*To type a five-line paragraph **without** error and in **two** minutes.*

requires perfect typing. If you were willing to accept a lower standard, such as

*To type a five-line paragraph with no more than **five** errors and in **five** minutes.*

you would plan less practice for the trainees. To reach a standard of "no more than five errors and in five minutes" would take x minutes of practice; to attain a higher standard of "without error and in two minutes" would take x + y minutes practice time.

As a general rule, let the standard accepted at the workplace dictate the level of difficulty of the standard in your training objective.

Let's return to our other example of a behavioral objective:

To list and explain the safety rules that apply when using a grinding machine.

Here is a rewrite that incorporates standards of excellence:

To list and explain without error and in five minutes five of the safety rules that apply when using a grinding machine.

The Conditions

The final component of a training objective describes the conditions under which the trainee is expected to perform. By including conditions in a training objective, you tell the trainee what resources he or she will have and in what environment he or she can expect to be tested. It helps you to define the resources you must prepare before the session. In the typing objective, for example, the trainees should know whether the typewriter is standard or electric, as each requires different skills.

However, listing all the conditions may become a little pedantic if some of them are self-evident. Including "a table and chair will be provided" adds little to the effectiveness of the training objective. Thus, the decision on what conditions to include in the objective depends, to a large extent, on the situation. It is probably better to err by being a little too specific rather than omitting important conditions. Here are some typical examples of conditions:

- Given a standard set of…

- Without the aid of mathematical tables…

- Using an electronic calculator…

✔ Checkpoint: The Training Objective

Identify what is wrong with the following training objectives.

1. To be aware of the eight safety rules for operating the Duplex Series 121 cutting machine in three minutes.

_____

_____

_____

2. Using an HP30 calculator, compute the mean and standard deviation of the given raw data in seven minutes.

_____

_____

_____

3. Using a capstan lathe, turn down the provided 41/50 steel torsion bar to a four-inch diameter shaft with a tolerance of $\frac{1}{1000}$ inch.

_____

_____

_____

4. Fire five rounds at the 50-yard target with no misses in 30 seconds.

_____

_____

_____

5. Given an Apple II computer, a table, and chair, enter the given raw data into the Visi-calc program without error and in nine minutes.

_____

_____

_____

Indicate true (T) or false (F), or fill in the blank.

6. Training objectives come directly from the training needs analysis. _____

7. By specifying a terminal behavior as the end result (objective) of the training session, you create a specific and real target at which to aim. _____

8. The three components of a training objective are:

   - Statement of terminal behavior

   - Statement of the standards

   - Statement of _____

9. An effective statement of terminal behavior uses an abstract verb. _____

10. In a theory-session model, you must "force" the trainee into an activity that demonstrates how well he or she has grasped the ideas. _____

11. Including a statement of standards makes the training objective more ambiguous. _____

12. Standards can generally be divided into three types: quality, quantity, and _____ .

13. Setting the degree of difficulty automatically helps to define the amount of session time needed to achieve that standard. _____

14. Including conditions in a training objective tells the trainee how long he or she has to complete the task. _____

15. It is pedantic to describe the make/type/model of machine in the training objective. _____

■ **Checkpoint Answers**

1. Uses the abstract "to be aware of." It should be changed to an action verb such as "to list" or "to explain" so that the behavior can be observed.   2. Needs a qualitative standard on how many errors are acceptable; for example, "with no more than two errors."   3. Needs a time standard to indicate how long the task should take.   4. The type of firearm to be used needs to be identified; for example, "a Walther P38 pistol."   5. The use of "a table and chair" in the conditions is pedantic; the trainee could reasonably assume that these would be provided.   6. T   7. T   8. conditions   9. F   10. T   11. F   12. time   13. T   14. F   15. F

Checklist: Writing Training Objectives

☐ Do I have a clear idea of what the trainees must *do* at the end of the session?

☐ Have I used an action verb to describe this behavior?

☐ Have I included standards of satisfactory performance on the job?

☐ Have I provided the resources that the trainee must have to satisfactorily perform the behavior?

☐ Can I readily test the behavior to specified standards under specified conditions?

☐ Do objectives include behaviors or skills that I do *not* wish to develop in the trainees?

☐ Do objectives exclude behaviors or skills that are crucial to adequate performance?

SUMMARY

We must write clear and useful training objectives. We start by analyzing the tasks in a job and describing these as behaviors. The behaviors become the sources for writing training objectives. A training objective has three components: statements of behavior, standards, and conditions.

Chapter 7 Doublecheck

1. Why do we use the word *terminal* in the phrase *terminal behavior statement*?

   _____

   _____

   _____

   _____

2. List the three components of a training objective.

   _____

   _____

   _____

   _____

3. Why is a statement of standards needed in a training objective?

   _____

   _____

   _____

   _____

4. What additional information does the statement of conditions in a training objective provide for the trainee? For the trainer?

   _____

   _____

   _____

   _____

   _____

   _____

5. Tell what difference it would make in your session if you were given this training objective:

   Given an R15 portable dwell-meter, set the points of a 1974 Volkswagen 1500 automobile within a tolerance of 1 degree and in 15 minutes.

   rather than the following objective:

   Given an R15 portable dwell-meter, set the points of a 1974 Volkswagen 1500 automobile within a tolerance of 5 degrees and in 45 minutes.

   _____

   _____

   _____

   _____

   Develop improved versions of each of the following objectives (if required).

6. Given a basic instructional manual, develop an appreciation of music in 45 hours of study.

   _____

   _____

   _____

   _____

   _____

7. To be able to repair a model B1 two-way radio.

   _____

   _____

   _____

   _____

   _____

   _____

8. To be able to solve five quadratic equations in five minutes.

_____

_____

_____

_____

_____

As a trainer, you are required to provide instruction in the following tasks. Write a training objective for each.

9. Mail sorting.

_____

_____

_____

_____

10. Operating an accounting machine.

_____

_____

_____

_____

■ Doublecheck Answers

1. Because it is what the trainees have to be able to do at the end of the session/program. It is a specific and real target at which to aim.

2. A statement of terminal behavior; a statement of standards; a statement of conditions.

3. A statement of standards identifies how well the trainees must perform the terminal behavior. It overcomes any ambiguities that may arise concerning what is expected of trainees.

4. It tells the trainee what resources he or she will have to complete the terminal behavior and in what environment he or she can expect to be tested. It helps you, the trainer, to define what resources must be prepared before the session.

5. The session would be longer as the first training objective has much higher standards than the second. This would mean that the practice time needed by the trainees would be much longer to achieve the higher standard.

6. No action verb; for example, "Given a basic instructional manual for 45 hours of study, explain the importance of melody and rhythm in music."

7. No conditions; for example, "Given basic repair kit and circuit chart…" No standards; for example, "in two hours."

8. No conditions given, but it would most probably be pedantic to do so. The objective as it stands is quite satisfactory.

9. Given standard-size letters, sort 50 letters into their correct destinations in 80 seconds with no more than five errors.

10. Given a standard NCR accounting machine, correctly add a column of 100 figures in 30 seconds.

8
CREATING THE SESSION PLAN

Key Concepts

- *The need for a plan.* A session plan is an essential foundation for a successful session. Without a plan, structure tends to become disjointed.

- *Write a clear plan.* Use a procedure in clarifying and preparing the plan, and document the plan clearly.

- *Time.* Carefully plan the times of segments of the session. Allow enough time to prepare an adequate plan.

Learning Objectives

After you have completed this chapter, you should be able to

- List the advantages of using a session plan.

- Write a session plan.

- Realistically relate time to the session plan.

ADVANTAGES OF A SESSION PLAN

A session plan is your road map—it reminds you where you want to go and how you have decided to get there. Here are some of the basic advantages of using a session plan:

1. Reminds you of the content of the session, helping you to keep on course.

2. Reminds you of the techniques to use in the session; for example, questions, summaries.

3. Shows you where to pick up and continue the session, if you deviate from the planned session.

4. Helps you to "time" the session—and to finish on time.

5. Indicates what visual aids you need to present a particular point as well as when you need them.

HOW TO WRITE A SESSION PLAN

Of course, you begin work on the session plan only after you have clarified and written the training objective(s). Use the following five-step procedure:

1. Grade the session content into *must* know, *should* know, *could* know.

2. Arrange the content in logical order.

3. Select basic resources.

4. Select training techniques.

5. Estimate segment times.

Step 1: Grade the Content

Usually, you are faced with trying to present a lot of information in a very limited amount of time. Grade this information into three ranks:

1. What the trainees *must* know. This is the material essential to the achievement of the objectives. Without it the trainee would fail. (Must-know material is sometimes listed as *key points*.)

2. What the trainee *should* know. This is the material that gives the trainee a clear understanding (reasons for doing). It fills in the gaps and answers a fairly wide range of questions.

3. What the trainee *could* know. This is the material that is interesting and relevant but not essential for a clear understanding.

With the total amount of information graded in this way, you then incorporate the information that is critical (*must* know), and the remainder (*should* know and *could* know) you include depending on its importance and the time available. Make your motto

"Present a little and present it well."

You may often feel a strong urge to cover a large amount of material very quickly, but resist this urge. It is better to select a relatively small unit of information, present it so that the trainees will understand it, and then check to ensure that the trainees have remembered it.

Step 2: Arrange the Content

Arrange the content in logical order so that the trainees can easily assimilate it. This needs more attention in a theory session because the task breakdown specifies the logical order for a skill session. This logical order is achieved by

1. Identifying the current knowledge of the trainees.

2. Presenting the new information in easily "digested" steps.

3. Moving from the "known" to the "unknown." When the "unknown" becomes "known," move on to the next "unknown."

Step 3: Select Resources

Select basic resources, such as the training room, projector, and charts. (Resources are covered in more detail in Unit V.)

Step 4: Select Training Techniques

Decide which training technique (telling, questioning, role playing) is best for demonstrating each point within each logical step.

Step 5: Estimate Time

Estimate how much time each part of your presentation will need. Check to be sure that the sum of these times does not exceed the total time allowed for the session. If it does, cut out some of the information content of the session. Eliminate the *could* know first and then the *should* know. Don't cut down the time for activities that you have designed for checking the trainee's understanding. You can revise the estimated times after a dry run and/or each actual presentation of the session.

HOW TO ORGANIZE A SESSION PLAN

Initially, you can use the layout on pages 91–92. With experience, you can modify this layout to suit your own situation and preferred style. In any case, use a layout that aims at completeness and clarity, so that if you suddenly become unavailable, another trainer can substitute for you at short notice and need no more guidance than your plan to successfully run the session. Try to express your main points succinctly, and do not include unrealistic times and techniques. Take a few moments now to review our suggested layout.

At the top of the page, write in the title of the training program. (This is also the filing key.) Then give the session title (and don't forget to name each session so that it summarizes the session content). Then give the session objective. (Don't forget to include the standards and the conditions.) List the visual aids you will use, as you can then do a quick check just before the session to ensure that you have all the resources you need. Finally, describe any special actions you have to take before the session (for example, placing a chart stand in a particular place or having a special piece of equipment ready). This information provides the context and background for the session and creates a historical record for your study and resource file.

Now look at the columns. You see four columns: Time, Modus Operandi, Main Points, and Details. The usefulness of your session plan is largely determined by how well you fill out these columns. Consider the following points as suggestions that can make your session plan more useful.

Time. When you are preparing the session, calculate times by starting at 0 minutes. Next, enter in the Time column the ending time of the first segment (for example, 4 minutes). This is also the starting time of the second segment. Then enter the ending time of the second segment (for example, a 4-minute segment would end at minute 8). Continue in this way to the end of the session. When you know the actual starting time of the session, write in the actual times. During your session, you can then check at a glance (and without doing any mental calculations) whether you are ahead of, on, or behind time.

Modus operandi. Specify how you intend to get your material across to the trainees. Common entries would be "chalkboard" (and then a note in the Details column about that part of the chalkboard plan); "question/s" (and then the actual question/s in the Details column); "trainee examples" (and then some examples in the Details column in case the trainees' examples are not satisfactory); and "activity" (given in the Details column). List every training technique you plan to use at the appropriate place in the column, with the details in the Details column. (Some trainers use capitals or different colored inks to highlight questions, activities, and so on.)

Main points. The basic entries in this column would be the stages of the session as outlined in Chapters 3 and 4: introduction, body, and conclusion, each with its sub-headings. For each stage, list the key points. You may also want to show (clearly identified) the *should/could*-know material that you can include or delete as time allows.

Details. Here you include everything to be said or done in the session. Once you have written and become familiar with your session plan, you should need to refer to the Details column only occasionally while running the session. It is there as a reserve memory bank and a guide to anyone else who must use your plan.

A session plan for a theory-session model follows on pages 93–94.

SESSION PLANNING SHEET

Program Title _____

Session Title _____

Total Time _____

Objective(s) _____

_____

_____

Visual Aids _____

Special Actions Before Session _____

_____

_____

_____

_____

Time	Modus Operandi	Main Points	Details
0 minutes			

Time	Modus Operandi	Main Points	Details

SESSION PLANNING SHEET

Program Title _Management Development_

Session Title _The Control Function_

Total Time _50 minutes_

Objective(s)
1. Describe the 4 components of a control system.
2. List and explain the specifications for control systems.

Visual Aids
1. Board
2. Overhead projector

Special Actions Before Session _none._

Time	Modus Operandi	Main Points	Details
0 minutes		INTRODUCTION	
		1. Interest and Motivate	Without controls, end up like this (cartoon
	overhead projector		on overhead transparency).
	Question	2. Check understanding	What do we mean by a "control system"?
		3. Orient	Control systems ensure that the planned
			target is achieved.
	Chart	4. Preview	In this session, we will cover these
10 minutes			training objectives
		BODY EXPLANATION No. 1	
	chalk board		PREDETERMINED STANDARD
	overhead		. The objective determined in the
	projector		planning function.
			-- A target at which to aim.
	Chalkboard		SENSOR
	overhead projector		- Gathers the information.
	Chalkboard		COMPARATOR.
	overhead projector		- compares the gathered information with
			the planned objective.
		Should know	(is the study of the relationships, i.e.,
			ratios, graphs, etc.).

Time	Modus Operandi	Main Points	Details
	Chalkboard		CORRECTIVE ACTION.
	overhead		- differentiate between symptoms and causes.
	projector		- looking at alternative courses of action.
20 minutes		could know	(Captain QVEEG vs. Will Rogers approach.)
		Activity No. 1	
	Clean Chalkboard		← Note.
21 minutes	Question		Ask to turn to clean page on their notebooks. Then ask them to explain (in writing) the 4 components.
	Question		When finished writing, call on 4 trainees to read out what they have written — one for each component.
35 Minutes			
		SUMMARY No. 1	
	Chalkboard		Write the 4 components on the chalk-board again and briefly explain them.
	Question		Are there any questions on the components of a control system?

A session plan for a skill session would be less detailed as the task breakdown provides most of the content. Consider the skill "to light a match." It would have the following task breakdown and session plan.

Task Breakdown

Objective: To light a match.

Steps	Explanatory points
1. Take the matchbox in the left hand.	So that the "striking edge" is accessible.
2. Push the inside container out.	Only half-way.
3. Select a match.	Grasp the match half-way down the shank.
4. Close the inside container.	For safety, so that the remaining matches do not ignite.
5. Scrape the matchhead against the "striking edge."	A sharp action, but not so violent that you break the match.
6. Extinguish the match when its purpose has been fulfilled.	To avoid burns and unwanted fires.
7. Dispose of dead match.	Ensure that it is disposed of safely.

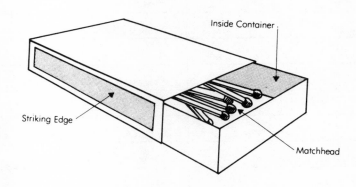

Inside Container

Striking Edge

Matchhead

SESSION PLANNING SHEET

Program Title ___ Camping Out ___

Session Title ___ Lighting a Match ___

Total Time ___ 15 minutes ___

Objective(s) ___ Given a matchbox and some matches, light a match while observing all safety procedures. ___

Visual Aids ___ None ___

Special Actions Before Session ___
1. 6 Boxes of matches
2. Portable fire extinguisher
3. Receptacles for dead matches

Time	Modus Operandi	Main Points	Details
O minutes		Introduction	- Why matches are needed - alone, no shops
			- Uses - camp fires, gas lights.
			Stress need for safety - grass and
			forest fires.
2 minutes			- Preview session.
		BODY	
2 minutes		1. Show	Demonstrate how is done.
2¾ minutes			
3 minutes		2 Show & Tell	"Will now demonstrate more slowly."
	Task Breakdown		- go through step-by-step, referring to task breakdown.
4½ minutes			- emphasize safety points.
		3. Check of Understanding	- Close matchbox & clear dead matches away.
			- ask trainees to tell me what to do (ensure that each has a turn).
6 minutes		PRACTICE	Provide each trainee with
			1. A box of matches.
			2. A receptacle for dead matches.
			3. A copy of the task breakdown.
			(N.B. Check to insure nothing flammable

Time	Modus Operandi	Main Points	Details
			is in vicinity.)
			Ensure every trainee is supervised well.
12 Minutes			
		Conclusion	
	Task Breakdown		- Briefly review steps referring to the task breakdown.
	Question		- Ask if trainees found anything DIFFICULT.
			- Any new or DIFFERENT techniques.
15 minutes			- Emphasize safety.

✔ Checkpoint: The Session Plan

Code the activity with the letter of the correct planning step.

A. Grade the content.
B. Arrange the content.
C. Select resources.
D. Select training techniques.
E. Estimate time.

1. Label this information "must know." _____

2. Choose a slide series. _____

3. Cut out the "could-know" information first. _____

4. Label this information "should know." _____

5. Identify the current knowledge of the trainee. _____

6. Move from the known to the unknown. _____

7. Draw a flowchart. _____

8. Use a dry run. _____

9. Use role plays. _____

10. Depend on questions from the trainees. _____

■ **Checkpoint Answers**

1. A   2. C   3. E   4. A   5. B   6. B   7. C   8. E   9. D   10. D

A GUIDE TO PREPARATION TIME

The session plan, then, is the complete guide to the purpose, content, and techniques of a training session. Bearing this in mind, you must allow yourself, and insist on, adequate session preparation time. As a rough guide, when session objectives are clear, when you are familiar with the content, when the training techniques will be standard, and when you have not prepared or run this session before, allow a minimum of two time units of preparation to one time unit of training session. If you have run the session before and it does not require a major re-working, a ratio of 1:1 (or perhaps even less) may be suitable. At the other extreme, when a trainer must start from scratch with respect to objectives, content, and techniques, a ratio of 10:1 is not uncommon (and 20:1 or 30:1 is occasionally necessary). Remember, time invested in getting something to work effectively is seldom wasted.

Checklist: How to Write a Session Plan———————————————————

☐ Have I specified *must*-know, *should*-know, and *could*-know material?

☐ Does the session develop in a logical order?

☐ Have I specified training techniques and aids?

☐ Are my time estimates realistic?

☐ Have I included a detailed introduction and conclusion?

☐ Is the session plan a complete guide to the purposes, content, and techniques of the training session?

☐ Would another trainer be able to successfully run this session at short notice on the basis of my session plan?

SUMMARY

A session plan is like a road map. It reminds you where you want to go and how you have decided to get there. We can use a five-step procedure to formulate our plan, and we must evolve a good layout in order to document our plan. Session plans are also useful for planning time.

Chapter 8 Doublecheck

1. List and describe the five steps for writing a session plan.

Step 1 _____

_____

_____

_____

Step 2 _____

_____

_____

_____

Step 3 _____

_____

_____

_____

Step 4 _____

_____

_____

_____

Step 5 _____

_____

_____

_____

2. Explain how you use the headings Time, Modus Operandi, Main Points, and Details to ensure that the session plan is complete and clear.

_____

_____

_____

_____

_____

_____

_____

_____

3. List the advantages of using a session plan.

_____

_____

_____

_____

_____

_____

_____

_____

■ Doublecheck Answers

1. The five-step procedure for writing a session plan is:

   Step 1. Grade the content into *must* know (material essential to the achievement of the objectives), *should* know (material that gives the trainee a clear understanding), and *could* know (material that is interesting and relevant but is not essential to a clear understanding).

   Step 2. Arrange the content in a logical order so that the trainees can easily assimilate it. This is a matter of identifying the current knowledge of trainees, present the new information in easily digested steps, and moving from the "known" to the "unknown."

   Step 3. Select the basic resources needed.

   Step 4. Select the training technique that best demonstrates each point within each logical step.

   Step 5. Estimate how much time each part of your presentation will need. Check to be sure that the sum of these times does not exceed the total time allowed for the session.

2. **Time.** When you are preparing the session, start at 0 minutes. Then enter the ending time of the introduction and the beginning and ending time for each step of each segment of the session. If you know the actual starting time of the session, write in the actual times.

   Modus Operandi. This is where you specify how you intend to get your material across to the trainees. Common entries would be "Chalkboard," "Question," and "Task breakdown."

   Main Points. The basic entries in this column would be introduction, body, and conclusion, each with its sub-headings.

   Details. Include everything to be said or done in the session.

3. The advantages of using a session plan are:

   • Reminds you of the content of the session.

   • Reminds you of the techniques to use in the session.

   • If you deviate from the planned session, it shows you where to pick up and continue the session.

   • Helps you to time the session—and to finish on time.

   • Indicates what visual aids you need to present a particular point and when you need them.

9
DEFINING MEASUREMENT CRITERIA AND TOOLS

Key Concepts

- *Outcomes*. Changes (results) from training that we can measure on different levels and in different areas.

- *Micro level*. Events and activities close to the training session.

- *Macro level*. Events and activities on an organizational level.

- *Measurement criteria*. We can define criteria in four areas: reactions, learning, behavior, and results.

- *Measurement tools*. A variety. Includes documentation from other organizational areas as well as tests composed by the trainer.

- *Tests*. These fall into two categories, subjective and objective, and must have two characteristics, reliability and validity.

Learning Objectives

After you have completed this chapter, you should be able to

- Measure outcomes to assess training impact.

- Write effective tests.

- Analyze the test situation.

- Explain how to grade a test.

MICRO/MACRO LEVELS

"Well, I've finished running the program. I know it went fairly well, so I can't see any sense wasting time and effort measuring outcomes to prove it."

Unfortunately, the attitude underlying this statement is not uncommon among trainers. But the claim that no outcomes were measured because measuring was not necessary will not get accepted. The name of the game is *measured results* (outcomes). You must define measurable outcomes in areas such as trainee performance, organization benefits, and effective use of resources, and you must show that these have been achieved in order to maintain your standing (and sometimes survival) in the organization.

The measurement of training outcomes occurs at both *micro* and *macro* levels. On the micro level (which we discuss in this chapter), we examine the training outcomes of a training program or even a training session. It has twin goals:

1. To assess the trainee development level at the end of the program.

2. To provide feedback on program content and techniques.

Thus, performing micro-level measurement is an important part of conducting a training program.

Measurement at the macro level (which we examine in a later chapter) is more likely to be the responsibility of senior trainers or the training manager. This level of analysis takes micro-level measurements as raw material, combines these with other data, and attempts to establish the benefits that the organization obtains from training. Such analyses are used to evaluate the training function, and they have an important bearing on the resources allocated to it.

Let's look now at the measurement of training outcomes at the micro level.

MEASUREMENT CRITERIA

D.L. Kirkpatrick in *A Practical Guide to Supervisory Training and Development* suggests that we should define criteria in four areas of outcomes:

1. Reaction

2. Learning

3. Behavior

4. Results

1. Reaction

Simply stated, how did the trainees react to the program or session? Did they like it? Did they hate it? We can measure this level quite easily through questionnaires or interviews during and immediately after the program. Trainees should feel that the program met their needs. If they feel it did not, then they are not likely to be motivated for further training. Moreover, the training experience could actually have been dysfunctional. This and the relative ease of measuring reaction supports evaluating this area of outcomes. But remember, *liking* a program does not guarantee that learning has occurred. So trainee reactions are really of secondary interest to the organization.

2. Learning

How much of the program content have the trainees absorbed and remembered? This can be measured relatively easily by performance or by written tests during and after the program. Note that the demonstration of learning does not guarantee that new learning will later be applied on the job.

3. Behavior

This is the payoff from training: Has the on-the-job behavior of the trainee improved? In relation to this job, is production up, waste down, equipment failure down, absenteeism down, cost down, interaction improved, morale better? Measuring behavior is more difficult than measuring reaction and learning, but we can do it through records of production, quality control, cost, and payroll, and through regular performance appraisals conducted and reported by supervisors. These measures applied *after* training parallel fairly closely the measuring criteria applied during the training needs analysis *before* training. The measuring activity is a golden opportunity for the trainer to get line management and supervision involved in what is, after all, one of their responsibilities—developing the human resources of the organization.

4. Results

Has the performance of the organization improved? Here we are looking at the same factors mentioned in the behavior area, but rather from the organizational or aggregate point of view. For the organization, this is the payoff from training.

Comment

As you work down the areas of measurement as we have listed them, the data generated from measuring become progressively more valuable but the effort required to do the measuring becomes greater, and the data more susceptible to contamination. In spite of this, you should attempt to show outcomes of training in the results area (or at least in the behavior area) rather than concentrating exclusively on the less important, but easier to measure, reaction and learning areas. By demonstrating results that have organizational value, you can enhance your function and position in the organization. The information you accumulate will also encourage regular and effective reviews of programs and will be valuable in planning your own professional development.

MEASUREMENT TOOLS

Now that we have defined some measurement criteria and areas, what tools do we measure with? Let's work with the four areas.

1. Reaction

As we have mentioned, in the reaction area the measuring tool may be a questionnaire that asks trainees for the good and bad points of a day or a session, what they liked and did not like, and so forth. Alternatively, the same questions may be asked of trainees in a less systematic fashion in informal interviews. We suggest a brief questionnaire daily, together with whatever you may gather during informal conversation with trainees. Observe the level of active participation by trainees, as this can indicate their reaction. On page 107 is a sample reaction questionnaire.

You can follow up with a more general questionnaire at the end of the program. Here you are looking for an overall reaction to the whole program. This information is useful when reviewing and/or modifying programs. Look at the questionnaire on page 108.

2,3. Learning and Behavior

In the behavior area, you can refer to the standard performance appraisals or reports conducted by the organization, for they become measuring devices if they are task-related and are performed systematically and reliably. For measuring in the learning area, standardized tests are a potentially useful form of measurement for some programs. You can purchase them if you are training in a widely recognized content area. It is much more likely, however, that as a trainer you will have to construct your own tests of training outcomes in relation to learning and behavior.

4. Results

In the area of results, you can use as measurement tools official reports and records, either of production, quality, waste, maintenance costs, absences, or others. Most organizations have these figures available or at least have the raw data from which they can be calculated. Keep an eye on these. Look for changes in results in groups, sections, or departments that have recently had training and look especially for changes that do not show up for other similar groups, sections, or departments. A change that shows up as a contrast between groups may be a result of training (provided everything else about the groups has been more or less equivalent).

DAILY QUESTIONNAIRE

Trainee's Name: _____

Date: _____

	RATINGS	Excellent	Good	Satisfactory	Marginal	Poor
Session Title: _____	Content	☐	☐	☐	☐	☐
_____	Presentation	☐	☐	☐	☐	☐
Session Title: _____	Content	☐	☐	☐	☐	☐
_____	Presentation	☐	☐	☐	☐	☐
Session Title: _____	Content	☐	☐	☐	☐	☐
_____	Presentation	☐	☐	☐	☐	☐
Session Title: _____	Content	☐	☐	☐	☐	☐
_____	Presentation	☐	☐	☐	☐	☐
Session Title: _____	Content	☐	☐	☐	☐	☐
_____	Presentation	☐	☐	☐	☐	☐

What was the high point of the day? Why?

_____

_____

_____

_____

_____

What was the low point of the day? Why?

_____

_____

_____

_____

_____

_____

PROGRAM EVALUATION SHEET

1. What were the objectives of this program?

   a. _____

   b. _____

   c. _____

2. Did these objectives reprsent the true training needs on your job?

1	**2**	**3**	**4**	**5**
Not at all	A little	A medium amount	Well represented	Exactly represented

3. How well did the program achieve its stated objectives?

1	**2**	**3**	**4**	**5**
Not at all	A little	Satisfac-torily	Very well	Exactly

4. What could be left out of the program? _____

   _____

5. What could be given less time? _____

   _____

6. What could be included in (added to) the course? _____

   _____

7. What could be given more time? _____

   _____

8. Were you able to relate the program content to what you already know?

1	**2**	**3**	**4**	**5**
Not at all	A little	A medium amount	Mostly	Always

9. Were you given sufficient opportunity to ask questions?

1	**2**	**3**	**4**	**5**
Not at all	A little	Sufficient	Slightly too much	Much too much

10. Which training techniques used on the program were effective? ineffective? ____

    _____

11. Please make any other comments you feel are appropriate.

    _____

    _____

    _____

✔ Checkpoint: Measurement Criteria and Tools

Classify each criterion with the number that identifies the area to which it applies. The areas are

  A. Reaction
  B. Learning
  C. Behavior
  D. Results

1. Did the trainees like the program? _____

2. For this trainee, has the production rate changed? _____

3. How much of the program content has this trainee absorbed? _____

4. For this department, has the production rate changed? _____

5. Let's use a questionnaire. _____

6. Let's use a test. _____

Indicate true (T) or false (F).

7. At the micro level, measurement of training outcomes might entail measuring the impact of a training session. _____

8. Measurement at the macro level can have an important bearing on the kind of resources allocated to the training function. _____

9. Questionnaires have no value as measurement tools. _____

10. Interviews are too open-ended to use as measurement tools. _____

11. For measurement in the learning and behavior areas, you can use performance appraisals. _____

12. For measurement in the results area, you can use reports and records of an organizational scope. _____

■ **Checkpoint Answers**

1. a   2. c   3. b   4. d   5. a   6. b and c   7. T   8. T   9. F   10. F   11. T   12. T

WRITING AND USING YOUR OWN TESTS

When measuring training outcomes in the areas of reaction and learning, you may find it expedient and effective to compose your own tests to fit the circumstances of your programs and your trainees.

Objective/Subjective Test Style; Test Formats

First decide what style of test is best. Can you use an objective test (where answers, responses, or activities are basically right or wrong and you need no interpretation in grading), or do the objectives of the training necessitate a subjective test? (For example, if the program requires integration and synthesis of material, you may want an essay question.) If you use a subjective test, you must of course cope with the possibility of grader bias.

How about the format? Should you use a performance, oral, or written format for the test? The following table shows some of the more common alternatives.

	Performance	Oral	Written
Objective	Make or do something to a clearly specified standard.	Repeat word perfect. True-false oral.	Multiple choice. True-false. Matching. Completion. Short answers.
Subjective	Make or do something *without* a clearly specified standard.	True-false oral. Repeat in own words. Interview.	Short answers. Essay.

Except in the specific instance of training programs with objectives that emphasize integration and synthesis, we strongly recommend that you use objective tests. In addition, since most commercial and industrial training is directed toward improving performance on the job, we suggest that you choose performance tests. A performance test is always preferable to a test of knowledge, since even a knowledgeable trainee may not apply the information to the job.

Now the advantages of training objectives become obvious. If you have specified a behavior, to a standard, under specific conditions in the training objective, you will have little difficulty in formulating a test. For example, the objective

To type a five-line paragraph without errors within two minutes.

formulates its own test. As a general guide when constructing a test, ask yourself

Can I use this test to accurately measure performance as specified in the objective?

Reliability and Validity

A test, no matter what format it uses, must have two characteristics: reliability and validity.

1. Reliability means that the test produces results that are consistent over time, assuming no new learning has occurred between testings. To increase reliability, make test items clear, concise, and complete. Also, be sure that the test can be easily administered and has a scoring system that provides fair and accurate grading (to minimize grader variation).

2. *Validity* means that the test actually measures what you want it to measure. With this in mind, design tests that relate directly to the training objectives (which preferably means tests that relate directly to on-the-job behavior).

Other Suggestions for Accuracy

Here are some additional suggestions for increasing the probability of measuring outcomes accurately.

Performance tests. Always include a clear statement of the standards required so that the trainee knows what he or she has to achieve and so that you have a yardstick for scoring the performance. Provide *all* the materials reasonably needed by the trainee, and insulate the trainee temporarily from those aspects of his or her job that could interrupt or distract his or her attention. Alternatively, if the training objectives require the trainee to deal with these pressures and problems at the end of training, then incorporate "average" interruptions, distractions, and pressures into the test.

Oral tests can easily degenerate into unreliable, impressionistic, and even prejudiced assessments unless you take certain steps. For example, prepare the questions in advance and then ask every trainee the same question in the same way. Immediately record a score for each answer. Determine this score by comparing the answer with predetermined, written criteria that define what is expected in the answer. (Do *not* mark if you have only a generalized impression of a trainee.) Be a skilled verbal communicator and listener. Do not badger or put unnecessary pressure on a trainee, unless it is your legitimate objective to examine the reactions of the trainee to stress.

Essays are relatively easy to construct and administer, but they are difficult to score reliably. Use them where an objective of the training program is analysis, or synthesis, or evaluation. If you propose to use essay questions, always write a detailed answer first. Then write a clear, concise question that includes enough cues to the trainee to elicit your "ideal" answer. Your answer then becomes a comparison point that promotes consistent grading. Utilize trainee numbers rather than names to reduce the possibility of grader bias. Grade one question for all trainees before grading other questions so as to promote consistency of grading within each question.

Short answers are basically mini-essays, so the suggestions for essays apply here as well. Short answers range in style from "Write a short paragraph about..." to "List the steps taken in the...procedure." The major advantage of short answers is that their smaller scope (compared to essays) allows for greater consistency of grading because of less subjectivity on the part of the grader. For example, a short answer will usually contain between two and four main points that are relatively easy for a grader to identify; an essay, however, may contain six or eight main points, with numerous potential sub-points for each.

Multiple-choice items pose a question (the *stem*) and provide alternative answers (usually four) from which the trainee chooses one. This type of question is best suited to measuring knowledge and comprehension, although you can also use it to test application and analysis of material. Multiple-choice tests are difficult and time-consuming (and therefore costly) to construct. You can save some time by choosing questions from the instructor's handbooks that often accompany standard textbooks or from other sources. Scoring is fast and objective. If you wish, you may adjust trainees' grades to allow for the possibility of guessing the correct answer. Apply this formula:

$$\text{Adjusted Score} = R - \frac{W}{n-1}$$

R = number of answers correct
W = number of answers incorrect
n = number of alternative answers

We do not find this procedure particularly useful, since it merely reduces the grade a trainee obtains (to a negative quantity in some instances, which the trainee finds difficult to accept). It also does not change the order of merit of trainees relative to each other. If you choose to use a correction procedure, you should inform trainees so that they can modify their answering strategies accordingly.

In writing your own multiple-choice items, use the following points as a guide:

1. Keeping the alternative answers as short as possible by including as much of the item as possible in the stem.

2. Use the minimum number of words necessary for clarity and understanding.

3. If possible, avoid statements phrased in the negative.

4. Make all alternative answers appear equally likely to the reader. (Do not use alternatives that are obviously incorrect.)

5. Make alternatives grammatically parallel and consistent with the stem.

6. Vary randomly the placement of the correct alternative within each set of alternative answers.

True-false questions give a 50 percent probability of a correct answer, even with a guess, so the usefulness of this style of question in formal assessment is limited. True-false items often prove useful, however, in quick trainee-scored tests designed to give trainees a rough measure of their learning.

Matching items test knowledge of the relationships between items of information, objects, people, tools, and so on. For example:

kookaburra   Mauritius
sparrow   Australia
dodo   North Africa
toucan   Europe
    South America
    New Zealand

As in the example, one column should contain more items than the other, so that the last pair is not obtained through elimination. Also, a matching exercise should always be complete on one page.

Completion items provide a statement with a *key* word or phrase missing. The trainee must insert the appropriate word or phrase to complete the statement. For example:

Objective written tests may use multiple choice, true-false, matching, and _____ items.

Take care to word the statement so that there is only one correct answer.

THE TESTING SITUATION

Having determined the outcomes of the training that we are interested in testing, and having defined the measurement criteria and written the test, our next step is to administer the test. We need to consider four important points:

1. Anxiety

2. Instructions

3. Environment

4. Materials

Test time is an anxiety-provoking time for trainees. Be aware of this, give as much information as possible, and be understanding about the occasional "exam nerves" outburst.

Always provide full and clear *instructions*. Specify the date, time, and place of the test, what the trainees can and/or should bring to the test with them, how long the test will last, the format of the test, and what the test will require the trainees to do.

Provide a test *environment* that is comfortable (heat, light, noise, ventilation, seating). Also provide sufficient bench or desk space to allow the trainees to spread equipment, papers, and so on conveniently.

Finally, have ready all the *materials* that trainees may need during the test session. Paper, pens, tools, and water are obvious examples. Headache tablets and towels are less obvious but often useful items to have available. Be sure that backup supplies of materials and tools are available in case any of those initially supplied to trainees prove to be sub-standard.

A little thought and preparation in these matters will assist the trainee in maximizing performance.

SCORING A TEST

The final step is scoring the test.

First, as the grader, be aware of your own expectations (or biases) in relation to length of answers, conciseness versus fullness of expression, neatness of work, use made of tools, acceptable margins of error, and degree of application of training content sought. In fairness to trainees, we suggest that you make these expectations known to trainees before test time. Also, beware of the "halo" effect. We all have our special interests and points of view, and you may give trainees who emphasize these higher scores if you are not aware of them.

Score test items according to a plan. This applies particularly to the more subjective types of questions. Without an answer plan to act as a standard, the very effort of scoring the first five answers can begin to affect the grader's attitude and consistency.

For subjective tests, grade one item for all trainees before starting to grade another item. As we have noted, this can help you to maintain a consistent standard for each question for all trainees.

Finally, when grading, avoid looking at the trainee's name. Or better still, use numbers on tests rather than names. Although he or she may try to avoid it, no grader can *guarantee* that his or her personal opinion of a particular trainee will not affect the score. Therefore, avoid identifying an answer with a trainee until you have completed the grading.

In conclusion, we must point out that this chapter is a *summary* of only the points we regard as most important to remember when working with measurement instruments. You can find numerous books (mainly in the field of education) on these topics if you wish to extend your knowledge and skills in this area. The topic is also a perennial favorite for seminars that aim to promote professional development in practicing trainers. (Remember also that we include in Chapter 26 an introduction to evaluation of training outcomes at a macro level.)

✔ Checkpoint: Writing and Using Your Own Tests

Indicate true (T) or false (F).

1. A subjective test is one where you need no interpretation in grading. _____

2. It is best to use objective tests to measure integration and synthesis of material. _____

3. A performance test is formulated by a good training objective. _____

4. In an oral test, each trainee should be asked the same question in the same way. _____

For each question, choose the correct alternative.

5. A reliable test is one that

   a. Actually measures what you want it to measure.
   b. Contains questions appropriate to the program.
   c. Gives results that are consistent over time.
   d. Is accepted by management as a meaningful test.

6. Essay questions are

   a. Easily constructed and scored.
   b. Difficult to administer.
   c. Suited to assessing recall of factual material.
   d. Used in assessing integration of material.

Match the items that belong together.

7. a. Oral test _____   1. Is useful in quick trainee-scored tests.
   b. Short answer _____   2. Requires a skilled listener.
   c. Essay _____   3. Is difficult and time-consuming to construct.
   d. Multiple-choice _____   4. Insert the appropriate word or phrase.
   e. True-false _____   5. Is especially suited to checking knowledge of relationships.
   f. Matching test _____
   g. Completion test _____

Fill in the missing words.

8. Check the test _____ to ensure trainees are comfortable.

9. Trainees may behave differently at test time because they are _____.

10. In subjective tests, there is always the possibility of grader _____.

Checklist: Measuring Training Outcomes

Did I

☐ Investigate and assess the usefulness of *all* outcome measures available in each of the reaction, learning, behavior, and results areas?

☐ Choose objective measures where possible?

REACTION QUESTIONNAIRES

Did I

☐ Obtain quantitative data (for example, ratings) from the questionnaire?

☐ Ask trainees to express opinions in their own words?

☐ Use the questionnaire to cover all matters about which I need information?

PERFORMANCE TESTS

Did I

☐ Base the performance test directly on the training objectives?

☐ Provide all the materials reasonably needed by the trainee?

☐ Decide how much "real life" job pressure to include in the test?

ORAL TESTS

Did I

☐ Prepare all questions in advance?

☐ Prepare written answers as criteria in awarding grades?

☐ Develop a system for immediately recording each answer?

☐ Use the communication and listening skills needed?

ESSAY AND SHORT ANSWER TESTS

Did I

☐ Choose an essay to assess appropriate objectives (such as analysis, synthesis, or evaluation)?

☐ Write a clear, concise question that includes enough cues to elicit an appropriate answer?

☐ Write an "ideal" answer, or a *detailed* grading plan?

☐ Plan to identify trainees by numbers instead of names?

☐ Plan to grade one question for all trainees before grading the next question?

☐ Consider my own expectations (or biases) on each question?

☐ Make my expectations known to the trainees?

MULTIPLE-CHOICE TESTS

Did I

☐ Choose multiple-choice to assess appropriate objectives (such as knowledge or comprehension)?

☐ Justify the time and cost of constructing a multiple-choice test?

☐ Consider applying a correction factor for guessing?

☐ Inform trainees of this decision?

☐ Keep the alternative answers as short as possible?

☐ Avoid statements phrased in the negative?

☐ Make all alternative answers appear equally likely to the reader?

☐ Make all alternatives grammatically parallel and consistent with the stem?

☐ Vary randomly the placement of the correct alternative?

TRUE-FALSE TESTS

Did I

☐ Choose true-false for appropriate reasons (as for quick feedback to trainees)?

☐ use the minimum number of words necessary for clarity and understanding?

☐ Avoid statements phrased in the negative?

MATCHING TESTS

Did I

☐ Choose matching to assess appropriate objectives (such as relationships)?

☐ Include more entries in one list than in the other?

☐ Complete each matching question on a single page?

COMPLETION TESTS

Did I

☐ Choose completion to assess appropriate objectives (such as knowledge or comprehension)?

☐ Omit *key* words or phrases?

☐ Check that there is only one correct answer for each omission?

☐ Include enough cues to elicit the correct response?

THE TESTING SITUATION

Did I

☐ Plan to cope with anxiety shown by trainees?
Provide full and clear instructions about:

☐ Date, time, and place of the test?

☐ What the trainees can/should bring to the test with them?

☐ How long the test will last?

☐ What the test will require trainees to do?

Check that the test environment is comfortable regarding:

☐ Temperature?

☐ Light?

☐ Noise?

☐ Ventilation?

☐ Seating?

☐ Size of work space?

Acquire all the materials that may be needed, including:

☐ Paper and pens?

☐ Tools?

☐ Raw materials?

☐ Water?

☐ Medication?

SUMMARY

A trainer must be able to show measurable outcomes in areas such as trainee performance, organization benefits, and effective use of resources in order to maintain standing in the organization. We can devise measurement criteria that apply to different areas and different levels. Measurement tools include documentation from other organizational areas as well as questionnaires and tests composed by the trainer.

Tests fall into two categories, subjective and objective, and in format may be performance-oriented, oral, or written. Before using a test, the trainer should analyze the test and grading situation.

Chapter 9 Doublecheck

1. Give one example of each of the following types of test.

   Objective performance test _____

   Objective written test _____

   Subjective oral test _____

   Subjective written test _____

   Objective oral test _____

   Subjective performance test _____

2. As an official at an athletics meet, I decide to check the sex of competitors by counting the fingers on each competitor's left hand. Comment on the reliability and validity of this test.

   _____

   _____

   _____

   _____

3. Why are the following test items less than perfect?

   a. Sweep the floor. _____

   _____

   _____

   b. Write an essay on engineering. _____

   _____

   _____

   c. In an oral test, the trainer says, "You should know the difference between weezles and woozles." _____

   _____

   _____

d. William the Conqueror's real name was

1. William Normandy.
2. William Tell.
3. William Rocquefort.
4. Billy the Kid.

_____

_____

_____

e. In some situations, _____ tests are better than _____ tests because

they allow greater _____ of _____ by the trainees.

_____

_____

_____

4. You are designing an introductory level skills program for filing clerks, and you decide to measure the outcomes of training. What measures, do you think, are appropriate at each of the following levels?

Reaction: _____

Learning: _____

Behavior: _____

Results: _____

■ Doublecheck Answers

1. a. Make or do something to a clearly specified standard.
   b. Multiple-choice, true-false, matching, completion, short answer
   c. True-false oral, repeat in own words, interview
   d. Short answer, essay
   e. Repeat word perfect, true-false oral
   f. Make or do something without a clearly specified standard.

2. Assuming I can see reasonably well and can count accurately, the reliability of this test should be perfect. Its validity, however, is doubtful.

3. a. No standards of performance or conditions are stated.
   b. The question gives no cues about what is expected. The grader must therefore accept anything "reasonable" and will not be able to grade to any clear plan.
   c. If this is a statement, it is making an assumption that may be incorrect, hence invalidating subsequent questions that build on the statement. If it is a question, it is putting undue pressure on the trainee by inferring he or she is "not good" if he or she doesn't know the difference.
   d. Billy the Kid is a throwaway, not a real alternative. William Tell is probably in the same category. This leaves a 50 percent chance of a guess being correct. (Note: The authors claim no knowledge of William's real name. Alternatives 1. and 3. were simply created for this exercise.)
   e. Too many key words missing, leaving several possible correct answers. The question does not give the trainee enough cues concerning what answers are required.

4. *Reaction.* Stated liking or disliking of program by trainees. Level of active participation. Trainee suggestions for improving program.

   Learning. Written test of procedures, etc. Simulated performance test.

   Behavior. Filing errors (incorrect insertion, incorrect storage, incorrect recall action) and filing times.

   Results. Customer complaints attributable to poor filing. Number of "lost" files. Time that "lost" files are missing. Efficiency (files handled per unit time) of paper flow.

10
GETTING TRAINING TO WORK

Key Concepts

- *Need for follow-up*. Performs a support service basic to the training function. Helps trainees to transfer learning to the job.

- *Encapsulation*. A training failure that occurs when the training experience is enclosed, as in a capsule, and not applied to the work situation. Can be caused by lack of on-the-job rewards.

- *Follow-up activities*. A basic strategy for combatting encapsulation by bringing rewards to the trainee after the training program.

Learning Objectives

After you have completed this chapter, you should be able to

- Explain the concept of encapsulation.

- List the kinds of follow-up activities suitable for a follow-up program.

- Design a follow-up program.

That's right! The chapter title does have two meanings, and both are relevant. At one level, we mean the process by which the trainee transfers learned material from the training situation back to the job. At the second (and consequent) level, the title indicates that it is only when learning is transferred to the job that training has any value through productive organizational outcomes.

For training to be worth anything at all, learning that occurs off the job must be implemented when the trainee returns to the job. Assisting the trainee to implement new learning should be regarded as an integral part of conducting training activities, a sort of after-sales service. In just the same way as you expect a surgeon to regularly check on the postoperative needs of a patient, so a trainer should expect to assist in meeting the post-course needs of trainees. These activities are collectively known as follow-up of training, and aim to prevent encapsulation of learning.

ENCAPSULATION

Often trainees will learn material in the training program but fail to improve their performance on the job. This phenomenon is known as *encapsulation of training*. The training experience is enclosed, as in a *capsule*, and not applied to the work situation. The condition may be caused by a supervisor's or peer's resistance to change, inflexibility in the system, a lack of motivation, a poorly designed learning experience (that does not facilitate transfer of learning to the job), or the inability of a trainee to cope with the tension produced by change. Whatever the cause, encapsulation is one of the major reasons that training fails to produce results.

We can to some extent explain the problem of encapsulation by examining the effect that reward systems have on learning. We all indulge in certain behaviors because these behaviors are rewarded. The basic idea of a training program is to impart new behaviors to the trainee, and during the training program, the trainer can manipulate rewards to establish new behaviors. However, often there are no rewards in the trainee's working environment to reinforce the extension of these new behaviors beyond the training program. In fact, sometimes these new behaviors are punished (for example, sarcastic comments from a defensive supervisor).

Reducing Encapsulation

To reduce encapsulation, your main weapon is a comprehensive, planned follow-up program. The basic strategy of follow-up programs is to bring rewards to the trainee after the training program. You mainly achieve this by assisting the trainee to experience success in his or her attempts to apply the new learning on the job.

Let's look first at various activities that you can incorporate into a follow-up program and then at how you can implement a follow-up program.

FOLLOW-UP ACTIVITIES

We feel that the following activities are potentially useful in follow-up.

Action Plan

During training, have each trainee (with your assistance) develop a plan to utilize aspects of the training on his or her job. Each trainee might identify three or four practical ideas presented during the program that he or she feels are applicable to his or her work situation. The trainees should consider the costs and benefits of utilizing each idea and then develop strategies and a timetable for the implementation of these changes. This action plan should then be discussed with the trainee's supervisor (and approved by him or her). In effect, it would become part of the trainee's job description when the trainee returns to work.

The major advantages of an action plan are these:

- It directly relates training to the job.

- It can be structured so that the trainee can evaluate his or her own success at implementing training.

An example of an action plan developed out of a safety program for supervisors might be to identify, investigate, and eliminate three safety hazards in the immediate work area within one month, in addition to performing normal duties.

Individual Project

A project is similar to an action plan, but it is usually broader in scope. Completion of the project may be the trainee's entire "job" for a considerable period after the training course. For example, you may give a supervisor who has just completed a safety program a project that includes an immediate survey of the entire work area in order to identify hazards. He or she may then systematically take steps to eliminate existing hazards and formulate rules and procedures to minimize the likelihood of accidents. In effect, the trainee becomes a safety officer for a period of weeks, or even months. Having completed the project, he or she returns to a standard supervisory position where safety is only one of his or her responsibilities.

To complete an assigned project, a trainee must review, consolidate, and apply material learned during training. The trainee is then more likely to use this learned material when he or she returns to his or her own job. In addition, you can use the on-the-job project to measure learning and also to generate tangible benefits (for example, a lower accident rate) for the organization.

Group Project

A group project is similar to an individual project, except here several trainees cooperate in the project. This follow-up activity is particularly useful where one of the objectives of training is the development of interpersonal skills.

Group projects have been used widely in relation to management training. For example, junior managers who have just completed a course on planning may be formed into a task force planning the introduction of a new product. The organization receives a plan of action relating to a real business problem, and the trainees have applied their new learning in an intrinsically satisfying way.

Individual Guidance and Coaching

Potentially, this is one of your most potent follow-up techniques. Its effectiveness, however, depends almost entirely on the coaching skill of the trainee's supervisor, who is usually given the role of coach because of limitations on the official trainer's time. As a result, this potentially very effective method of follow-up will fizzle out if the supervisor is an inadequate coach or does not have the time to coach.

Note that individual guidance and coaching is not the same as "looking on," where a trainee watches what to do and then does it. Guidance and coaching involves progression through a thoroughly planned set of learning experiences with a coach-to-trainee ratio of 1:1. This type of training is often used at upper levels of organizations where individuals are appointed to "understudy" the occupants of key positions by working through a carefully selected set of projects, programs, and other learning experiences.

If you have sufficient time, you can assume some aspects of the coaching role through a series of scheduled visits and inspections. If used primarily for teaching rather than evaluating, this is useful, but not as effective as "full-time" coaching by the supervisor.

Formal Sessions

This kind of session is a mini-program. Run it some time after the training program. You can use it to re-examine material that trainees have reported as difficult. Or you can use it to motivate the continued use of the concepts and skills learned in the main program. It can serve as a useful review of the original program, but it may not adequately serve the individualized needs of trainees.

Seminars and Guest Speakers

In seminars, you can bring trainees together to extend their knowledge on topics of mutual interest. You can have them prepare seminar papers themselves, or you can invite a guest speaker. Success depends on the effectiveness of the speaker and the importance of the topic to the trainees. For example, customer services programs utilizing transactional analysis (TA) characteristically omit much of TA theory. Often, however, enough is included to "whet the appetite" of trainees, and trainers find that follow-up seminars on further aspects of TA may be useful. These extend the trainees' knowledge while reiterating the core concepts of the training.

Workshops

Workshops are very popular and often effective ways of following up training. At regular workshop meetings, trainees take turns presenting their current work problems. Group members draw on the training materials plus their own experience to propose solutions to the problems. Workshops thus reinforce concepts and skills learned in training and contribute significantly to the reduction of organizational problems.

Trainers often follow up sales training programs with formal or informal workshops. The following is an example of a workshop dialogue.

Scene: Training Room. Two Salespersons (A and B)

A: I've been asked to talk about a work problem, so I chose this one. I had a terrible customer yesterday morning. He wouldn't make up his mind. I didn't know what to do.

B: "Did you try—?"

A: "Yes, and it made no difference."

B: "OK. Well, another thing I've used is—."

A: "That's interesting. Remember that the trainer said something about that in our program? Did it work for you?"

B: "Well, it seemed to. I hadn't thought of it like that, but I suppose I did do what the trainer suggested."

A: "I've got to remember to try that next time!"

B: "Me too."

Comment

The choice of the follow-up activities depends a lot on your training situation. We suggest that a combination of action plan, project, coaching, and/or workshops is likely to produce good results because in these the trainee is actively learning about immediate work problems. Mature trainees will often be able to give you sound guidance on what type of follow-up they would find most useful.

✔ Checkpoint: Follow-Up Activities

Indicate true (T) or false (F), or fill in the blank.

1. Encapsulation refers to a training failure in which a trainee seems unable to transfer a learned behavior to the job situation. _____

2. The basic strategy in combatting encapsulation is to bring _____ to the trainee on the job.

3. Resistance to change is a significant cause of encapsulation. _____

4. An action plan focuses on a few practical ideas developed by the trainee for application on the job. _____

5. An action plan permits a trainee to evaluate his or her own success at _____ training.

6. A project is similar to an action plan but narrower in scope. _____

7. Group projects are particularly useful when one of the training objectives is the development of interpersonal skills. _____

8. Coaching is an ineffective follow-up activity if performed by someone other than the trainer. _____

9. Scheduled visits to the workplace by the trainer can support the coaching role. _____

10. Formal follow-up sessions are particularly sensitive to the individual learning needs of trainees. _____

■ **Checkpoint Answers**

1. T   2. rewards   3. T   4. T   5. implementing   6. F   7. T   8. F   9. T   10. F

IMPLEMENTING FOLLOW-UP

Trainers often find that the implementation of a follow-up training program is beset with difficulties. While each situation requires its own specific strategies, we offer the following suggestions.

First, convince top management of the value of training (including follow-up). Keep in mind that training should be seen to have management's support. This will not eliminate obstructions based on precedent or cost, but it will reduce them.

Second, inform all trainees and their supervisors of the follow-up requirement well before the commencement of a training program. This allows the supervisor to plan work allocation to accommodate the follow-up activity. Through discussions, set a "psychological contract" in which both the trainee and the supervisor are aware of and accept the requirements placed on them by the follow-up activity.

Finally, it is sometimes possible to minimize the time and resource cost of follow-up training by selecting as trainees individuals who are motivated to apply new approaches to their job and who have in the past shown persistence and even tenacity in aspects of their performance. Such individuals are less likely to encapsulate their training in the face of contrary pressures and will need less support through follow-up activities.

A warning about the last suggestion is in order, however. Note that while selecting trainees this way will reduce the costs and problems of follow-up, it runs counter to the requirements of a scientific evaluation of training effectiveness. As a trainer, you will have to weigh the costs and benefits and base your decision on the method of selecting trainees according to the requirements of your situation.

Checklist: Planning Follow-Up Activities

Did I

☐ Minimize all external factors that contribute to encapsulation of training?

☐ Provide resources to allow follow-up activities for all training programs?

☐ Plan follow-up activities as part of the development of the initial program?

☐ Inform supervisors about both the training program and the follow-up activities? Negotiate suitable arrangements with them? If necessary, invoke the support of top management?

☐ Minimize factors internal to the program that might contribute to the encapsulation of training? Attempt to involve trainees in actively preparing to meet their perceived work problems?

☐ Consult with trainees regarding the nature of the follow-up activities?

☐ Organize and implement the follow-up activities, again involving trainees in actively solving their perceived work problems? Utilize appropriate principles of learning?

☐ Promote, and be available for, continued trainer-trainee contact? Visit the workplace, and involve the supervisor in on-the-job coaching, if possible?

SUMMARY

Follow-up activities are a necessary support to training. They help the trainee to apply the training on the job and reduce the possibility of training encapsulation. We have described a variety of follow-up activities suitable for an effective follow-up program. The trainer must analyze the training and at-work situations to define an appropriate program.

Chapter 10 Doublecheck

Indicate true (T) or false (F), or fill in the blank.

1. To help support follow-up activities, try to convince _____ management of the value of training.

2. Inform all trainees and their supervisors of the follow-up requirement _____ the commencement of the training program.

3. A trainer must learn to assess the training situation and then tailor follow-up strategies to fit it. _____

4. What is encapsulation of training?

   _____

   _____

   _____

   _____

   _____

5. Encapsulation will be reduced if trainees are given rewards for applying their learning to the job. List some rewards that may be effective.

   _____

   _____

   _____

   _____

   _____

6. List ways in which an action plan is superior to a formal session for follow-up.

   _____

   _____

   _____

   _____

7. What is coaching?

_____

_____

_____

_____

_____

8. How would you implement follow-up?

_____

_____

_____

_____

_____

■ Doublecheck Answers

1. top

2. before

3. T

4. A training failure that occurs when training is learned but is enclosed (as in a capsule) and not applied to the work situation.

5. Encouragement from the supervisor. Recognition of good work by the supervisor or peers. Achievement in the form of successfully completing a project. Extra money as a result of increased production. Being asked to help others with on-the-job training.

6. The trainee is actively involved. The trainee is working on a real problem of his or her own choosing. The trainee obtains feedback on his or her performance. The activity may produce immediate tangible benefits for the organization. The trainee's supervisor becomes involved.

7. On-the-job learning where one coach supervises the progression of one trainee through a thoroughly planned set of learning experiences.

8. Get top management's acceptance of follow-up as an integral part of training. Plan follow-up as an integral part of training programs. Inform supervisors and trainees of follow-up requirements well in advance. Get supervisors involved in follow-up activities.

III. TRAINING TECHNIQUES

11 QUESTIONS

Key Concepts

- *Value of questions.* Questions are essential tools in promoting learning. Skill in using questions is basic to good teaching and communication.

- *The question-and-answer dynamic.* Exchanges between trainer and trainee are formed by a dynamic relationship between asking, listening, and responding.

- *Kinds of questions.* We divide questions into two broad categories, open and closed.

- *Funnel-shaped questioning.* This involves using gradually more closed questions to arrive at a specific answer.

Learning Objectives

After you have completed this chapter, you should be able to

- Explain the question-and-answer dynamic.

- Recognize and use basic questioning techniques.

- Demonstrate skills in listening.

THE QUESTION-AND-ANSWER DYNAMIC

Questioning is one of the most basic and important skills that you can use. Good questions make the difference between passive trainees learning poorly and active trainees learning for themselves. Questioning is a particularly appropriate technique when you are working with mature learners, who often bring to a training session useful skills and/or information that they are willing to share if you encourage them. You can also use questions to direct and control a discussion.

Questioning is a dynamic that develops through exchange. The trainer asks a questions and the trainee listens. The trainee then responds and the trainer listens. The trainer then responds. This completes the exchange.

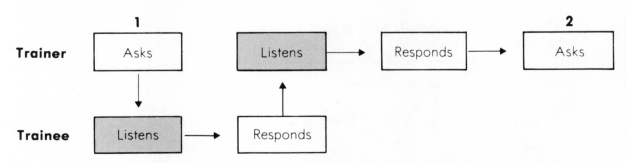

In this chapter, we will first examine the construction of questions and how to *ask* them. We will then suggest how to *listen* in order to encourage the trainee in his or her response. Finally, we will consider how the trainer can respond in order to promote learning.

THE TRAINER ASKS A QUESTION

Open vs. Closed Questions

Questions are usually divided into two broad categories that form a continuum from open to closed and from general to specific.

Open (General)   **Closed** (Specific)

Whether a question is "open" or "closed" depends on how wide the area is from which the trainee can answer. For example, the question

"What are the causes of industrial conflict in the United States?"

is quite open because the trainee can draw from a wide area of information in order to answer. But the question

"How many days of industrial conflict were there during the last financial year in the United States?"

is relatively closed because there is a limited area from which to draw an answer.

Should You Plan Questions?

We are often asked whether the trainer should preplan questions and write them into the session plan, or whether the trainer should allow the questions to be spontaneous. The answer is *both*!

It is quite easy to plan and design questions, either singly or in a series, to start each explanation step and to uncover items within each explanation step. In fact, we recommend that you make a habit of writing out questions in all your session plans. Use questions often. However, use spontaneous questions as well. They can arise out of the texture of the session and allow the trainee to inductively think out the information. This is immeasurably better than your simply giving the information to the trainees. Never pass up an opportunity to allow the trainees to work out their own answers.

During the question-and-answer exchanges, the questioning takes on what is called a *funnel* shape as the answers become more definitive. The first question is usually planned and open (and often starts the explanation step of a session segment). The next question may not necessarily be planned in detail and may be partly the result of the answer to the first question. This question is less open, with the series of questions continuing to the final closed question, which should produce a clear and specific answer.

Funnel-Shaped Series of Questions

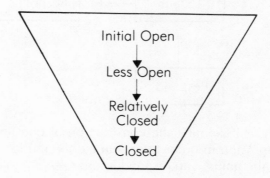

Initial Open

↓

Less Open

↓

Relatively
Closed

↓

Closed

A special use of the funnel-shaped series is a sequence of steering questions that lead a trainee down a trainer-guided path to a specific conclusion. This would be used to assist a trainee to "discover" material that more open techniques have not generated.

Questioning Techniques

We can divide questioning techniques into any number of types based upon how the questioner phrases the question. We have found that the following types are most helpful to trainers. The question type signals the technique.

The overhead question. This is undoubtedly the technique most commonly used by trainers. The essential features are

1. Ask the question.

2. Wait for a trainee to volunteer an answer.

In effect, you leave the question hanging over the trainees' heads. This technique stimulates thought and, because the trainees are unsure of who is to answer, tends to make the entire group think. For example:

"What are the functions of a management control system?"

The direct question. The essential features are

1. Name the person to answer.

2. Pause. (Count to 2.)

3. Ask the question.

This technique helps to discipline the "talker" or the "sleeper," and you can also use it for the "shy person." By stating the name first, you ensure that the person hears the question, and so you avoid potential embarrassment. For example:

"John." (Pause.) "What do you check before setting up the milling machine?"

The combined question. In order to gain the involvement of trainees but avoid a lengthy pause while trainees wait for someone else to volunteer and answer, you can use a combined question. You first pose the question to the entire group and then pick one trainee to answer. The essential features are

1. Ask the question.

2. Pause. (Count to 3.)

3. Name a person to answer.

For example:

"What are the basic components of an Apple II computer?" (Pause.) "Tom."

The relay question. Quite often, of course, the trainees will ask *you* a question. Remember, we have said previously that it is better that the trainees discover information for themselves than for you to give it to them. You can use the relay question to give trainees the opportunity to discover information already available within the group. The essential features are

1. A trainee asks the trainer a question.

2. The trainer relays this question back to the group.

For example:

> Tony: "What is the purpose of the records register?"

> Trainer: "Pat, what do *you* think is the purpose of the records register?"

The rhetorical question. The rhetorical question needs no answer. It is fairly clear that the person who posed the question is going to supply the answer, or, alternatively, feels that the answer is so obvious that is needs no elaboration. For example:

"What is wrong with the world today?"

"Who would like to finish the session early?"

We strongly suggest that you avoid overusing this kind of question; use one or two in a session to promote a little variety.

Do's

1. Distribute your questions equally among the trainees.

2. Use the direct question for the inattentive person.

3. Use easy questions at the start of the session (to get the group used to answering questions successfully) and for the shy or quiet person (to encourage participation).

4. Include questions (fully expressed) in your session plan.

5. Rephrase your question if a trainee does not understand it. Try to avoid the temptation to answer the question yourself. You can rephrase a question with simpler words, relating it more directly to an idea the trainee already understands, expanding it with some explanation, or breaking it down into component stages or questions that can be answered sequentially. Alternatively, you could redirect the question to another trainee.

Don'ts

1. Don't question the group in a regular order (for example, from right to left around the room).

2. Don't use long, involved questions.

3. Don't use leading questions. These you can often identify because they can start or end in "don't you?" For example:

> "You always identify your sales target first, don't you?"

The leading question provides the answer and therefore has little use as a learning device. Don't confuse this kind of question with the useful kind that leads a trainee to discover information or concepts.

4. Don't overuse yes/no questions. These give limited response variety and have a 50/50 chance of being answered correctly. You can effective use a yes/no question to get a "sleeper" involved initially. Then you can ask the sleeper to justify his or her answer.

5. Don't use ambiguous questions. These are questions that are open to different interpretations. They usually generate confusion and/or argument.

✔ Checkpoint: Questioning Techniques

Indicate true (T) or false (F), or fill in the blank(s).

1. Questions are usually divided into two broad categories that form a continuum from open (_____) to _____ (specific).

2. You should only use planned questions. _____

3. An open question often starts the explanation step of a theory-session segment. _____

4. The essential features of the overhead question are to ask the question and then wait for a trainee to volunteer an answer. _____

5. The relay question is used to involve the shy person. _____

6. The rhetorical question needs no answer. _____

7. Use difficult questions at the start of a session. _____

8. Rephrase your question if a trainee does not understand it. _____

9. Don't question the group in a regular order. _____

10. Don't use leading questions. _____

■ **Checkpoint Answers**

1. general, closed   2. F   3. T   4. T   5. F   6. T   7. F   8. T   9. T   10. T

THE TRAINER LISTENS

In the training situation, you must listen *actively*. You have three important goals to achieve while listening:

- To identify the meaning of what the trainee is saying.

- To encourage the trainee by indicating that he or she has your attention.

- To promote listening and listening behavior by everyone in the group.

Listening, then, is an active, goal-directed process that must be practiced to achieve competence.

1. To Listen for Meaning

There is a tendency among trainers to "help" trainees answer questions by putting words (hints) "in their mouths." The problem with this tendency is that if you do it, you assume that you know what the trainee wants to say before he or she has *actually* said it. A more productive approach is to allow the trainee to have his or her say first and then to check that you have really understood the meaning by feeding back for verification a summary of the main points of the answer. This process is called *reflecting* (or *reflection*), and it tends to markedly decrease misunderstanding.

2. To Encourage the Trainee

While listening to a response, use non-verbal messages to indicate to the speaker that he or she has your attention. The primary way of doing this is to face the speaker and maintain appropriate eye contact. The amount of eye contact that is "good" varies between individuals, but we suggest that you take your cues from the speaker. Be prepared to look at the speaker's eyes (or nose, if you find eye contact stressful) while he or she is looking at you. As soon as he or she glances away, you can do likewise, while being ready to re-establish eye contact if the speaker looks back at you.

In addition, you can use non-verbal signs of approval (for example, smiles or nods) at appropriate places to indicate that you are paying attention and to reward the trainee for having attempted to answer.

3. To Promote Listening and Listening Behavior

One way of promoting listening and good listening behavior is to ask the trainee who is answering to speak up. Another is to ask everyone else to be quiet. Phrase these requests carefully so that the obvious intention is to promote learning. Adult learners will often reject an autocratic approach.

A less obvious but very useful tactic is to actually move away from the speaker. As long as you indicate that you are still paying attention (by maintaining eye contact), the speaker will usually compensate for the increased distance by speaking more loudly, thus allowing the entire group to hear the response.

An additional useful tactic is to make a habit of asking a trainee in the group to comment on an answer that another trainee has just given. The expectation that you may ask for comments on answers will do much to promote listening behavior.

THE TRAINER'S RESPONSE

Assume that you have asked a question and a trainee has answered. The way in which you comment (provide feedback) on that answer will influence how much the trainee learns from the question-and-answer exchange, and will affect the likelihood of that trainee's answering questions in the future. The future answering behavior of other trainees will also be affected.

Use the following guidelines for effective responses to assist you in maximizing learning and motivation.

In your response, highlight both good and poor parts of an answer. Analyze good parts to establish the reasons for their "goodness" and to create positive motivation in the trainee. Analyze poor parts in order to establish specific reasons for, or areas of, failure. The trainee may be able to do this with the help of appropriate questions from you. Other trainees may also help with comments.

Make your comments on poor answers answer-oriented rather than person-oriented. For example,

"That's right as far as it goes, but I think there's something missing…" *rather than*

"You left out an important point there, John."

Similarly, when the trainee answers by performing a physical activity, make your comments performance-oriented rather than person-oriented. For example,

"The gasket blew because it wasn't aligned correctly with the guides…" *rather than*

"The gasket blew because you were too lazy to align it with the guides."

Make your comments on poor answers quite specific, and suggest strategies for improvement based on techniques or concepts already mastered by the trainee. If the trainee can diagnose these him- or herself, so much the better.

In your response, *be* realistic and objective, and try to ensure that your response is *perceived* as realistic and objective. The trainee will reject responses not meeting these criteria.

Follow feedback from you to the trainee with an effective listening behavior, so that the trainee can express his or her own perception of the learning problem. Remember, mature trainees have opinions about their learning, and they like to have their opinions taken into consideration.

Modify your response to suit the situation. In particular, individualize feedback to meet the different needs of each trainee. For example, some trainees "fold up" under very mild criticism, while other trainees have a "tough skin" and are unaffected by even sharp criticism.

Finally, always try to reinforce the behavior of attempting to answer a question. Do this quite apart from the acceptability of the content of the answer. For example,

"Thanks for that answer, Tammy. Now let's look at what you have said…"

This rewarding of the behavior of answering is very important, especially when the content of the answer is wrong or partly wrong. If you simply deal with the wrongness of the content without rewarding the behavior of answering, trainees will soon learn non-answering behavior. Even highly developed questioning skills will then be useless.

✔ Checkpoint: The Trainer Listens and Responds

Indicate true (T) or false (F), or fill in the blank.

1. In the training situation, the trainer must listen _____.

2. The trainer must identify the _____ of what the trainee is saying.

3. The trainer must encourage the trainee by indicating that the trainee has the trainer's _____.

4. The _____ must promote listening and listening behavior.

5. Never use non-verbal signs to encourage trainees in answers. _____

6. Mature learners tend to like autocratic approaches. _____

7. Eye contact helps to establish a listening-responding relationship. _____

8. The trainer's response should highlight both the good and the poor parts of the trainee's response. _____

9. A trainer should make sure that his or her comments on poor answers are answer-oriented rather than person-oriented. _____

10. A trainer's comments on poor answers should be specific. _____

■ **Checkpoint Answers**

1. actively   2. meaning   3. attention   4. trainer   5. F   6. F   7. T   8. T   9. T   10. T

Checklist: Questions

Questioning

☐ Did I include questions in my session plan?

☐ Did I too often find myself giving a direct answer to a trainee's question? (Use relay question.)

☐ Do most trainees switch off as soon as I ask a question? (Use combined questions, with less predictability of whom you will ask to answer.)

☐ Are there *long* pauses before questions are answered, or do I frequently have to rephrase a question? (Questions may be too difficult or complex.)

☐ Do I find that no interest exists in answering questions? (Poor trainee motivation. Look again at introduction to session.)

☐ Do some trainees answer very infrequently? (Use direct easy questions.)

☐ Do some trainees want to answer every question? (Use direct question.)

Listening

☐ Do I use non-verbal signals to indicate that I am paying attention to a speaker?

☐ Do all trainees listen to answers to questions?

☐ Do I use "reflection" to check that I have accurately understood the meaning of an answer?

Responding

☐ Do I give trainees comments on both good and poor parts of answers?

☐ Are my comments answer-oriented rather than person-oriented?

☐ Are my comments specific, realistic, and directed toward improving learning?

☐ Do I reward answering behavior, independent of the content of the answer?

SUMMARY

Questioning and questioning skills are essential to promoting good learning. We divide questions into two broad categories, open and closed. These categories roughly correspond to general and specific. Questions prepared for sessions should be explored thoroughly for potential answers, and the session plan should take account of these.

Questioning techniques are many, but we can characterize a few according to the kind of question each requires, such as the overhead question, the direct question, and the combined question.

When listening, the trainer should listen actively and encourage the trainee to realize that he or she has the trainer's attention. The trainer should also encourage good listening behavior in the group.

Chapter 11 Doublecheck

1. Read the questions and then identify in the blank the type of question. Then describe the effect of using the question.

   a. "Do we have any idea what that action cost us?" (Pause.) "Yes, we do." _____

   _____

   _____

   b. "I think that these points are the best, don't you?" _____

   _____

   _____

   c. "What use is wet sand in the metal casting process?" (Pause.) "Alan?" _____

   _____

   _____

   d. "Did you only find one solution to the problem?" _____

   _____

   _____

   e. "Julie, why do bees sting?" _____

   _____

   _____

   f. (Joe) "Why?" (Trainer) "Can anyone suggest a solution to Joe's problem?" _____

   _____

   _____

2. What goals should the trainer have while listening actively to the trainee, and how can the trainer achieve these goals?

   _____

   _____

3. Indicate whether the following trainer responses are effective or not. If not, explain why. How could the response be improved?

a. "You just don't seem to be able to understand. The computer terminal drops out because you don't seem to be able to use the program correctly!"

_____

_____

_____

_____

b. "You are correct in saying that planning is the primary management function. However, you should also recognize that the planning function overlaps with the control function. This is explained in Chapter 10 of the textbook."

_____

_____

_____

_____

c. "Well, the answer doesn't cover all the points. This is what was left out…"

_____

_____

_____

_____

■ Doublecheck Answers

1. a. Rhetorical. May gather interest. Does not produce response.

   b. Leading. Everyone agrees (at least on the surface). Doesn't promote thought.

   c. Combined. Gets all trainees to think about the question.

   d. Ambiguous. Produces more confusion and pressure than it's worth.

   e. Direct. Other trainees may not think about question. Gets Julie's attention.

   f. Relay. Relay and overhead. Gets the trainees to continue the quest for information.

2. a. To listen for meaning to decrease misunderstandings in communication. This is achieved by *reflecting* (or *reflection*), where the trainer listens to the trainee first and then checks to make sure that the meaning has really been understood by feeding back to the trainee for verification a summary of the main points of the answer.

   b. To encourage the trainee by using non-verbal messages to indicate to the speaker that he or she has the trainer's attention. This can be achieved by facing the speaker, maintaining appropriate eye contact, and using signs of approval (such as smiles and nods).

   c. To promote listening and listening behavior by carefully phrasing requests for the trainee to speak up or for other trainees to be quiet. Another useful tactic is to ask a trainee in the group to give comments on an answer that another trainee has just given.

3. a. Not effective. It is person-oriented rather than answer- and performance-oriented. A better approach would be: "The computer terminal drops out because the program is not being used correctly."

   b. This is quite an effective response, as it highlights both the good and the poor parts of the answer. It is also quite specific on the poor part and suggests where the missing information can be found.

   c. Not effective. It does not reinforce the behavior of attempting to answer the question. However, it is answer-oriented rather than person-oriented. It could be improved as follows: "Thanks for the answer, Angelo. You covered most of the points. Are there any additional points that could be made?" Notice how the trainer does not give the additional points but tries instead to extract them from the other trainees.

12
HOW TO TRAIN ON THE JOB

Key Concepts

- *On-the-job training.* Has both advantages and problems, compared with other training techniques. Is frequently preferable to off-the-job training.

- *Skill-session model.* Has an introduction, a body, and a conclusion and is based on a task breakdown.

- *Shaping.* Administering rewards for successively closer approximations to a desired behavior.

- *Reward schedule.* Plan rewards for maximum effectiveness.

- *Modeling.* We learn from watching others.

Learning Objectives

After you have completed this chapter, you should be able to

- Describe three causes of ineffective on-the-job training.

- List the advantages of on-the-job training.

- Explain the process of shaping.

- Explain reward schedules.

- Explain modeling.

- Write a plan for an on-the-job training session.

THE CONTEXT OF ON-THE-JOB TRAINING

Learning is a life-long experience. No matter how good our staff members are, they will at times come across some aspect of the job that they have not experienced before. As managers or supervisors, we must ensure that staff members are given the information and skills to deal with any unknown aspect of a job. When this training is given at the workplace by the manager, supervisor, or co-worker, we call it *on-the-job training*. Unfortunately, on-the-job training is often ineffective because

- The trainer (the supervisor or co-worker) does not have enough time.

- The trainer does not accept the responsibility to assist when asked.

- The trainer does not have the necessary training skills.

These problems relate more to the management of training than to on-the-job training techniques. With proper management, these problems can be minimized. On-the-job training then becomes a powerful tool for learning because of the following advantages:

- Immediate application of learning to the job.

- A strong emphasis on skill development.

- A trainer to trainee ratio of 1:1 (usually). This allows the trainer to give close attention to, and individualized feedback on, the trainee's performance. The trainer also has greater flexibility in the content and pace of training.

- A continuing daily relationship between trainer and trainee. This helps the trainer to monitor performance and to offer appropriate rewards over an extended period of time.

ON-THE-JOB TRAINING

Training on the job is almost always skills training; thus the skill-session model described in Chapter 4 is a good guide for on-the-job training. Let's review the skill-session model.

The Skill-Session Model

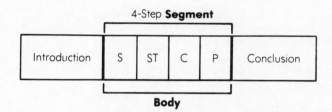

Task Breakdown

Your first step in preparing for on-the-job training is to analyze the task the trainee is to learn and to construct a task breakdown. The task breakdown lists the steps in performing the task and includes explanatory points where appropriate. It also specifies the content and sequence of the session plan for on-the-job training.

The Session

Next, you plan your training session. Following the skill-session model, you would construct a plan as follows.

Introduction

1. Orient the trainee to the session. Show how this session relates to the job or to other training sessions.

2. Motivate. Explain why this skill (and session) is important.

3. Check current knowledge of the trainee so that you don't repeat what the trainee already knows or miss anything he or she needs to know.

4. State objectives in order to give the trainee something to aim at.

Body

1. Show (S). Do the task to standard, giving the trainee a mental picture of what he or she has to do.

2. Show and tell (ST), one step at a time, following the task breakdown. Follow correct methods and emphasize safety.

3. Check understanding (C) of the trainee. Question the trainee, or perform the task to the trainee's instructions.

4. Practice (P). The trainee performs the task under your supervision. Correct errors, emphasize safety, give constructive feedback. Practice should take half of the session time.

Conclusion

1. Review the steps and key points of the session.

2. Give particular attention to difficult steps.

3. Check for any new techniques the trainee may have found.

4. Emphasize safety and standards of performance.

5. Answer any remaining questions.

6. Finish the session.

After the Session

One of the advantages of on-the-job training over every other training technique is that the trainer (that is, manager, supervisor, or co-worker) and the trainee remain in close contact for a prolonged period after the training. This gives the trainer every opportunity to monitor performance and to offer appropriate rewards on a continuing basis—which is the ultimate in follow-up of training. Since ongoing rewards are one of the virtues of on-the-job training, let's look at some important principles for administering rewards.

Shaping. Technically, shaping is the administering of rewards for successfully closer approximations to a desired behavior. In practice, it means that on the trainee's first attempt at a task, you reward any reasonable effort. As the trainee has more attempts, you expect him or her to come closer to success, and so you give rewards only for better attempts. You are gradually increasing the standard the trainee must achieve before you give a reward, until eventually the task must be done expertly before a reward is forthcoming. You have shaped the trainee's behavior to the desired standard.

Shaping can be readily seen if you observe parents and their young children. For example, when a baby at age twelve months says "Ma," the mother gives plentiful rewards (smiling, touching, hugging, attention) and happily accepts being called "Ma." In a few months, however, the mother can be observed saying "Mom, not Ma," and remaining relatively unresponsive until the baby offers a sound closer to "Mom" than "Ma." Rewards are given for closer approximations to "Mom" until, at age two years, rewards are given only for a clearly enunciated "Mom."

In a similar way, someone just starting a job is initially rewarded for performance that would usually be regarded as sub-standard. With experience on the job, the required standard is progressively raised and rewards are given accordingly.

Reward schedule. After you have established the desired behavior through shaping, do you have to reward the trainee every time the behavior occurs? This is neither practical nor efficient. You must continue to give rewards in some way, however, since unrewarded behavior will cease (extinguish). We suggest that you gradually move from a "one piece of behavior to one reward" ratio (1:1) to a 2:1 ratio, to a 5:1 ratio, and so on. In this way, you get more of the behavior for each reward. You can make your rewards even more effective by making their occurrence slightly unpredictable. For example, if you are operating on a 10:1 ratio, you might give the reward after the behavior has occurred 8 times, then after another 13 times, then after another 9 times, and so on. Alternatively, you might reward on a time basis, for example, about every half day.

Note that when the trainee has mastered the behavior, he or she may be able to assess his or her own performance and may become self-rewarding (providing, for example, a sense of achievement). Such trainees will often become relatively independent of rewards provided by the supervisor.

In summary, the on-the-job trainer plans the rewards to be given after training as well as planning the training session itself.

MODELS

Another aspect of learning that on-the-job trainers in particular must be aware of is the idea that we learn from watching others. This process is called *modeling*.

The skill-session model includes a Show step, where the trainer performs the task. The trainees then model their behavior on the trainer. This is the reason why it is so important to perform the task to standard in the Show step.

The trainer is not the only model available. An expert worker will often make a good model for trainees. Alternatively, the model may be on film or video-tape, so that the trainees can see the task repeated *exactly* as often as necessary. Think carefully about the model you show your trainees, especially in relation to the following factors that determine the probability of the model's being copied by trainees.

1. The status of the model.

2. The attractiveness of the model.

3. The rewards the model is seen to receive.

An additional important factor that influences copying involves the rewards you offer to trainees and the way in which you give them. In summary, if you are going to use a model, take the time necessary to make it a good model that will be copied by trainees.

✔ Checkpoint: On-the-Job Training

Answer true (T) or false (F), or fill in the blank.

1. On-the-job training may be ineffective because the trainer does not have enough time. _____

2. On-the-job training is almost always skills training. _____

3. The task breakdown lists the _____ in performing the task.

4. On-the-job training involves a short contact period between the trainer and the trainee. _____

5. The on-the-job trainer can offer appropriate rewards on an ongoing basis. _____

6. Learning from watching others is called _____.

7. The _____ segment in the skill session is designed to demonstrate a model performance.

8. Expert workers make good models. _____

9. If unrewarded, a behavior will _____.

10. If a trainee can assess his or her own performance, he or she may become _____.

■ **Checkpoint Answers**

1. T   2. T   3. steps   4. F   5. T   6. modeling   7. Show   8. T   9. extinguish (or cease)
10. self-rewarding

EXAMPLE OF A SESSION PLAN

Objective: Given a properly connected video monitor and video-cassette recorder, load and play a prerecorded video-tape without error.

Task Breakdown

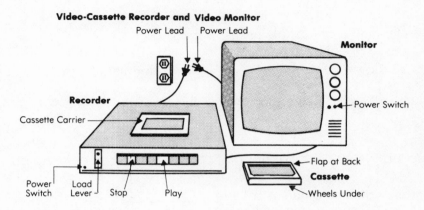

Step	Explanatory points
1. Plug power leads into wall socket.	Ensure that wall switch is "off".
2. Turn on wall switch.	
3. Turn on power switches on equipment.	Push both switches in until they click.
4. Pull load lever down.	Cassette carrier will rise.
5. Place cassette in carrier.	Make sure wheels are down and flap is at back.
6. Raise load lever.	Cassette carrier will lower. Ensure that fingers are not caught.
7. Press "Play".	Picture should appear on monitor after about 30 seconds.
8. At end of program, press "Stop".	

Action before session: Make an appointment for a 15-minute learning session. Have equipment ready. Have task breakdown for trainees.

Details of session: (see page 153)

Action after session: Check with the trainee in two days. Reward good performance. Then check again in a week (and after that, whenever you remember to do so). Encourage the trainee to get a sense of achievement from performing the task so that he or she becomes self-rewarding.

SUMMARY

On-the-job training can be very effective if planned carefully and implemented properly. It is based on the skill-session model, with particular attention given to shaping, rewards, and models.

Time	Modus Operandi	Main Points	Details
0 minutes	say	INTRODUCTION	So you want to learn to operate the video gear. that's terrific! You'll be even more indispensable around the place!
	Question		What do you know about the video gear now?
	Say		o.k. Today I want to show you how to load and play a cassette.
2 min.		BODY	
	DO	Show	I want you to watch while I do the whole thing. (DO TASK AS PER BREAKDOWN.)
	say		Now that you've seen what the whole thing is, let's break it down into parts and look at them closely.
	say & do	Show & Tell	(GO THROUGH STEPS AND EXPLANATORY POINTS FROM JOB BREAKDOWN.)
		Check understanding	Now let's see if you remember that. You tell me what to do and I'll do it. (CORRECT AS REQUIRED)
6 min.		Practice	Now I'd like you to do it several times while I watch. Here's a task breakdown to help you. (USE SHAPING, ESPECIALLY FOR SPEED OF PERFORMANCE. EMPHASIZE SAFETY.)
17 min.	Question	CONCLUSION	Can you review what we've done? Anything difficult? Can you see any better ways of doing it?
	say		Finally, remember the safety points.

Chapter 12 Doublecheck

1. What are the advantages of on-the-job training?

   _____

   _____

   _____

   _____

   _____

2. List the stages of each segment of the skill session.

   Introduction _____

   _____

   _____

   Body _____

   _____

   _____

   Conclusion _____

   _____

   _____

3. What is *shaping*?

   _____

   _____

   _____

   _____

   _____

   _____

4. Why use reward schedules?

_____

_____

_____

_____

_____

5. What factors affect the probability of a model's being copied by trainees?

_____

_____

_____

_____

_____

■ Doublecheck Answers

1. Immediate application of learning to the job. A strong emphasis on skill development. A trainer:trainee ratio of 1:1, allowing individual attention. A continuing daily relationship between trainer and trainee.

2. **Introduction.** Orient, motivate, check knowledge, state objective.
   Body. Show, show and tell, check understanding, practice.
   Conclusion. Review, difficult steps, new techniques, safety and standards, questions, finish.

3. Administering rewards for successively closer approximations to a desired behavior.

4. It is neither practical nor efficient to reward the trainee whenever the behavior occurs. Using a reward schedule, you get more of the behavior for each reward. Rewards are even more effective if they are given on a slightly unpredictable schedule.

5. The status of the model. The attractiveness of the model. The rewards the model is seen to receive. The rewards offered to trainees for copying the model.

13
HOW TO PREPARE
AND LEAD A DISCUSSION

Key Concepts

- *Discussion planning.* A discussion is not an open forum. It requires a leader and planning.

- *Discussion circumstances.* We must analyze the training situation carefully to determine whether or not the circumstances are appropriate for a discussion.

- *Session plan.* The structure and process of the discussion become part of the session plan. We have three kinds of plans: content-focus, broad-focus, and strategy-focus.

- *Discussion conduct.* The discussion leader is basically a guide. The trainer should show and generate enthusiasm and help to stabilize and direct the question-and-answer dynamics.

Learning Objectives

After you have completed this chapter, you should be able to

- Explain what a discussion is and is not.

- Explain when you should use a discussion.

- Describe the kinds of session plans you can use when preparing a discussion.

- Explain how to conduct and how to cope with the problems characteristic of a discussion.

WHAT A DISCUSSION IS AND IS NOT

"I haven't had time to do any preparation, so I'll run this morning's session as a discussion." This comment is not uncommon. But it reveals misconceptions about what a discussion is and is not. A discussion is far from being an easy way out. It must be planned, and the planning must be done with care. The greater degree of unpredictability in both the content and the process of a discussion requires you to

1. Anticipate and think through all the issues that could be generated in the discussion.

2. Decide how you can use the issues toward achieving your training objective.

When you apply the theory- or skill-session model, the structure of the body segment incorporates feedback to the trainer. However, when you use a discussion technique, you substitute a discussion for the body segment, and during the discussion you must consciously search for behavioral feedback so that you can judge whether the trainees are moving toward the session objective. Preparing and running an effective discussion is therefore at least as difficult as planning and running a more formal session.

Another misconception is the idea that a discussion tends to wander, with no clear objective. Let's dispel this idea immediately. A trainer chooses to use a discussion as a training technique because the trainer thinks it will help to achieve a specific training objective. You use a discussion to promote learning, not to relieve the tedium of other training techniques.

WHEN SHOULD YOU USE A DISCUSSION?

You may need to evaluate several factors in the training situation in order to determine whether or not a discussion is suitable. You can use a discussion

1. When your training objective incorporates either thinking and reasoning critically, exhibiting independent thinking, or improving communication and/or social skills.

2. When benefits may be gained through trainees' "discovering" content for themselves. Using this approach improves recall and motivates future learning in some trainees.

3. When the group size is appropriate. This may vary from 4 (where everyone knows something about the topic and will contribute) to 15 (where some trainees have little knowledge of the topic and you need little depth in the discussion). On most occasions, 6 to 8 participants is optimum.

4. When you want to monitor individual progress. A discussion provides an opportunity to give individual attention and to promote remedial learning if necessary.

5. When you want to form or change attitudes. Personal involvement in a group and public commitment to opinions become powerful agents for changing attitudes, and a discussion can promote both involvement and commitment.

6. When trainees have some knowledge of the topic. (Discussion of mutual ignorance will not enlighten anyone.)

7. When content covered per unit time is not critical. A discussion is seldom time-efficient. The justification for using a discussion is that the *quality* of learning counterbalances the additional time that learning may require.

8. When you are skilled in leading discussions.

Each time you consider using a discussion as a training technique, assess the training situation in relation to these factors.

PREPARING A DISCUSSION

You begin the discussion when you start planning it. We have already emphasized the importance of planning a discussion. Now let's examine how we plan it.

1. Decide your objective for the session. What specific learning outcomes should the session achieve?

2. Decide whether in the current training situation a discussion is the appropriate technique to achieve the objective.

3. Write a session plan. Most plans include:

   Outlines of the major content areas you want to cover and a likely time allocation for each area.

   Questions you can use to direct the discussion to these areas.

   Visual aids and when to use them.

Summary points.

Connections between different areas of the discussion.

Connections between the discussion and the job world.

There are three types of discussion plans: the content-focus, broad-focus, and strategy-focus.

The Content-Focus Plan

The amount of detailed content you write into your session plan will vary according to your objective, your clarity in defining the content of the discussion, and your confidence in your skills as a discussion leader. If the content of the discussion is well defined, or if you are not confident of your discussion-leading skills, then you can prepare a detailed session plan. See Session Plan Example 1 on pages 161 and 162. The session plan format is based on the format in Chapter 8. It has been modified by omitting the Modus Operandi column since discussions are based entirely on questioning.

The Broad-Focus Plan

As you become more confident in your discussion-leading skills, particularly in your ability to generate appropriate questions on the spot and your ability to flow with and effectively use contributions made by trainees, your discussion plans will usually become less detailed, as in Session Plan Example 2. Turn to Example 2 now (page 163). Note that

- A behavioral objective is still given.

- Timing is carefully planned.

- Introduction and conclusion are still outlined in some detail.

- Thought has been given to the content areas that are most likely to emerge.

Some consideration has also been given to questions that may tap the desired content, but the plan has been written to enable the skilled discussion leader to create on-the-spot questions that fit with the discussion as it develops.

The Strategy-Focus Plan

For some training situations, the actual *content* of the discussion may receive little planning effort. For example, if the objective is to modify attitudes, the skilled discussion leader will carefully plan the *process* of the discussion in order to build up a total experience for the participants that is likely to produce changes in attitudes. Session plan Example 3 (page 164) is of this type. Achieving the objective in this type of discussion depends on how well the trainer can guide the verbal interaction. The trainer should understand and be able to use principles of group dynamics and appropriate questioning techniques. Note that the format of the session plan remains the same. However, since the time needed to perform each step is difficult to predict, no attempt has been made to subdivide the total time.

Comment

The three types of discussion planned in Examples 1, 2, and 3 form a progression ranging from least to most difficult to conduct. We suggest that beginning trainers build up experience on the "preplanned in detail" (content-focus) type of discussion before moving on to the more difficult types. Specialized development in relation to group processes, questioning skills, and structured learning experiences may be advisable before a trainer becomes heavily involved in leading attitude-change discussions (strategy-focus). No matter which type of discussion you use, here are some tips:

1. For good motivation, choose topics that are recognizably important to trainees.

2. Master all relevant content yourself. (Explore any additional material that you think may be introduced by the trainees, even if it is not part of the session plan.)

3. Choose topics that trainees have some knowledge of. (You can build the discussion directly on a previous session, or set reading assignments or written reports before the discussion.)

SESSION PLANNING SHEET

Program Title __Training Officers Course__

Session Title __Using Principles of Learning__

Time Allowed __40 min__

Objective(s): __Following an introduction to the principles of Learning, trainees will list 5 principles and describe ways of using each principle to improve Learning__

Visual Aids Needed __chart paper and pens__

Action before Session ____

Time	Main Points	Details
0 minutes	ENTER: Introduce, Orient, Motivate, Review	I've just outlined the Theory of Planning. Now we will take several of the principles and show how they can be applied to improve Learning - how you can use them to make Training effective.
		First, a review. Can you tell me the 10 principles of Learning outlined in the previous session?
1 Min.		WRITE OUT THE PRINCIPLES PROPOSED) 1 PER SHEET OF CHART PAPER. IF EXACT NAME NOT GIVEN, REFER TO THIS

Time	Main Points	Details
		OTHER TRAINEES. IF A PRINCIPLE IS OMITTED, LEAD UP TO ITS "REDISCOVERY" BY DESCRIBING THE PRINCIPLE IN USE (TO JOG MEMORIES) OR BY REFERRING BACK TO A SPECIFIC EVENT IN THE PREVIOUS SESSION (e.g. "REMEMBER WHAT _ SAID ....").
5 min	BODY:	We can only deal with 5 or so in the time available. So each of you pick the 5 that you would like to during as practical training tools.
		Count votes & indicate which 5 will be dealt with in the session.
		Remember, I recommend that individually each of you should do for the 5 principles voted on what we are about to do for the 5 principles voted on. This is very important.

Time	Main Points	Details
		OF THE 10 PRINCIPLES
		LISTED BELOW DISCUSS ONLY
		THE 5 CHOSEN BY TRAINEES
		USE UP TO 5 MINS. EACH.
		RECORD ON THIS CHART
		PAPER SUGGESTED WAYS OF
		USING EACH PRINCIPLE.
8 MIN.	1. Whole or part	Q. How can you divide a
		block of material into parts?
		A. Logical steps
		A. Separation of information
		segments by applications
		or practice.
		Q. How can parts be unified
		into a whole?
		A. Activities requiring the
		integration of the parts.
		SUMMARIZE, THEN SHIFT CHART
		PAPER TO WALL
	2. Spaced learning	Q. How can we avoid
		massed learning?
		A. Rest breaks.
		A. Interspersed theory
		and activity sessions.
		SUMMARIZE THEN SHIFT
		PAPER TO WALL
	3. Active Learning	Q. (To cost a non-participant
		involved) John, what do
		you think will promote
		active learning?
		A. Questions

Time	Main Points	Details
		Assignments, projects, activities.
		A. Discussion
		Note how often activities appear
		on the list.
		SUMMARIZE, THEN SHIFT PAPER TO WALL
	4. Feedback	Q. How can trainees be
	THE 'PLAN' WOULD CONTINUE ON IN THIS STYLE, WITH FULL DETAILS OF QUESTIONS, AND ANSWERS, FOR ALL 5 PRINCIPLES.	
33 min.	(conclusion)	SUMMARIZE THEN SHIFT PAPER TO WALL
		Can anyone have anything that they
		would like clarified?
		IF SO CLARIFY (USING OTHER TRAINERS)
		IF resolved.
	Review	Now let's review this session.
		First we listed all 10 principles
		on learning, then we voted to examine
		5 of them. We suggested practical ways
		of using each of these 5 and wrote
		the suggestions on chart paper.
	Test	Now I'll give you self-feedback, see how
		many of the suggestions you can
		write down without using the chart
		papers to jog your memory.
		ALLOW 3 MINS. DISCOURAGE PEEKING
		AND LOOK AT WHAT EACH TRAINEE
		CAN REPRODUCE (FEEDBACK FOR me).
		OK. Compare what you wrote with
		what's on the wall. Remember to
		do this whole revision for the
		other 5 principles of learning.
	(2 mins.)	We will follow up this material
		when we start learning a session
40 min.	Finish	tomorrow. I'll see you then.

SESSION PLANNING SHEET

Program Title __Supervisory Development__

Session Title __Causes of Poor Performance__   Time Allowed __30 min.__

Objective(s) __List 4 possible major causes of poor performance at work, and list symptoms of each cause.__

Visual Aids Needed _____   Action before Session _____

Time	Main Points	Details
0 minutes	INTRO:	Interest - only 50% to 70% of work time is productive.
		The appropriate performance of this level — what would just 10% would be astronomical.
	Motivate	
	Orient + objective	In this session, we'll list 4 causes of poor performance at work and their symptoms. In subsequent sessions, we'll look at ways of alleviating each cause.
3 min.	BODY: Deal first with 1. motivation	OPEN QUESTION: From your experience, what causes poor performance? Do you have any idea how you couldn't cure poor? Why do they feel this way? Do they get adequate rewards? What are some symptoms of their problem?

Time	Main Points	Details
8 min.	SUMMARIZE	OPENING QUESTION — If people want to work well, but still don't perform, what might be wrong?
		How does this contribute to poor performance?
(5 min. for each of 3)	accept + discuss list. 3 of following to emerge: 2. poor job design 3. poor supervision 4. lack of ability or skill 5. group norms 6. Organizational systems	Ask in relation to each: What are some of the symptoms of this problem?
		SUMMARIZE AFTER EACH SEGMENT.
		MENTION THAT THERE MAY BE OTHER CAUSES AND THAT TRAINEES SHOULD INVESTIGATE THESE FOR THEMSELVES.
25 min.	CONCLUSION:	Any points of clarification? Summarize and test by asking the group to list the 4 causes identified and to paraphrase the discussion thereon. Point the way to future sessions.
30 min.		

SESSION PLANNING SHEET

Program Title _Management Development_

Session Title _The People Part of Management_

Time Allowed _Up to 90 min._

Objective(s) _To change the negative attitude of task-oriented managers toward the "non-productive" people aspects of the manager's task._

Visual Aids Needed

Action before Session
1. Obtain suitable case study. 2. Ensure a mixed group, that is some slightly task-oriented managers and some effective "task-and-people-oriented" managers.

Time	Main Points	Details
0 min.	INTRO	Announce purpose — to discuss case study. Distribute case study (which should be about one page) and circulate then manage using a considerable amount of time in a "people" problem with living success. Allow time for participants to read them.
7 min.	BODY	Take discussion through the following process. 1. Identify decision of strain/support to the case. 2. Analysis of responsibilities and differences 3. Identification / underlying attitudes (stereotypes).

Time	Main Points	Details
		4. Check confrontation of inappropriate attitudes. 5. Assist with development of modified attitudes. 6. Organise group support to modified attitudes. 7. Organise help in applying modified attitudes. (action plan).
Up to 90 min.	CONCLUSION	Review discussion. Give assurance of continued support. Make appointments to follow up on action plans.

164

✔ Checkpoint: The Discussion, When to Use and How to Plan

Indicate true (T) for false (F), or fill in the blank(s).

1. Before conducting a discussion, a trainer must anticipate and think through all the issues that may arise during the discussion. _____

2. We should allow discussions to wander. _____

3. A discussion is a good technique if your objective is to teach communication skills. _____

4. A discussion is a good technique if your objective is to teach social interaction. _____

5. A discussion is not a good technique for encouraging trainees to discover information. _____

6. A discussion provides an opportunity to give _____ attention.

7. A discussion provides an opportunity to promote _____ learning.

8. A content-focus plan is appropriate when you can define the _____ of the discussion.

9. A broad-focus plan is appropriate when you are confident of your _____ skills.

10. A strategy-focus plan is appropriate when your objective is to change _____.

■ **Checkpoint Answers**

1. T   2. F   3. T   4. T   5. F   6. individual   7. remedial   8. content
9. discussion-leading   10. attitudes

CONDUCTING A DISCUSSION

Using Questions

Basically, in a discussion you are a guide. You should show enthusiasm for the topic and for trainees' contributions. At the beginning, you should generate trainee enthusiasm with an interest-getting question, a trigger film, a news report, a case situation, or even an outlandish statement. In addition, you should generate contributions by posing questions. Questions should be

- Initially thought-provoking and open-ended, allowing several possible responses.

- Directed initially at the whole group.

- Redirected to individuals chosen randomly if no one has volunteered an answer after several seconds.

- Rephrased (or re-expressed in "component-part" questions) if you get no answer to the original question.

You can also use questions to tactfully handle incorrect answers. You can

- Ask for clarification.

- Ask for rephrasing in an acceptable form.

- Indicate partial correctness before asking for comments on incorrect aspects.

- Use probing questions to lead a trainee to "discover" the wrongness of an answer.

- Ask other trainees to comment.

Guidelines

Here are some general guidelines for conducting the discussion and maintaining interest and a cooperative atmosphere.

1. Keep the discussion on a clearly defined topic. You can do this by keeping the session objective firmly in mind (even displaying it in front of the group). You can use summaries to emphasize and focus on what has been covered and what is left to be covered. When your objective is to change attitudes, keep the discussion on target by moving through your planned discussion process.

2. Arrange the seating so that each participant can see all the others. This arrangement allows better use of non-verbal cues.

3. Try to create an atmosphere of cooperation and support in which trainees feel free to contribute. Use first names. Reward positive contributions, both at the time they occur and afterward, by attributing them to their source when you are summarizing. Reward mutual support activities by trainees.

4. Summarize during and at the end of the discussion in order to emphasize major points and to evaluate progress toward the objective.

5. Continually observe trainees for feedback that indicates their degree of understanding of the discussion. (For example, look for frowns, nods.)

6. Encourage the behavior of answering questions by rewarding answers before dealing with the rightness or wrongness of the content of the answers. (For example, "Thanks for giving us that information, Kylie. Let's think about it in relation to...".)

Visual Record

If it is possible, it is usually a good idea to create an ongoing visual record as a discussion progresses. The main benefits are

- Every trainee can see at a glance the main points covered so far. This prevents backtracking, and also points the way ahead. The discussion will be much more focused.

- The act of writing a contribution into the record is a simple and a powerful reward, providing the trainee feels the contribution is his or hers. To encourage this ownership, use the trainee's own word(s) if possible. If not, obtain the trainee's agreement to the word(s) you finally record.

- The need to summarize contributions into short phrases (for recording purposes) encourages attentive listening and reflection of content, which often serves the important purpose of thoroughly clarifying meaning for every participant in the discussion.

The problems that can be created by producing a visual record are

- The "power of the pen"; that is, the person who holds the pen obviously has significant power to shape the discussion.

- The act of recording a point may disrupt the flow of the discussion.

- The need to summarize contributions into short phrases (for recording purposes) may bog the discussion down.

The major methods of producing a visual record of the discussion are as follows:

- Whiteboard/chalkboard. Try to bring the board up close, so that it is almost a member of the group. The major problem is that the trainer must continually jump up and down to record items, or must stay standing (and so be a little removed from the group). A possible solution is for the trainer to stay seated with the group, while a trainee acts as scribe.

- Flip paper. Generally has the same benefits and problems as a board, but, because of its smaller size, is usually easier to manage. As sheets are filled, they can be stuck to the wall to form a complete record.

- Overhead transparency. Simply write on an acetate sheet on the overhead projector, which is left on for the duration. This is probably the easiest method to manage, because a room can usually be arranged to allow the trainer to sit beside the projector. Problems includes distracting hand shadows (which can be masked if necessary) and a strict limit on the amount of information that can be displayed at one time. A major disadvantage is that each trainee can be given a photocopy of each acetate sheet as their personal record of the discussion.

PROBLEMS AND SOLUTIONS

Here are four problem situations that can occur during discussions. Imagine that you face each situation in a discussion group you lead. Then write down either the solution that you would probably try or the solution you have observed other trainers try. Compare your solutions with ours and note carefully any new approaches. The four situations are:

1. Discussion gets out of control or off the topic.

2. Group or individual does not contribute.

3. Persistent objector or disrupter in the group.

4. Lack of preparation by trainees.

Here are some possible solutions.

1. *Discussion gets out of control or off the topic.*

   Summarize.

   Interrupt and ask a question concerning the topic.

   Use physical movement (e.g., stand up) or eye contact to dominate the group.

   Use a series of probe questions to relate the material back to the topic.

   Cut the discussion and move on to new material.

2. *Group or individual does not contribute.*

   Use a question that you know someone can answer.

   Use simple questions initially, building up slowly to more complex ones.

   Float a provocative or outlandish statement to be attacked.

   Avoid putting an individual on the spot, unless all else fails.

   Provide rewards for attempted answers. Seek non-verbal cues that indicate interest in the topic, and then invite an interested trainee to comment. (If the trainee is interested, he or she is unlikely to feel "on the spot.")

3. *Persistent objector or disrupter in the group.*

   Probe this person's statements, requesting justification or explanation.

   Encourage other trainees to comment on the disrupter's contributions.

   Reward contributions, omitting aggressive intentions, so that information becomes acceptable.

   Use group pressure on this person. Allow other trainees to tell the disrupter he or she is annoying them. Alternatively, watch for non-verbal signals among other trainees, verbalize those signals, and ask the group to confirm your statement of group feelings. Use physical movement or eye contact to dominate this person.

4. *Lack of preparation by trainees.*

   Seek to prevent this situation by using early sessions to establish an expectation that preparation will be done. For example, discuss preparation when you establish a psychological contract. Structure sessions so that trainees who do not prepare will feel that they have missed something important. For example, a discussion based on a technical article that a trainee has not read will have little meaning for the trainee. Unprepared trainees will not learn much from the session, but they may prepare for the next session.

Make the preparation interesting.

Use trainee participation (which is partly determined by the quality of preparation) as an assessment device.

Ask the trainees why they have not prepared.

Briefly summarize material that they should have prepared; then proceed with the session. (The trainees should learn the content of the session reasonably well, but they will also learn that they don't have to prepare for subsequent sessions.)

Comment

A discussion is likely to be an effective training technique when you establish appropriate objectives, plan thoroughly, use good questions, and reinforce suitable responses.

✔ Checkpoint: Conducting a Discussion

Indicate true (T) or false (F), or fill in the blank.

1. In a discussion, the leader is a _____.

2. You should always indicate quickly and strongly that an incorrect answer is wrong. _____

3. _____ are useful in keeping a discussion on the topic.

4. Being able to see the other people in a discussion is not important as long as everyone can hear. _____

5. Attributing material to its source is one way of _____ contributions.

6. If a discussion is off the topic, use a series of _____ questions to relate the material back to the topic.

7. Use a question that you know someone can answer if the group will not _____.

8. Use simple questions initially to build up a history of successfully answered questions. _____

9. Group pressure can control a persistent objector. _____

10. When setting a psychological contract, avoid discussion of preparation so as not to de-motivate trainees. _____

11. A visual record is too much trouble to be worthwhile using in a discussion. _____

■ **Checkpoint Answers**

1. guide   2. F   3. Summaries   4. F   5. rewarding   6. probe   7. contribute   8. T   9. T
10. F   11. F

Checklist: How to Lead a Discussion

Situation

☐ Is the group size suitable?

☐ Do participants have some pre-knowledge of the subject?

☐ Will all participants be able to see each other?

Leader's Preparation

☐ Do I have clear objectives?

☐ Do I have a "plan" for the learning experience?

☐ Do I have all information relevant to the learning experience at my disposal?

Introduction

☐ Is the introduction motivating, interesting?

☐ Do I show enthusiasm for the topic?

☐ Is the topic clearly stated?

Body

☐ Can I keep the discussion on the topic?

☐ Am I ready to promote participation by all group members?

☐ Can I control disruptions?

☐ Am I ready to reward positive contributions?

☐ Am I ready to reward mutual support activities by group members?

☐ Am I ready to use feedback from group members?

Conclusion

☐ Is my conclusion an overall summary?

☐ Does the conclusion relate the discussion to the objectives?

☐ Do I have summaries at strategic points in the discussion?

☐ Do I need more summaries?

A more extensive checklist in the form of a Discussion Feedback Sheet follows. You can use this form as it is or modify it to suit your requirements. It can be used as a detailed checklist before the session, or an observer can complete it to give you feedback after the session.

SUMMARY

A discussion requires a plan. The trainer, as discussion leader, is basically a guide. When considering a discussion, he or she must first define the objective, then analyze the training situation to decide whether a discussion is suitable, and lastly compose a session plan.

DISCUSSION FEEDBACK SHEET

Name _____ Date _____

Title of Session _____

Directions: Listen carefully to the session; then put a check mark in the column indicating your opinion on each question.

	No	?	Yes	N/A

Objectives
1. Did the learning experience convey information?   1
2. Did the learning experience promote critical thinking?   2
3. Did the learning experience promote improved communication skills?   3
4. Did the learning experience promote attitude change(s)?   4

Situation
5. Was the group size suitable?   5
6. Did the participants have some pre-knowledge of the subject?   6
7. Were all participants able to see each other?   7

Leader's Preparation
8. Did the leader appear to have clear objectives?   8
9. Did the leader appear to have a "plan" for the learning experience?   9
10. Did the leader have all information relevant to the learning experience at his/her disposal?   10

Introduction
11. Was the introduction motivating, interest gathering?   11
12. Did the leader show enthusiasm for the topic?   12
13. Was the problem (topic) clearly stated in the introduction?   13

Body
14. Did the leader keep the discussion on the topic?   14
15. Did the leader promote participation by all group members?   15
16. Did the leader control disruptions?   16
17. Did the leader reward positive contributions?   17
18. Did the leader reward mutual support activities by group members?   18
19. Did the leader perceive and use feedback from group members?   19
20. Was an effective visual record of the session created?   20

	No	?	Yes	N/A

Conclusion

21. Did the leader conclude the discussion with an overall summary? — 21
22. Did the conclusion relate the discussion to the objectives? — 22
23. Did the leader use summaries at strategic points in the discussion? — 23
24. Could the leader have used more summaries? — 24

Questioning Techniques

Did the leader use the following questioning techniques successfully?

25. Overhead — 25
26. Direct — 26
27. Combined — 27
28. Seeking group comment — 28
29. Dealing with unanswered questions — 29

Did the leader show listening behaviors?

30. Giving attention — 30
31. Reflecting meaning — 31

Did the leader respond to answers effectively?

32. Rewarding answering behavior — 32
33. Dealing positively with incorrect answers — 33

Other

34. Did the leader utilize non-verbal communication? — 34
35. Did the leader utilize group influence and pressure constructively? — 35
36. Did any group member feel attacked, put down? — 36
37. Was there an overall atmosphere of cooperation and support? — 37
38. Was the verbal communication satisfactory? — 38
    If "?" or "No," specify
    Volume   Pace   Pauses
    Clarity   Rhythm   Other _____
39. Were there any distracting mannerisms? — 39
    If "?" or "Yes," specify
    "Ah-has"   Finger or pen tapping
    Headscratching   Lip wetting or biting
    Ear pulling   Pacing
    Eye rubbing   Cloud gazing
    Toe tapping   Other _____

(*Continued.*)

Further comments _____

_____

_____

_____

_____

_____

_____

_____

_____

_____

Chapter 13 Doublecheck

The following is a session plan for a discussion. Read the plan and then list and briefly describe the ways in which the plan is deficient.

Discussion — Personal Safety Equipment: The Total Package

Time: 40 min.

Introduction

Body: Get items on list via questions.
       What is the function of each item?
       Any relevant personal experiences?

                         helmet
                         eyes
                         gloves
                         clothes
                         shoes

Conclusion

_____

_____

_____

_____

_____

_____

_____

■ Doublecheck Answers

1. Objective: No objective is given. From the content, we can assume it is aiming at imparting knowledge rather than changing attitudes.

2. Audience: No specification of audience (program).

3. Time: Total time given, but isn't broken down into segment times.

4. Visual aids: No mention of aids, which could easily be used in this situation.

5. Introduction: No suggestions about interesting or motivating the trainees, or relating the discussion to their experience.

6. Body: Content list is incomplete considering the title reference to "the total package." Some questions are listed, but no planned backup questions are provided. No reminder of summaries.

7. Conclusion: No reminder of appropriate sub-headings.

14
HOW TO PREPARE AND GIVE A LECTURE

Key Concepts

- *Lecture planning.* A lecture is not a speech. We must research, plan, and shape a lecture to a session objective.

- *Lecture circumstances.* We must analyze the training situation carefully to determine whether or not the circumstances are appropriate for a lecture.

- *Lecture structure.* We modify the session model by dropping the activity step from the body segment.

Learning Objectives

After you have completed this chapter, you should be able to

- Explain what a lecture is and is not.

- Explain when you should use a lecture.

- List the advantages and disadvantages of the lecture.

WHAT A LECTURE IS AND IS NOT

As a training technique, the lecture has been rather maligned. We see a dull speaker droning on while an audience nods. *But that's not a lecture.* That's simply a speaker talking to himself.

In fact, a lecture is a dynamic learning process requiring audience participation and exciting visuals.

The Structure

Let's recall the structure of the theory session from Chapter 3.

E = Explanation
A = Activity
S = Summary

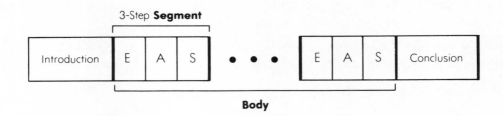

177

When you use a lecture, you modify the basic segment of the body by omitting the activity step. So, in the structure for a lecture, EAS becomes ES. Thus we have a two-step segment: explanation and summary. This modification also enables you to pack more information into the time available.

Like every training method, the lecture is effective only if you use it in the appropriate manner to achieve appropriate objectives. You have two prerequisites for preparing and delivering an effective lecture. First, research and plan it. Second, deliver it under good environmental circumstances so that its advantages are maximized and its disadvantages are minimized. (We'll explain this shortly.)

PREPARING A LECTURE

The Introduction

Use the same basic guides as when you are preparing for the theory session. First check current knowledge. This may seem a little more difficult in the lecture, but you can prepare an "audience analysis" before the session. Then

1. Try to interest the trainees. (This is perhaps more important than usual, for if you do not gain a high initial interest, your task becomes more difficult because you lack the activity step.)

2. Orient the trainees.

3. Motivate the trainees.

4. Preview the information covered in the lecture. (You can outline the structure of the lecture.)

The Body

Divide the body of the lecture into logical, easily assimilated two-step segments. Accompany each segment with visual aids and get the trainees to participate if possible. You can use the board, the overhead projector, and charts. Charts are particularly good. Their neatness and ordered presentation enhance the well-structured path of the lecture.

Getting trainees to participate is a little more difficult. Here are some suggestions:

1. Use a question-and-answer period. This often is set apart after the conclusion, but you can use the questions and answers as a way to create the summary after each explanation step.

2. Ask for examples from the trainees in order to explain or exemplify particular points.

3. Have the trainees fill out a questionnaire before the session begins. The questionnaire responses may be used to demonstrate important points in the lecture.

4. Incorporate into the lecture experiments or demonstrations to establish points. Volunteers from the audience may take part in these.

5. Finally, use plenty of examples with which the audience can identify. This process of adopting examples as "their own" incorporates some of the aspects of active learning.

The Conclusion

In the conclusion, you should review the main items of the lecture. Questions should already have been answered during the question-and-answer periods.

1. Motivate the trainees to use or at least to understand the content of the lecture.

2. Preview future sessions and provide a link with them.

3. Leave the trainees in no doubt that you have finished the lecture.

The Session Plan

On pages 181–182 is a session plan for a lecture on the basic principles of accident prevention. It is based on the assumption that the lecturer has a good knowledge of the subject, and it therefore does not provide too many content details. A lecturer who is less knowledgeable on the subject or is less confident may prefer to have a more detailed plan.

WHEN SHOULD YOU USE A LECTURE?

Any technique has advantages and disadvantages. It's up to you to make the most of the former and the minimize the latter.

In general, the lecture is most useful when you are presenting facts, information, or opinions in an organized manner and when trainee activities are not essential. It is also suitable when you have a large population of trainees (more than 20) and a short amount of time. Two important and related variables are trainee motivation and maturity. When trainees are mature and motivated, they will often learn information and ideas as readily from a lecture as from any other format. Less mature trainees, however, tend to learn better with more individualized formats.

In conclusion, problems attributed to the lecture technique are often related to the lecturer rather than the technique. You can overcome many of the disadvantages of the lecture by making the material meaningful and by being sensitive to the reactions of the trainees.

Advantages of a Lecture

1. Low cost.

2. Most adults have been taught by this method and are therefore familiar with it.

3. Ease of administration.

4. Direct and clear (if well done).

5. Conserves time.

6. Information presented in orderly fashion.

7. Can accommodate a large audience.

8. Training aids are easy to include and use.

Disadvantages

1. Basically, creates one-way communication.

2. May result in passive learners who do not have the opportunity to clarify material.

3. Insensitive to individual differences.

4. Does not provide immediate feedback to the learner.

5. Can be dull, boring.

6. Lacks group activities.

7. Effects on audience not easily determined.

8. Requires speaking ability.

9. Most people are not auditory learners and are easily distracted unless visual aids are utilized.

SESSION PLANNING SHEET

Program Title: _Safety on the Shop floor._

Session Title: _Basic Principles of Accident Prevention_

Total Time: _50 minutes_

Objective(s): _To explain the 4 basic principles of accident prevention_

Visual Aids: _____

Special Actions Before Session: _Write session title at the top of the board. Set up prepared chart with 4 basic principles._

Time	Modus Operandi	Main Points	Details
0 minutes	overhead projector	Introduction	
		1. Interest	– Show latest accident figures of factory. – We cannot continue with such high figures.
	overhead projector	2. Motivate	– Show transparency: "Accident prevention is MY responsibility." – This has to become our motto.
	Point to session	3. Orient	– A knowledge of the principles of accident prevention will help us achieve the motto. – In this lecture, I propose to cover the following basic principles of accident prevention:
			1. Safe working conditions.
			2. Safe working habits.
			3. Employee participation.
			4. Corrective action when rules ignored.
		4. Review	
	refer to prepared chart	Body: Explanation	Safe Working Conditions
	Questionnaire	Questionnaire	– Before the session you completed a questionnaire where you suggested means

Time	Modus Operandi	Main Points	Details
	overhead projector		Of ensuring safe working conditions. This transparency summarises most of them. (Explain each one)
	Switch off overhead projector		– As managers, it is our duty to ensure that these means of ensuring safe working conditions are carried out.
	Question		– Are you ... (any questions or comments?) (Deal with each question in turn)
		Summary No.1	Let's look again at the listed means of safe working conditions. (Read off transparency.)
	write 88% on board	Explanation No. 2	Safe Working Habits. Heinrich considers that 88% of all accidents result primarily from unsafe acts.
			THE PLAN WOULD CONTINUE IN THIS STYLE, WITH AN ASSESSMENT FOR EACH REMAINING BASIC PRINCIPLE OF ACCIDENT PREVENTION.
	Point to board	Summary No.3	It is therefore important that we take immediate corrective action when these are ignored.
		Conclusion	
	Switch off projector	1. Motivate	– I refer again to the latest accident figures in our factory. – These figures must come down.
	Point to chart	2. Review	– One way to achieve this is to actively follow these 4 basic principles.
		3. Future Session	The next 3 sessions look at practical ways of using these 4 principles.

Time	Modus Operandi	Main Points	Details
	overhead projector	9. Finish	— To finish: I would like to remind you of this motto: "Accident prevention is my responsibility." — Thank you for your attention — After the break, we will have a short question-and-answer period.

✔ Checkpoint: The Lecture, When and How

Identify which part of a lecture session the item belongs to. Use the letter I for *introduction*, B for *body*, C for *conclusion*.

1. Point to a chart to emphasize a fact. _____

2. Try to get the trainee's interest. _____

3. Ask for examples from the trainees to stress a point. _____

4. Preview future sessions and provide a link with them. _____

5. Orient the trainees. _____

Indicate true (T) or false (F).

6. In general, the lecture is most useful when presenting facts, information, or opinions in an organized manner. _____

7. One of the advantages of a lecture is low cost. _____

8. One of the disadvantages is that immediate feedback is lacking. _____

9. An advantage is that it tends toward one-way communication. _____

10. An advantage is that most adults have been taught by this method and are therefore familiar with it. _____

■ **Checkpoint Answers**

1. B   2. I   3. B   4. C   5. I   6. T   7. T   8. T   9. F   10. T

Checklist: How to Conduct a Lecture

SITUATION

☐ Are facts, information, or opinions to be presented in an organized manner?

☐ Are trainee activities *not* essential?

☐ Is there a large population of trainees?

☐ Are trainees motivated and mature?

LECTURER'S PREPARATION

☐ Do I have clear objectives?

☐ Are the advantages of the lecture technique maximized and the disadvantages minimized?

☐ Have I researched and planned the lecture?

INTRODUCTION

Did I

☐ Check the current knowledge of the trainees?

☐ Grab the interest of the trainees?

☐ Orient the trainees to the subject in general?

☐ Motivate the trainees?

☐ Preview the information to be covered?

BODY

☐ Did I divide the body into logical, easily assimilated two-step segments?

Explanation Steps

☐ Did I get the trainees to participate?

Did visual aids have

☐ Sufficient impact and imagination?

☐ Sufficient variety?

☐ Correct use?

Summary

☐ Were summaries presented at appropriate places in the session?

CONCLUSION

Did I

☐ Review the main items?

☐ Motivate the trainees to use or at least understand the content of the lecture?

☐ Preview future sessions and provide a link with them?

☐ Leave the trainees in no doubt that I had finished?

SUMMARY

A lecture is not a speech. It must be researched, planned, and shaped to the session objective. As when planning the discussion, we must analyze the trainees' situation carefully to determine whether or not the circumstances are appropriate for a lecture. We should know the distinctive advantages and disadvantages of the lecture format.

Chapter 14 Doublecheck

1. What specifically should you do in the introduction of the lecture?

_____

_____

_____

_____

2. How can you get trainees to participate during the body of the lecture?

_____

_____

_____

_____

3. What should you do in the conclusion of the lecture?

_____

_____

_____

_____

4. When should you use a lecture? Why?

_____

_____

_____

_____

5. List the advantages and disadvantages of a lecture.

Advantages	Disadvantages
_____	_____
_____	_____
_____	_____
_____	_____
_____	_____
_____	_____
_____	_____
_____	_____
_____	_____
_____	_____
_____	_____
_____	_____

■ Doublecheck Answers

1. Try to interest the trainees. Check trainees' current knowledge. Orient the trainees. Preview the information to be covered in the lecture.

2. Use a question-and-answer period. Ask for examples from the trainees in order to explain or exemplify particular points. Have trainees fill out a questionnaire before the session begins, and use the responses during the lecture. Incorporate into the lecture experiments or demonstrations to establish points. Use plenty of examples with which the trainees can identify.

3. Review the main items. Motivate the trainees to use or at least to understand the content of the lecture. Preview future sessions and provide a link with them. Leave the trainees in no doubt that you have finished the lecture.

4. The lecture is most useful when you are presenting facts, information, or opinions in an organized manner; when trainee activities are not essential; when you must cover a large population of trainees in a short time; when trainee motivation and maturity are high.

5. *Advantages:* Low cost. Most adults familiar with it. Ease of administration. Direct and clear. Conserves time. Information is presented in an orderly fashion. Large audience. Training aids easy to include and use.

   Disadvantages: One-way communication. May result in passive learners. Insensitive to individual differences. No immediate feedback to the learner. Can be dull, boring. Effects on audience are not easily determined. Requires speaking ability. Most people are not auditory learners.

IV. ADVANCED TECHNIQUES

15
THE CASE STUDY AND THE ROLE PLAY

Key Concepts

- *Advanced techniques.* Techniques that extend the repertoire of the trainer beyond the theory and skill sessions, the discussion, and the lecture.

- *Case study.* A problem statement (often in a narrative form) that uses a realistic situation to develop problem-solving skills.

- *Role play.* A training technique in which the trainees act (or play) the roles of the characters in a case study.

Learning Objectives

After you have completed this chapter, you should be able to

- Describe the case study and the role play.

- List the advantages and disadvantages of each.

- Explain when you should use the case study and role play.

- Discuss how you should conduct a case study and a role play.

- List and describe the steps for writing a case study and a role play.

INTRODUCING OTHER TECHNIQUES

"What other training techniques can I use?" Quite a logical question for a trainer who wants to be as effective as possible. So far we have covered the theory and skill sessions, the discussion, and the lecture. These are the basic techniques that every trainer should be able to use with confidence and skill. Unless a trainer has a thorough grounding in these basic techniques, he or she should not use more advanced techniques.

BASIC OR ADVANCED

As well as the experience of the trainer, there are at least five other variables that should be examined when deciding whether to use a basic or advanced technique. These are:

- Whether the trainers have the motivation to put in the additional energy that the advanced techniques usually require.

- Whether the trainees have a sufficient level of maturity to accept the less structured nature of the advanced techniques.

- The complexity of the topic. Those topics that have one-answer solutions (e.g., how to complete a form) are most probably better learned by the basic techniques. The advanced techniques are more suited to areas where there are many possible solutions (e.g., supervisory and management development).

- The time available. The advanced techniques tend to require more time.

- The return on investment. Because of this additional time investment, the objectives that have to be achieved should be at a deeper level (e.g., explain the "why" as well as the "how" or "identify a problem-solving process"). Additionally, when the commitment of the trainees is important, a high time investment may be justified.

In this chapter, we will discuss two of the most common advanced techniques—the case study and the role play.

THE CASE STUDY

A case study is a description of an event that involves some problem or problem situation. The description often has some narrative element together with sufficient background material to make the problem seem "real" and to allow the development of "real" solutions. The description usually has a narrow theme to ensure that the experience results in a specific educational outcome. The narrative is often followed by several questions for the trainees to ensure that this specific outcome is achieved. The case is usually presented in written form, although if appropriate, the trainer can use visual and/or audio inputs. The amount of detail may vary greatly; for example, many case studies involve about one-half of a printed page, but some can be as long as fifty pages. The case study involves some form of debriefing activity, often a small group discussion.

Example of a Case Study

Situation. As Lester Wong was returning from his coffee break at 10:45 A.M., he heard his phone ringing. Since he was expecting a call from an important client, he ran up the aisle as quickly as he could. As he entered the space between his desk and Joan Mack's desk, he tripped over a telephone cord that was suspended in mid-air between the desks. Just a few minutes earlier, Joan had shifted her telephone to Lester's desk so that she could talk to a client while she searched for some product information that was stored in Lester's filing cabinet. Although Joan had finished her call, she had not immediately returned the phone to her desk. Joan's phone is now out of order, and Lester has been taken to the local hospital to have stitches inserted in a head wound.

Questions

1. What unsafe acts can you identify?

2. What unsafe conditions were present?

3. What can be done to prevent the situation from recurring?

A discussion based on this case might have the following outline:

1. Unsafe acts

   a. Running.
   b. Shifting the phone so that the cord is suspended.
   c. Not returning the phone immediately after use.

2. Unsafe conditions

   a. If the cord is suspended, it is the wrong length.
   b. Filing reference material where it is not easily accessible to every user.

3. What can be done
   a. Lengthen cord so that it isn't suspended in mid-air.
   b. Shorten cord so that the phone can't leave Joan's desk.
   c. Store reference material where both Joan and Lester have easy access.
   d. Outlaw running in the office.
   e. Raise employees' awareness of hazards.

Advantages

The major advantages of the case study are:

- It encourages transfer of training by bringing the trainee closer to the "real" world.

- Specific theories and principles underpin most case studies but trainees "discover" these by examining a practical situation rather than simply being told about them.

- It encourages an exchange of ideas, opinions, and views between trainees thereby broadening each individual's perception and analytical process.

- The analytical process itself is emphasized (i.e., "discovered" and practiced by trainees) in addition to promoting recall of theories and principles.

- A manager must cope with a flow of information and a variety of problems on the job. Case studies tend to mirror this situation.

Disadvantages

As with most training approaches, the case study does have some disadvantages including the following:

- Because it focuses on a specific episode rather than the total situation, the case study tends to give a "tunnel view." Trainees will then fill in the background with their own individual past experiences. This can lead to widely differing solutions.

- As the people in the case study are not known personally, the trainee becomes somewhat detached because the events are happening to a stranger. This may lead to lack of commitment to solving the problem.

- In the longer, more complex case studies, the trainee can become frustrated with the sheer volume of information and the consequently slow pace of learning.

- The trainees concentrate on quick solutions rather than developing skills of analysis and application of theories.

When Should You Use a Case Study?

Use a case study when you think the trainees would be motivated by working on a "real" problem. For the case to appear "real," you must include enough data to allow realistic and meaningful conclusions. Here are other determining conditions.

1. When a training objective is to develop skills of analysis or to relate reported events to previously learned theories or concepts.

2. When the trainer has discussion, evaluation, and feedback skills.

3. When sufficient time is available for discussion of various problem solutions. The post-case discussion is probably the major factor in the learning effectiveness of

the case-study technique. Plan the discussion in advance in order to isolate and highlight the crucial points to be learned from this case.

4. The trainees have had sufficient time to read and digest the material.

CONDUCTING A CASE STUDY

When you have determined the objectives of the training session and have decided that the case-study method will achieve those objectives, you write or select an appropriate case study. Assuming that you decide to use an existing case, select one which meets the following criteria:

- The case seems "real."

- The data given allows the development of realistic solutions.

- The content of the case demonstrates the principles you wish to establish.

- The level of detail in the case study can be effectively dealt with in the time available.

When the case has been selected, then the information can be given to the trainees. The way the information is presented will depend on the case study. If it is a written case study, the trainees can be given the written material to read either before the session commences or during session time. One advantage of the written case study is that it is given to individual trainees who can then prepare it in their preferred way and at their own pace. If the case study depends on a film or video, then the trainees will most probably have to be briefed as a group.

Once the trainees have digested the information, they can then turn their attention to the questions. This activity requires the trainees to analyze and synthesize the information. Following their deliberations the trainees can then provide the answers. You have two options here:

1. The trainees can respond *individually*, either verbally or in writing. If the standard in the training objective specifies that *each* trainee has to demonstrate a certain level of skill, then you will have to opt for this alternative.

2. The trainees respond as a group, usually via a discussion. Even if it is to be a group discussion, you will find it helpful to have the trainees write down ideas individually first. The group discussion often enhances learning as the sharing of ideas provides a rich source of data and comparison.

When you are satisfied that the trainees have achieved the desired training objective, the usual concluding steps of review, clarification, and tying up loose ends can be covered. We recommend that the trainees be provided with a written summary of the main points. This summary can be pre-prepared, but there are advantages if the trainees can recognize the final printed summary as the one that developed out of the discussion. A half-day delay for typing and copying their own conclusions is usually acceptable to trainees.

THE ROLE PLAY

Role plays fall into two main categories. The first (called *preplanned*) is basically an extension of a case study. Here the problem is acted rather than just described. Trainees who are playing roles are given role descriptions (or briefings) while the other trainees are given detailed observation guides that indicate what they should look for during the role play. All participants receive a background statement. The roles that trainees are asked to play are clearly detailed and may be quite different from the trainees' usual behavior.

The second category of role play (sometimes called *spontaneous*) happens when a trainee is given a role in which he or she basically plays himself or herself, but "tries out" certain new behavior to expand his or her range of responses. For example, during a session on counseling, a role play may follow a discussion of empathy. A trainee is asked to act as a counselor and to display as much empathy as possible. In the absence of further role definition, the trainee will usually behave as he or she normally would, except for attempting to increase his or her empathetic behaviors. For spontaneous role plays, role briefings are minimal, but detailed observer's guides are required.

Example of a Role Play

Situation. A parent has come to school at the close of the day and demanded an interview with the teacher. The interview follows.

Role: Parent

You are the parent of a sixteen-year-old boy who has just received his high school report card. He is performing well in most subjects but has received a barely passing grade in science.

You believe your son is putting equal effort into all subjects, and his past academic performance is such that you are surprised at this low mark.

When questioned, your son says he does not feel comfortable with the science teacher and implies that he is being victimized because of a misunderstanding with the teacher at the beginning of the year.

You feel angry and decide to confront the teacher.

Role: Teacher

You are a teacher in a high school, teaching several subjects to different levels of students. Compared to other teachers, you have a fairly heavy work load this year.

You know that when under pressure, you occasionally become irate at students, but you believe that this does not influence the marks you give students, even though marks include a subjective estimate of the value of the student's contributions in class.

You have occasionally been the target of complaining parents in the past, but no more so than other teachers. The principal of your school respects and supports the integrity of the teachers but also wants students and parents to feel that justice is being done.

When confronted with angry parents, you try to calm them down and then solve the problem.

Observation Guide

- Observe the verbal and physical aggression.

- Observe reactions to aggression.

- Observe constructive attempts at problem-solving.

- Observe techniques for turning behavior from aggression to problem solving.

Discussion Guide

1. What parts of the interview were aggressive?

2. What reactions did this provoke? Why?

3. Was this aggression-reaction situation useful?

4. What parts of the interview were productive?

5. What was characteristic of these parts?

6. How was the transition from confrontation to a more cooperative situation managed?

7. Are these techniques applicable to other situations?

Advantages

Some of the major advantages a role play brings to a training session are:

- In common with the case study, the role play encourages transfer of training by bringing the training room closer to the "real" world.

- It is *action* oriented as the trainees observe and practice new ways of behaving. The technique demonstrates the difference between *thinking* and *doing* in that the trainee is required to carry out a thought or decision.

- It emphasizes that good human relations requires skill.

- The trainees come to understand the effects of their behavior on others.

- It can demonstrate that a person's behavior is not only dependent on his or her personality but also on the situation within which the incident takes place.

- It can create new insights by taking the trainee out of the usual sequential cognitive process and confronting him or her with new and more complex information.

The Disadvantages

You should be aware of the following problems that could occur with the role play:

- One of the major problems stems not from the role play itself but from its inept or inappropriate handling by the trainer causing negative reactions in the trainees.

- The trainees do not take the experience seriously and it degenerates into a farce.

- Irrelevant facts and issues are introduced disrupting the role play and its subsequent debriefing.

- The role playing becomes stilted because the trainees are not good actors or become self-conscious.

When Should You Use The Role Play?

You can use a role play in a number of situations and for a number of reasons:

1. When an objective is to change attitudes and/or behavior, understand the perceptions and feelings of others, or develop communication or interpersonal skills.

2. When the trainees would be motivated by working on a "real" problem.

3. When the trainer has observation, evaluation, discussion, and feedback skills. These are important in all role plays, but they are most important in the spontaneous variety. (We suggest you gain some experience with preplanned role plays before attempting to lead the spontaneous kind.)

4. When sufficient time is available for post-play analysis and discussion. To assist discussion, use observation guides for trainees not playing roles. Also, video-taping the role play can be very useful for later viewing and discussion.

CONDUCTING A ROLE PLAY

A standard pre-planned role play usually proceeds as follows:

1. The trainer introduces the role play, concentrating on setting the expectations of the trainees and promoting an atmosphere of trust. He or she checks that all trainees understand the background of the situation, that the role players understand their roles, and that the observers understand their guides.

2. The role play is enacted. The trainer encourages trainees to stay in-role (if necessary), checks that the observers are working, steps in if the role play goes off target or becomes too traumatic, and stops the play at an appropriate time.

3. The trainer conducts the post-play discussion, which is a critical stage in learning from a role play. First, trainees are "de-roled." This involves expressing feelings that are created in the role situation. This is an essential step if the role player is to objectively analyze information that will be fed back to him or her by the observers later in the discussion. The leader seeks answers from the group to a set of questions that should probe the information obtained by the observers. Crucial aspects of the learning experience are isolated and highlighted and may be related to an appropriate theory.

Combining The Case Study and The Role Play

One of the problems with long case studies is that some trainees can become bored. One way of overcoming this is to use the case study as a role play. This usually means that the case study has to be handed out some time before the session so that the trainees can assimilate the information. Then the trainees can be given specific roles within the case and be asked to develop the characters. Again, they may need to have a little time to do this. When each trainee feels comfortable in his or her role, the usual steps of conducting, "de-roling," and debriefing can be followed.

✔ Checkpoint: Conducting the Case Study and Role Play

Indicate true (T) or false (F), or fill in the blank.

1. Variables that should be examined when deciding whether to use a basic or advanced technique include trainee motivation, level of maturity of trainees, _____ of topic, _____, and return on investment.

2. The case study involves some form of debriefing activity, often a small group discussion. _____

3. Some major advantages of the case study include transfer of training, discovery learning, the exchange of ideas, the use of the _____ process, and the closeness to real-life management situations.

4. You should use a case study when the training objective is appropriate, the trainer has the skills, time is available for _____, and the trainers have sufficient opportunities to read and digest the material.

5. At the end of a session using a case study, the trainees should be provided with _____ .

6. Role plays fall into two main categories: the preplanned and the spontaneous. _____

7. The advantages of using a role play include transfer of training, _____ orientation, emphasis on skillful human relations, exploration of effects of trainees' behavior on others, recognition that this behavior is also dependent on _____, and the creation of new trainee insights.

8. You should use a role play when the training objective is appropriate, the trainees are motivated, the trainer has _____, _____, _____, and _____ skills, and sufficient time is available.

9. When conducting the post-play discussion, the trainer should ensure that the trainees are _____.

10. Trainees can become bored with long case studies. One way of overcoming this is to _____ .

■ **Checkpoint Answers**

1. complexity, time available   2. T   3. analytical   4. discussion   5. a written summary of the main points   6. T   7. action, the situation   8. observation, evaluation, discussion, feedback
9. de-roled   10. use the case study as a role play

WRITING A CASE STUDY OR ROLE PLAY

An alternative to using a published case study or role play is to write one yourself. In this way, you can ensure that the learning experience fits the training objectives and includes local material that will make the trainees feel comfortable.

We will first discuss writing a case study. The role play has a few additional considerations and these will be discussed at the end of the chapter. There are ten steps to writing a case study.

Step 1

Define the theoretical principles or skills you wish the trainees to learn. This gives the specific focus that will be emphasized in the case. It also specifies the overall aim of the case study.

Example: Define the customers and the customers' needs before making any business decision.

Step 2

Convert these theoretical principles into *training objectives* by describing the terminal behavior of the trainees that will indicate to you that they have grasped the theoretical principles. Add standard and condition statements if required.

Example:

1. Describe a customer need.

2. Explain how the decision made by the business owner is inappropriate.

Step 3

Define the population of trainees who will be using the case study. This definition should include their occupational background, culture, level of experience, and position in the company so that

- The case study can be worded at an appropriate level, and unknown jargon can be avoided.

- Attitudes and perceptions can be predicted.

- Any controversial areas not required in the case study can be avoided.

Example: Trainee managers who left high school last year and have each completed six months planned experience in three areas of the company. They have limited experience in business.

Step 4

Establish a situation that illustrates the theoretical principles or allows the trainees to develop the required skills. Brainstorm ideas, look at newspaper articles, think over your own experiences, interview other people; in general, create information. Continually focus on the training objectives to ensure that the information is relevant. Then use this information to create a short description of the situation.

Example: A business whose customers are only interested in cheap prices. The business has high overheads (possibly rental). The cheap prices do not cover these costs.

Step 5

Develop the symptoms. These are the basic building materials of the case. Create evidence that will give cues to the reader. The cues should not be so obvious that trainees are insulted, nor so obscure that they cannot be found. Provide facts, graphs, and statements from key characters that will lead the discerning trainee towards the training objective. During this stage you will need to develop the characters of the story. Make them real, with acceptable everyday names and ensure that they are human—not all bad or all good.

Example:

1. Main character: Peter is good at his trade. He decided to start up his own business a few months ago.

2. The business: an automotive repair shop.

3. The customers: mainly owners of second-hand car yards who must keep the costs on car repairs low to stay competetive.

4. How does Peter know his business is in trouble?

   - He cannot pay his bills.

   - His bank manager has advised him that he is well overdrawn.

   - Some of his creditors are complaining that his checks are being returned as unpaid.

5. He is in a modern workshop on a main road and consequently has high rental payments. He thought that the location of the workshop would attract the public. In reality, the car yards provide 80 percent of his income.

Step 6

Write the case study. Some specific points to think about include:

- Make the narrative as concise as possible by omitting unnecessary descriptions and by using graphs and figures.

- Case studies can date very quickly. Use periods of time (e.g., "one year") rather than dates (e.g., "September 1983").

- Remember the equal employment opportunity, safety, health, and other legislation. Ensure that you do not inadvertently transgress these requirements.

Example: Peter is an A-grade mechanic in his late twenties. He completed his apprenticeship and after working for the same company for ten years, he decided to start his own automotive repair business. He had always taken pride in his work, so he was very happy when he leased a clean modern workshop next to a busy main road. Although the rental payment was very high, he thought that he might attract a lot of work from the public with such a good location. Initially, he would have to rely on customers from second-hand car dealers who would not be interested in fancy locations. The work would be fairly mundane and it would be a lower return per hour, but he recognized that he had to start somewhere. Now, seven months later, he is wondering if he made the right move. He has been having some difficulty paying his bills, and three days ago his bank manager advised Peter that his bank account was badly overdrawn. To cap it all off, on the same day one of his main suppliers came in with one of Peter's checks that had "bounced." Peter's first reaction was that he should work more hours. However, his wife said "Fourteen hours a day is enough!" To see what other options he had, Peter reviewed his records for the last six months. He found that 20 percent of his income was coming from the public and 80 percent from used car dealers. "Well" thought Peter, "where do I go from here?"

Step 7

Check the written case with the training objective in Step 2 and the audience analysis in Step 3.

Step 8

Develop the questions. These should be based on the training objectives as they elicit the terminal behavior you will observe. Re-read the case study to ensure that it will lead up to the answers desired.

Example:

Question 1. Who are Peter's real customers and what is their need?

(Answer: Used car sales yards who need cheap repairs.)

Question 2. Why was Peter's decision to open in his present location incorrect?

(Answer: The rental was high. The second-hand car dealers are not interested in modern workshops on the main road, only in cheap jobs and cheap jobs do not pay high rental.)

Step 9

Prepare the debriefing activity. This will almost always take the form of a discussion, either trainer-to-trainee or in a small group. The questions at the end of the case will almost always define the structure and the process of the discussion, so little preparation is needed if you have good discussion leading skills.

Step 10

Test it! Preferably, use a sample of the trainee population for whom it was written. At the very least, allow some fellow trainers to read it. This will test it for consistency, completeness, and acceptability as well as ensuring that the desired answers to the questions develop logically from the material in the case and represent the terminal behavior required of the trainees.

Writing a Role Play

A role play is a case study plus. Usually, the trainer will provide a background statement, briefings for role players, and guides for observers whenever a preplanned role play is to be enacted. By definition, a spontaneous role play is not written beforehand, so the guides for writing a role play apply only to the preplanned type.

The background statement is basically a case study describing the situation and defining the problem, and should be written according to the guidelines outlined in the previous section. The guides for observers are equivalent to the questions at the end of a case study, and should be developed directly from the learning objectives you have specified for the role play. In this way, observers will be looking for behavior in the role players which directly indicates that the desired learning has actually occurred. The only skills required to write a role play which are not required to write a case study are those which relate to producing the actual briefings for role players.

When creating briefings for role players, consider the following points:

- Ensure that each briefing contains enough information to make the role appear "real."

- Write both positive and negative components into all roles. This closely resembles the complexity of reality, and also allows the players to identify more easily with their roles.

- The roles should be written in a way which virtually guarantees the production of the behaviors written into the observer's guide. This does not mean that the role briefings should be entirely prescriptive, but it does mean that each briefing should have a clear underlying theme (or themes) which directly relates to the content of the observer's guides.

- Depending on the acting ability of the target audience, decide on the amount of detail to be included in the role briefings. For experienced role players who also exhibit a wide range of behaviors in everyday interaction, you can safely give a fairly general description of the role (e.g., be aggressive) and allow the player to flesh out this skeleton with specific behaviors. However, for novice role players it is often advisable to offer suggestions on specific behaviors they might adopt while playing the role (e.g., be aggressive by raising your voice, or pushing the other person, or interrupting, or talking over the top of the other person).

The final step in writing a role play is to plan the debriefing procedure you will use at the end of the enactment. With a case study, this step is virtually automatic, because the debriefing will almost always be based on the end-of-case questions. With a role play, however, you must plan to accomplish several goals. First, players must be de-roled. Then observer's reports must be received and analyzed. The information thus collected should then be related to the learning principles identified at Step 1 in writing the case. Finally, some attention should be given to improving the behavior, including possibly a series of re-enactments of the role play in which various alternatives are tried and evaluated.

The debriefing is the critical part of every role play. It is at this stage that systematic learning occurs for most trainees, built on the experiential groundwork laid during the enactment. Consequently, adequate planning of the debriefing cannot be emphasized too strongly.

Following these procedures for writing case studies and role plays is useful for an experienced trainer and is strongly recommended for novice trainers. The procedures greatly increase the probability of the designed objectives being achieved, and also markedly reduce the probability of major pitfalls that from time to time bedevil case studies and role plays.

Checklist: The Case Study

☐ Did the case provide sufficient information for realistic analysis?

☐ Was the case analysis organized around a set of questions?

☐ Did I isolate and highlight crucial aspects of the case?

☐ Was appropriate theoretical material introduced in the discussions?

☐ Was there an attempt to state general principles developed out of the case?

Checklist: The Role Play

PREPARATION

Did I

☐ Choose a role play appropriate to the objective?

☐ Provide a statement of background?

☐ Provide briefings for role players?

☐ Provide observation guides for observers?

INTRODUCTION

Did I

☐ Set expectations for participants?

☐ Promote an atmosphere of trust?

ENACTMENT

Did I

☐ Encourage participants to take roles seriously?

☐ Step in if the interaction became too traumatic?

☐ Stop the role playing at an appropriate time?

POST-PLAY DISCUSSION

☐ Did I successfully de-role participants?

☐ Did I organize the discussion around a set of questions?

☐ Did I isolate and highlight crucial aspects of the role play?

☐ Was appropriate theoretical material introduced in the discussion?

☐ Was there any attempt to state general principles developed out of the role play?

Chapter 15 Doublecheck

1. What is a case study?

   _____

   _____

   _____

   _____

   _____

2. What should the trainer provide when a preplanned role play is being used?

   _____

   _____

   _____

   _____

   _____

3. List the steps in writing a case study.

   _____

   _____

   _____

   _____

   _____

4. When should you use a role play?

   _____

   _____

   _____

   _____

5. Identify the problems with how the following case study is written. (Don't try to solve the case questions.)

Case Study

Training Objectives of Case Study

1. To list the principles of learning that have not been used.
2. To understand how the training session could have been improved.

"Simple Simon was quite puzzled. He had quite enjoyed giving his theory session on 'Loading a 16mm projector.' He had stated his training objective early in the session. 'Given a 16 mm projector and a reel of film, load the projector in 3 minutes.'

He had explained everything quite clearly and had answered the spate of questions throughout the session quite well. In fact, his story about his trip to New York had created considerable positive reaction. However, none of his trainees had been able to load the projector. In fact, the last trainee had jammed the film in the projector and, despite all Simple's efforts, he still could not get it out. When Simple had left school in 1969, he tried to become a fireman. However, he found this not to his liking and after five years left the fire department to becomes a training officer. Now, two years later, he was beginning to think that he might not be a good training officer either."

Question 1. What did Simple do wrong?

Question 2. Referring to the principles of learning, discuss how this session could have been improved.

■ Doublecheck Answers

1. A statement of a problem with sufficient background data to seem real and to allow the development of a realistic solution.

2. A background statement, role descriptions, and an observer's guide.

3. a. Define theoretical principles.
    b. Convert into training objectives.
    c. Define population of trainees.
    d. Establish situation.
    e. Develop symptoms.
    f. Write case study.
    g. Check with objectives and audience analysis.
    h. Develop questions.
    i. Prepare debriefing activity.

4. A role play should be used when
    a. An objective is to change attitudes and/or behavior.
    b. Trainees would be motivated to work on a "real" problem.
    c. The trainer has the necessary skills.
    d. Sufficient time is available.

5. The problems are
    a. The second objective "To understand…" does not have an action verb.
    b. Simple Simon is not an acceptable name.
    c. Use of date "1969."
    d. Question 1 does not relate to an objective.

16
COMPUTER-BASED LEARNING

Key Concepts

- *Computer-based learning (CBL)*. Any form of learning that is delivered or managed by a computer.

- *Courseware*. The physical aspects of the training program. Disks and written material are examples.

- *Authoring system*. A sophisticated computer program that allows trainers with little knowledge of computers to create courseware.

Learning Objectives

After you have completed this chapter, you should be able to

- Define CBL, CAL, and CML.

- Outline the advantages and disadvantages of CBL.

- Evaluate off-the-shelf courseware.

- Create a CBL course in flowchart form.

- Describe the factors which might affect the implementation of CBL.

"I get so frustrated with this classroom learning. If I go fast enough to keep the bright trainees interested, everyone else gets lost. And if I go slow enough for everyone to stay in contact, half the group gets bored. I wish I could give each trainee the attention he or she requires, so that each person could progress at his or her own rate and get individual feedback on learning."

Utopia? Perhaps. But computer-based learning (CBL) has taken giant strides in the last ten years towards making the dream a reality.

Definitions

Before we look at CBL specifically, let's define some terms.

- Hardware is the actual equipment such as computer, disk drive, and monitor.

- Software is the computer program that controls and instructs the hardware.

- Courseware is the disk, booklets, and other materials which are the physical aspects of the training program itself.

It should also be noted that this chapter is different from the rest of the book, in which we have chosen to talk about training programs (a broader term) rather than training courses. In connection with CBL, however, we use the term "courses" because the term "programs" has a separate meaning in the technical language associated with computers.

WHAT IS CBL?

We have selected CBL as the broad term to cover any form of learning that is delivered or managed by a computer. The wide variety of terms in common use is summarized in the diagram below.

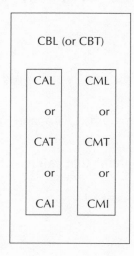

CBL (or CBT)

CAL	CML
or	or
CAT	CMT
or	or
CAI	CMI

A = assisted

B = based

C = computer

I = instruction

L = learning

M = managed

T = training or teaching

As indicated in the diagram, CBL can be divided into two major categories—computer-assisted learning (CAL) and computer-managed learning (CML). In this chapter, we will first describe CAL and CML, and then will look at the effectiveness of CBL, buying and creating CBL material, and implementing CBL.

Computer-Assisted Learning

Computer-assisted learning (CAL) occurs when a trainee accepts learning inputs from a computer. The computer may be a large mainframe device or a hand-held "games" machine or anything between these two extremes. Presently, the most frequently used machines are stand-alone micro computers of 64K to 640K RAM. These are sometimes networked to each other and/or to a mainframe computer to facilitate centralized distribution of learning material. More commonly, however, courses are distributed on floppy disks and individual trainees are free to learn wherever and whenever their stand-alone micro computer is available.

CAL may make simple or complex use of the computer. The types of learning activities that a computer is suited to are varied. In increasing order of learning sophistication, they are as follows.

1. Data reduction. This occurs when the computer is used to perform tedious and/or repetitive calculations, thus expediting other learning activities.

2. Drill (or practice). The drill is based on the assumption that certain principles or procedures are known to the trainee. Consequently, a drill program consists of question, answer, check answer, diagnose difficulties (if any), and prescribe the next question in view of the diagnosis. Spelling, math, and typing programs are usually of this type.

3. Tutorial. A tutorial program is similar to a drill, except that provision is made to give trainees additional information when they show they can answer certain questions. In a tutorial program, the computer is basically being used as a fancy page turner for a programmed instruction course.

4. Simulation. Simulation learning is qualitatively different from tutorial learning. A simulation is always based on a model of some process, equipment, or procedure. The learning objective is for trainees to learn the model via their experience of the simulation, and then to transfer their knowledge of the model to the real world. Simulation can clarify, simplify, speed up, or make safe trainee experience with a close approximation of the real task. Pilot training simulators and business games are common simulations.

5. *Problem solving.* Some CBL teaches a problem solving process. Trainees are required to develop strategies to solve a presented problem and receive scores based on the effectiveness of their strategy. Some arcade games have a significant problem solving component.

6. *Inquiry.* Based on advanced processing ability and data-base facilities, some programs receive trainee requests and produce "intelligent" answers. The trainee learns problem-solving skills plus the skill of diagnosing what information to seek when.

Computer-Managed Learning

Computer-managed learning (CML) is the ability of the computer to manage each trainee's learning activities in a way which optimizes learning. The major activities involved are as follows:

1. *Testing.* A computer is very efficient at selecting questions from a battery, administering a set of questions (a test), scoring the questions, giving feedback to trainees, and recording each trainee's results. This process is often integrated with the learning program, and becomes part of the total learning experience for trainees.

2. *Diagnosing.* Based on the results of a pretest, the computer can diagnose which units of the program particular students can bypass, because they already know the content of those units. Indeed, a student might bypass the entire program, reducing the time and energy expended and the boredom created for the trainee. Note also that the computer may direct trainees to learning programs other than CAL, such as having them view a video-tape, perform an experiment, or read an article.

3. *Reporting.* Through pre- and posttesting procedures, the computer can maintain a detailed record of each trainee's learning activity. As an example, records can include dates, time spent, pretest scores, units attempted, and posttest scores. Data on individual trainees can be made available to the trainees and/or to the trainer, and summary data (class averages, etc.) can be produced. In this way, the computer greatly assists the trainer with the otherwise complex task of keeping track of the individualized learning activities of a large number of trainees.

Linking CBL and CML

Most CBL programs use a combination of the CAL strategies outlined, and may also include some CML facilities. Our experience suggests that any course which limits itself entirely to one strategy is unlikely to produce the most efficient learning. The various learning objectives that are almost always present with any substantial course are most likely to be achieved using a variety of learning strategies, both within and outside the realm of CAL.

✔ Checkpoint: What is CBL?

Indicate true (T) or false (F), or fill in the blank.

1. Computer-based learning can be divided into two major categories—computer-assisted learning (CAL) and computer-managed learning (CML). _____

2. Computer-assisted learning occurs when a trainee accepts learning inputs from a computer. _____

3. Commonly, courses are distributed on _____ and individual trainees are free to learn wherever and whenever their stand-alone micro computer is available.

4. In increasing order of learning sophistication, the types of learning activities that a computer is suited to are data reduction, drill, _____, simulation, _____ and inquiry.

5. Simulation learning is qualitatively the same as tutorial learning. _____

6. With inquiry-based learning activities, the trainee learns problem-solving skills plus the skill of _____ what to seek when.

7. The major activities in computer managed learning are testing, _____, and reporting.

8. A computer is very efficient at administering a test, scoring a test, and giving feedback to trainees. _____

9. The computer can greatly assist the trainer with the complex task of maintaining detailed student records. _____

■ **Checkpoint Answers**

1. T   2. T   3. floppy disks   4. tutorial, problem solving   5. F   6. diagnosing
7. diagnosing   8. T   9. T

THE EFFECTIVENESS OF CBL

Recent books and journal articles report many advantages and disadvantages of CBL. We have organized the advantages and disadvantages under four headings: for learning, to trainees, to trainers, and to the organization.

Advantages

1. For learning

   a. Learning is individualized. Specifically, it is self-paced, provides variable entry levels, and provides variable learning routes. The latter two characteristics ensure that trainees learn only what they need and, in particular, are not forced to repeat material they already know.

   b. CBL provides regular, and often instant, feedback on learning performance.

   c. The two preceding characteristics tend to produce satisfaction with learning, which probably produces motivation for further learning.

   d. The interactive nature of CBL ensures active (at least to some degree) rather than passive learning.

   e. All trainees continue learning until all (with few exceptions) achieve competence.

   f. CBL allows a variety of teaching/learning strategies (e.g., simulation, problem-solving, drill), some of which may be difficult to set up and/or manage in a group learning situation.

   g. If CBL occurs on the job and/or is closely integrated with the job, transfer of learning problems are minimized.

2. To the trainee

   a. Usually, reduced time is spent to learn given material.

   b. Reduced time spent traveling to a learning center.

   c. Reduced dislocations to home life.

   d. Learning is self-paced, so the trainee has some control over the degree of boredom or stress experienced.

   e. Entry levels and course content are diagnosed to suit individual trainees.

   f. Trainees derive increased satisfaction and motivation from learning.

   g. Trainees become acquainted with computers in a relatively structured and "safe" computing environment.

3. To the trainer

   a. CBL provides more detailed and more accurate records of learning.

   b. CBL ensures increased control over what each trainee learns and how they learn it.

c. Trainers are less involved in presentations, giving more time for course development work and for individual attention to trainees. The trainer's role changes from instructor to guide and helper.

4. To the organization

   a. Average training time to achieve competence decreases.

   b. Travel time and costs decrease.

   c. On-the-job performance improves.

   d. Learning content is standardized and there is decreased variability in trainee scores. In many job situations, such standardization on the part of the human operators of complex equipment might be essential.

   e. Training can occur whenever it is needed. One person does not have to wait until enough trainees are available to justify the running of a course.

   f. Training is available to geographically scattered trainees. Learning is not something that occurs only in a centralized training center.

Disadvantages

1. For learning

   a. CBL cannot utilize all teaching/learning strategies. For example, a computer cannot give feedback on trainee practice if a modeling strategy is being used to develop interpersonal skills, and cannot monitor and/or modify group processes in a group discussion. CBL is therefore unsuitable for some training applications.

   b. Given the cost of developing CBL courseware, regular modification of material to update unstable content is not practical. The only possible exception to this is where a large central computer is being used for CBL, so that a change to the single central program directly modifies the content received by all trainees.

   c. If the actual operation of the hardware or courseware is complex (i.e., not user friendly), trainees may be so occupied making the system work that they have little spare capacity to devote to learning the content of the course.

2. To the trainee

   a. Some hardware/courseware is not user friendly.

   b. Trainees must possess the basic computer skills to operate the system.

   c. Some trainees do not like computers, even to the extent of developing computer phobia.

   d. Some trainees do not like the lack of interpersonal contact fostered by CBL.

   e. Trainees with low motivation may find it difficult to start and/or continue with a self-paced learning program.

   f. Where a computer has multiple users or uses, training may be a low priority use and consequently be continually interrupted or postponed.

3. To the trainer

   a. Since CBL provides individualized learning, it is often difficult to integrate CBL learning with group learning activities.

   b. Hardware incompatibilities dictate frustrating courseware incompatibilities.

   c. Even when using authoring systems, CBL courseware design requires complex and demanding skills. Trainers must undergo the stress of acquiring these skills, or make the stress-inducing decision to avoid them (and by inference be left behind professionally).

   d. CBL is seen as a direct threat to the employment security of some trainers.

4. To the organization

   a. CBL hardware is costly to acquire and update.

   b. CBL courseware is expensive to purchase or develop.

   c. Some CBL hardware (particularly peripheral equipment) is less than reliable in the hands of novice users.

   d. Competing uses for scarce hardware capacity often result in CBL receiving a low priority, and hence very restricted time allocations.

   e. In large, decentralized organizations, hardware incompatibility problems may be immense.

SELECTING CBL EQUIPMENT

The technical aspects of this topic are beyond the scope of this book. In fact, trainers often have little input into decisions concerning hardware because of one or more of the following:

1. The hardware is already there.

2. A "recognized expert" in the organization has final control over all computer purchases.

3. The hardware is primarily purchased for uses other than CBL.

4. Organizational policy on computer compatibility dictates certain purchases.

5. The purchase of hardware is based largely on economic (including "special deal") considerations.

In so far as you can influence hardware decisions, your order of investigation is courseware, then hardware. Your prime concern should be to acquire equipment which will run the best available (and/or predictable) courseware. Resist the temptation to go for the biggest or fastest computer simply because it is biggest or fastest. You might be embarrassed to discover that no courseware is available, or that the only courseware is of poor quality, or that there is good courseware which also runs efficiently on less expensive equipment. So evaluate courseware first, establish the requirements of the courseware, and then start looking at the hardware which meets the identified requirements.

SELECTING CBL COURSEWARE

Basically, evaluating a CBL course is exactly the same as evaluating a movie or a packaged training program on any topic. The basic questions are:

1. Does the course achieve its own objectives effectively?

2. Do the objectives of the CBL course dovetail well with the learning objectives of the trainees in my particular course or organization?

3. Does the course use its chosen medium/media to best effect?

4. Does the course use the most effective teaching/learning strategies for my context?

At a more specific level, several authors have provided detailed procedures for evaluating CBL courseware. The checklist below has been modified from Hofmeister and Maggs (1984).

Checklist: Evaluating CBL Courseware

☐ Are the course objectives fully and clearly defined?

☐ Are prerequisite knowledge and skills stated?

☐ Is the target audience clearly defined?

CONTENT

☐ Is the content presented clearly and logically?

☐ Are the structure and relationships of the content emphasized?

☐ Is the content consistent with the objectives?

☐ Are new terms explained?

☐ Are the terms used appropriate to the topic and the target learners?

DESIGN

☐ Does the program use effective teaching/learning strategies?

☐ Does the learner skip content that is already known?

☐ Does the program use the most effective display modes (color, graphics, sound)?

☐ Are displays clear?

☐ Are displays understandable?

☐ Are displays attractive?

☐ Does the program use the most effective learner response modes?

☐ Are detailed typing and complex keying minimized?

☐ Does the program contain appropriate previews and reviews?

☐ Does the program require sufficient activity by the learner?

☐ Is feedback to the learner constructive?

☐ Is feedback to the learner motivational?

☐ Can the content and design be modified to suit local needs?

COURSE MANAGEMENT

☐ Does the program include diagnostic and evaluative testing?

☐ Does the program keep records of trainee responses?

☐ Does the program produce summary statements indicating trainees' progress and class progress?

☐ Does the program suggest future learning activities for each trainee?

☐ Does the program provide both screen and printed out options for presentation of progress records?

USING THE PROGRAM

☐ Is the program "user friendly"?

☐ Are "HELP" procedures available at all times?

☐ Is the program reliable in normal use?

☐ Can trainees exit the program whenever they wish?

☐ Are non-computerized materials included in the course and are they:

- readily available?
- directly related to the course objectives?
- effectively presented?
- motivational?

✔ Checkpoint: Effectiveness of CBL and Selecting Equipment

Indicate true (T) or false (F), or fill in the blank.

1. One of the advantages of CBL is that it ensures passive learning. _____

2. Another advantage is that CBL allows a variety of teaching/learning strategies. _____

3. For the trainee, CBL can reduce time spent in learning given material and traveling to a learning center. _____

4. CBL can diagnose _____ and course content to suit individual trainees.

5. CBL gives the trainer more time for course development work and individual attention to trainees. _____

6. For the organization, a disadvantage of CBL is that training is not available to geographically scattered trainees. _____

7. CBL can monitor and modify group processes in a group discussion. _____

8. Trainees with low motivation may find it difficult to start and continue with CBL. _____

9. In so far as trainers can influence hardware decisions, the order of investigation is hardware then courseware.

10. When evaluating a CBL course, you should ensure that its objectives _____ with the learning objectives of the trainees.

■ **Checkpoint Answers**

1. F   2. T   3. T   4. entry levels   5. T   6. F   7. F   8. T   9. F   10. dovetail

AUTHORING SYSTEMS

The recent popularity of CBL is based largely on the availability of cheap, reasonable capacity micro computers and the advent of effective authoring systems. The ready availability of micros has made CBL accessible to a large population of trainees for the first time, and the existence of authoring systems has encouraged the generation of a much wider range of situation-specific courseware.

Prior to the existence of authoring systems, three major sets of skills were required to create CBL courseware. First, an expert in the subject matter (who may or may not have been a trainer) decided on the content of the course. Then an instructional design expert (usually a trainer) decided on the teaching/learning strategies to be adopted, the content that should be in each frame, and the sequence of (connections between) the frames. Finally, a programming expert coded the course into one of the standard computer languages. The process was a long and involved one if handled by a project group of three or more people. The alternative of having one person perform all three functions was seldom practical, because a single person possessing all these skills was a very rare individual indeed.

With the advent of authoring systems, things changed quite dramatically. The authoring system takes over the role of the programmer, allowing an author to create CBL courseware with virtually zero knowledge of programming. The creator of the courseware provides plain English instructions, which the authoring system converts into a program which allows the computer to function. Some authoring systems even provide assistance with aspects of the instructional design. The overall effect was that CBL created by one person rather than three became perfectly feasible, and, more importantly, many trainers who had previously been disqualified by their lack of knowledge of programming were now able to create CBL programs to meet the particular needs of their own organizations and trainees. As a result, the amount of available courseware (some good, some bad, most acceptable) increased dramatically.

The numerous authoring systems available have been reviewed elsewhere (e.g., Dean and Whitlock, 1983, p. 237–244; Hofmeister and Maggs, 1984, p. 10.1–10.15). We will briefly comment on the desirable characteristics of an authoring system.

- The system must run on the hardware you have available (assuming you already have hardware).

- Its cost per expected use should be reasonable.

- It should be flexible, allowing the design of courseware varying from drill through tutorial and simulation to inquiry.

- It should allow the use of other media, for instance, calling up video input at appropriate places if this is an effective instructional design.

- It should support color, graphics, and sound effects.

- It should support diagnostic and evaluative testing.

- It should maintain trainee records and provide individual and summary reports to the trainer.

When choosing an authoring system, assess your needs for the predictable future, and then rank order the criteria listed in order of their importance in meeting your diagnosed needs. Each available system can then be evaluated in terms of how well it fulfills your particular criteria. Finally, be prepared to spend at least half a day "playing with" each system, especially the larger ones. You can't expect to do a thorough review of a system in less time than that.

CREATING CBL COURSEWARE

In principle, the procedure for creating CBL courseware is exactly the same as the procedure for creating a good session plan. We will outline the procedure, list some guidelines on creating frames and accepting trainee input, and then give an example of a short CBL course (in flowchart form). Finally, costs of creating CBL courseware will be examined.

Designing Courseware

1. Identify the training need.

2. Develop objective (for the course).

3. Establish course content (or learning points).

4. Establish the logic of the content (what has to be learned before what).

5. Divide content into units.

6. Develop objectives for units.

7. Select appropriate teaching/learning strategies for units.

8. Divide units into teaching frames.

9. Write teaching frames.

10. Create testing (or criteria) frames.

11. Create feedback frames.

12. Create practice and/or application frames.

13. Create remedial frames and sequences.

14. Create review frames if necessary.

15. Create pretests and posttests.

16. Create introductory frames (course directions) and concluding frames.

17. Check the logic of frame interconnections and of the overall course.

To help the designer see the overall picture, especially with large courses, it is often useful to create a storyboard of the course in the same way as movie and video creators do. Frames (or screens) are written on large sheets of paper, and the connections (sequencing) between the screens are indicated by arrows. A very flexible alternative is to write frames on index cards, which can then be attached to a board on which the connecting arrows can be drawn. This allows quick and easy experimentation with the sequencing of frames until the most effective combination is discovered. The first product is a flowchart indicating all the frames and frame sequences in the course. A sample storyboard is given on pages 220 to 226.

Creating Frames

Frames in a CBL course are visual inputs to the trainee, so it is predictable that the guidelines for creating frames are essentially the same as the guidelines for creating overhead transparencies. Specifically,

• Ensure that the screen is not crowded.

• Use graphics (pictures, diagrams) where possible.

- Use clear, concise prose.

- Use signposts (headings, underlinings, symbols, colors).

- Use more frames with fewer words each in preference to fewer frames with more words each.

Additional guidelines specific to CBL frames are as follows:

- Don't put time limits on screens. Allow trainees to move forward at their own pace.

- Allow trainees to return to previous screens if they wish.

- During a teaching/learning sequence in a course, feel free to ask a question which is based on information which is still available on the screen. For testing frames, you will have to remove the relevant information before you can assess recall.

When writing a frame, remember that it has two goals. The first is to enable the trainee to effectively learn the content of the frame. The second is to motivate the trainee to continue with the course. Consequently, avoid the official, dry, boring prose that is the lifeblood of many organizations. With each and every frame, you must bring to bear training and communication techniques and skills which promote trainee interest and motivation. A variety of strategies and presentation styles, visually attractive inputs, effective feedback, and clear relevance to trainee concerns are some of the more important motivational techniques which you should strive to creatively incorporate in the design and writing of your CBL frames.

Accepting Trainee Responses

In order to achieve the objectives of the course, trainees must be encouraged to concentrate on the content of the course. If the CBL system or courseware is difficult or complex for the trainee to operate, attention is continually distracted from the learning process. Consequently, when creating CBL courseware, you should standardize and simplify the responses required of the trainee as much as possible. In computer jargon, make the course "user friendly." In particular,

- Clearly indicate how responses are to be given.

- Use a consistent format for questions.

- Use a consistent format for answers. For example, always use "yes" and "no" OR "Y" and "N"—never a mixture.

- Structure required trainee responses so that a minimum number of keystrokes is required. It is, however, better to use more keystrokes that have an obvious logic than to use fewer keystrokes based on a code system which has to be learned.

Cost of Creating CBL Courseware

Obviously, developing CBL courseware is a detailed, time-consuming, and therefore expensive process. When the necessity of trial running and then appropriately modifying a new course is taken into account, the hours required to create one hour of learning can be considerable.

In general, the development hours needed will depend on

- The complexity of the subject matter.

- The teaching/learning strategies involved (e.g., drill versus problem solving).

Sample Storyboard

(The beginning of a course titled "How To Make A Cup of Tea.")

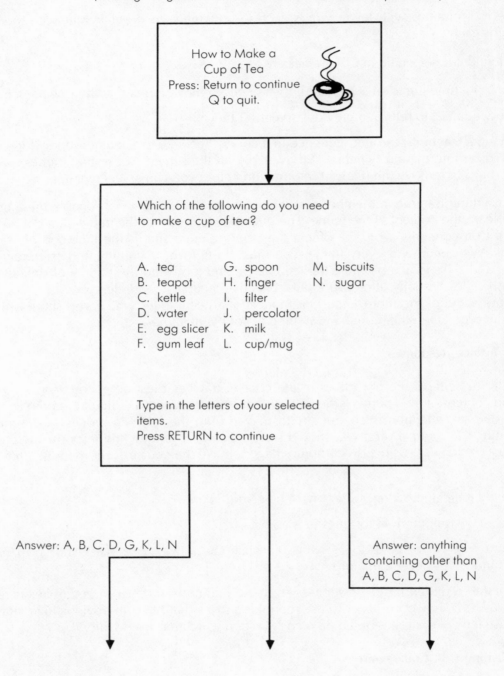

How to Make a
Cup of Tea
Press: Return to continue
Q to quit.

Which of the following do you need
to make a cup of tea?

A. tea	G. spoon	M. biscuits
B. teapot	H. finger	N. sugar
C. kettle	I. filter	
D. water	J. percolator	
E. egg slicer	K. milk	
F. gum leaf	L. cup/mug	

Type in the letters of your selected
items.
Press RETURN to continue

Answer: A, B, C, D, G, K, L, N

Answer: anything
containing other than
A, B, C, D, G, K, L, N

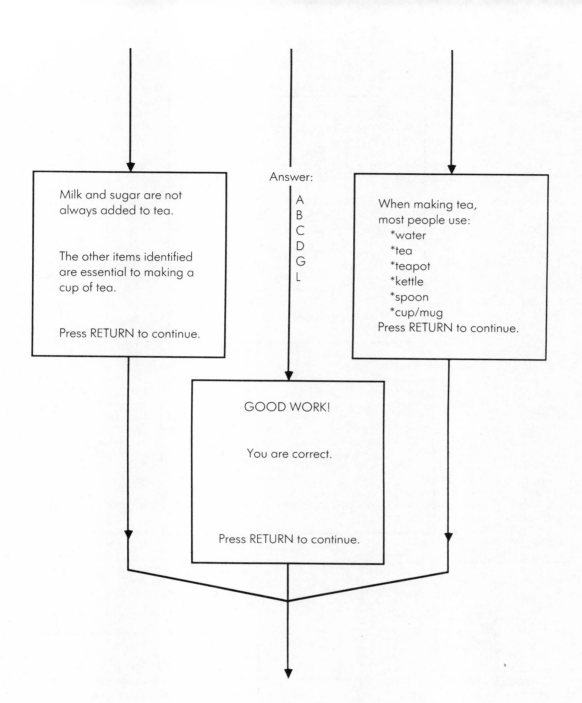

Milk and sugar are not
always added to tea.

The other items identified
are essential to making a
cup of tea.

Press RETURN to continue.

Answer:

A
B
C
D
G
L

When making tea,
most people use:
  *water
  *tea
  *teapot
  *kettle
  *spoon
  *cup/mug
Press RETURN to continue.

GOOD WORK!

You are correct.

Press RETURN to continue.

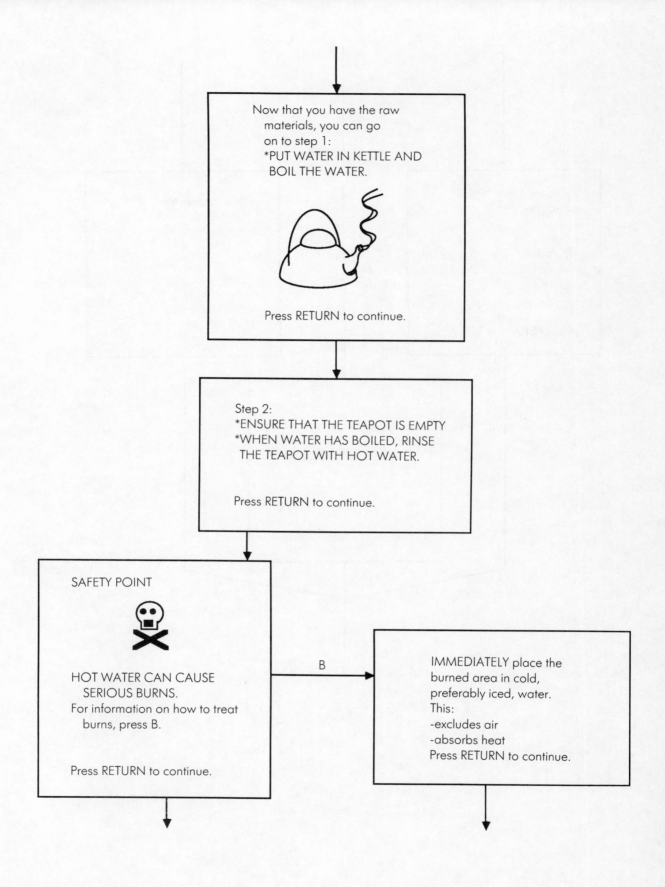

Now that you have the raw
materials, you can go
on to step 1:
*PUT WATER IN KETTLE AND
 BOIL THE WATER.

Press RETURN to continue.

Step 2:
*ENSURE THAT THE TEAPOT IS EMPTY
*WHEN WATER HAS BOILED, RINSE
 THE TEAPOT WITH HOT WATER.

Press RETURN to continue.

SAFETY POINT

HOT WATER CAN CAUSE
   SERIOUS BURNS.
For information on how to treat
   burns, press B.

Press RETURN to continue.

B

IMMEDIATELY place the
burned area in cold,
preferably iced, water.
This:
-excludes air
-absorbs heat
Press RETURN to continue.

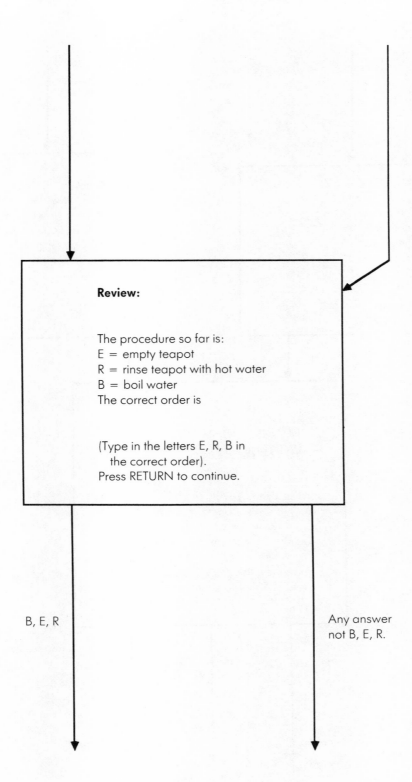

Review:

The procedure so far is:
E = empty teapot
R = rinse teapot with hot water
B = boil water
The correct order is

(Type in the letters E, R, B in
   the correct order).
Press RETURN to continue.

B, E, R

Any answer
not B, E, R.

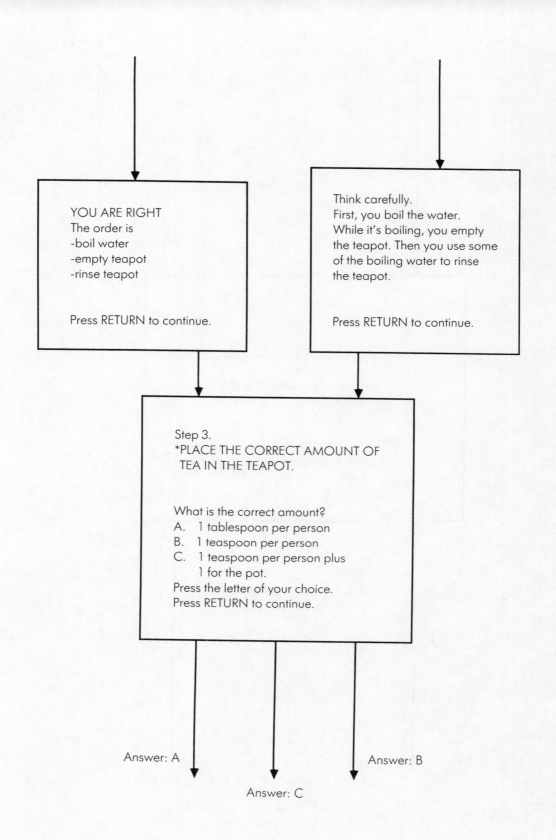

YOU ARE RIGHT
The order is
-boil water
-empty teapot
-rinse teapot

Press RETURN to continue.

Think carefully.
First, you boil the water.
While it's boiling, you empty
the teapot. Then you use some
of the boiling water to rinse
the teapot.

Press RETURN to continue.

Step 3.
*PLACE THE CORRECT AMOUNT OF
  TEA IN THE TEAPOT.

What is the correct amount?
A.   1 tablespoon per person
B.   1 teaspoon per person
C.   1 teaspoon per person plus
      1 for the pot.
Press the letter of your choice.
Press RETURN to continue.

Answer: A

Answer: C

Answer: B

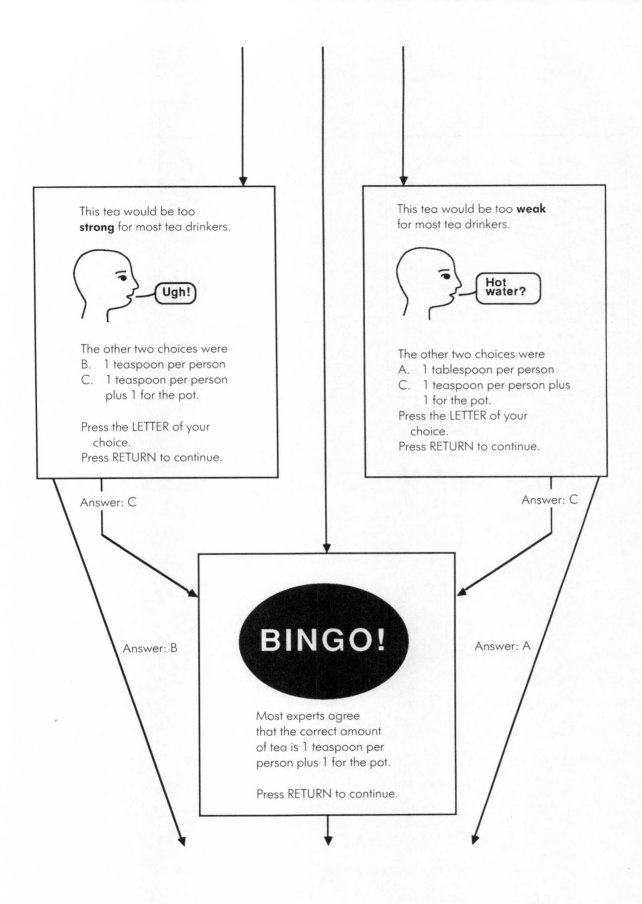

This tea would be too **strong** for most tea drinkers.

Ugh!

The other two choices were
B. 1 teaspoon per person
C. 1 teaspoon per person plus 1 for the pot.

Press the LETTER of your choice.
Press RETURN to continue.

Answer: C

Answer: B

This tea would be too **weak** for most tea drinkers.

Hot water?

The other two choices were
A. 1 tablespoon per person
C. 1 teaspoon per person plus 1 for the pot.
Press the LETTER of your choice.
Press RETURN to continue.

Answer: C

Answer: A

BINGO!

Most experts agree that the correct amount of tea is 1 teaspoon per person plus 1 for the pot.

Press RETURN to continue.

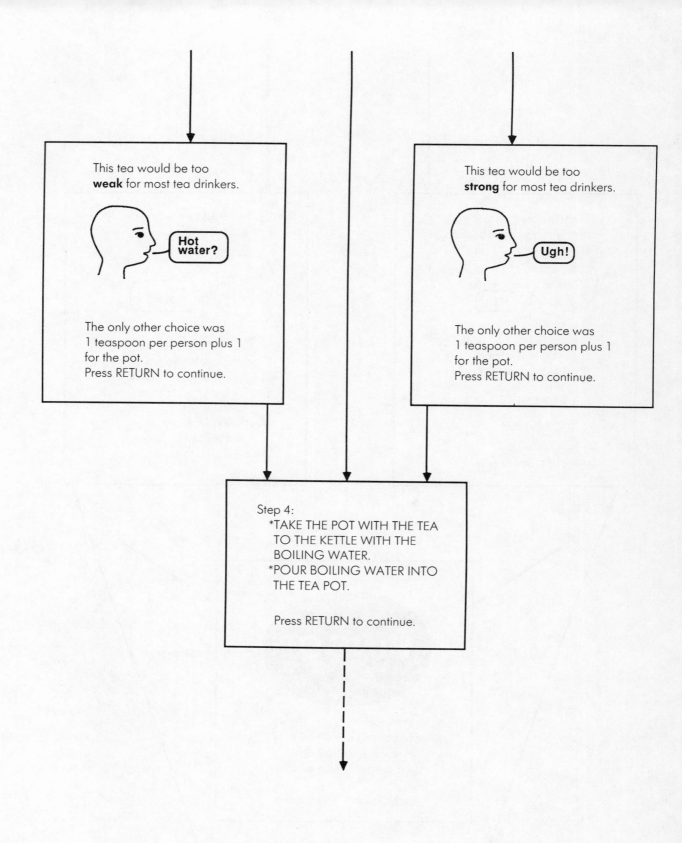

This tea would be too **weak** for most tea drinkers.

Hot water?

The only other choice was
1 teaspoon per person plus 1
for the pot.
Press RETURN to continue.

This tea would be too **strong** for most tea drinkers.

Ugh!

The only other choice was
1 teaspoon per person plus 1
for the pot.
Press RETURN to continue.

Step 4:
   *TAKE THE POT WITH THE TEA
   TO THE KETTLE WITH THE
   BOILING WATER.
   *POUR BOILING WATER INTO
   THE TEA POT.

   Press RETURN to continue.

- The complexity of the displays (graphics) required.

- The degree of branching used in the course.

- The skill of the courseware creator.

A skilled designer who is converting existing, well-organized, and straightforward content into a relatively simple drill or tutorial style CBL course may require between ten and forty development hours for each hour of final product. At the other extreme, an inexperienced designer who must organize new and complex content before converting it into a multi-branched simulation or problem-solving style CBL course may require up to 600 development hours for each hour of final course. An average expectation would be in the region of 150 to 250 hours of development for each hour of learning.

The consequence of these costs is that few organizations will provide the financial or people resources needed to create CBL courseware. Most users of CBL will buy their courseware "off the shelf." In some instances, standardized courseware may be "customized" by the supplier to meet the specific needs of the purchaser—for a fee, of course.

IMPLEMENTING CBL

Many factors affect whether a CBL implementation will be successful. Some of the more important factors are briefly discussed as follows.

Equipment Reliability

Users will very quickly tire of attempting to use a CBL facility if it frequently doesn't work or behaves unpredictably. For many users, learning the courseware is difficult enough. Problems with the hardware are likely to be the last straw.

Training

All staff members who are expected to use a CBL system should be trained in its use, rather than left to muddle through. This is particularly important when computers produce anxiety in many trainees. Frequently, trainees are uncertain about their ability to master the equipment's requirements, and sometimes a computer is considered to be a direct threat to a person's job. A carefully supervised introduction to CBL to guarantee successful first experiences with the system is a high priority requirement.

Documentation

Poor documentation is a never-ending problem for computer users, even users with years of experience. It is simply unrealistic to expect new CBL users to be willing or able to put up with confusing or inaccurate documentation.

User Involvement

Involving trainees in needs analysis, objectives setting, and even course design is a time-proven method of increasing trainee motivation to learn. User involvement in the design and implementation of CBL has been shown to have the same effects. In addition, involvement of the instructors that the CBL course will "replace" frequently converts them from potential negative influences into strong supporters of CBL systems.

Management and Supervisor Commitment

Senior members of the organization must be supportive of CBL. This is necessary to ensure that the CBL system receives the admittedly high level of resources that it requires. It is a truism that any under-resourced project is much more likely to be evaluated as failing. CBL is particularly prone to this problem because its high initial resource requirements mean that it is more likely than most projects to be under-resourced.

In addition to being supportive, it is also critical that senior members of the organization are *perceived* to be supportive. This is part of the leadership function. Where the supervisor leads, the subordinate will (other things being equal) follow. As the bottom line, if a supervisor is heard to say that a CBL course is good, trainees are more likely to react positively when they undertake the course.

Evaluation and Control

Since CBL is likely to be an expensive project, it is important that public evaluation of results be carried out and that appropriate control actions are seen to be taken by management. Under these circumstances, CBL will be seen as having to perform in the same way all other projects are expected to perform.

These strategies will circumvent or overcome some of the common pitfalls experienced by trainers while implementing CBL systems. The best CBL system in the world is worth nothing if it is implemented so poorly that nobody uses it. So think carefully about your implementation strategies, and even be prepared to divert some resources from the CBL system towards implementation activities. In this way, whatever system you do install will at least be used effectively.

✔ Checkpoint: Authoring Systems and Creating CBL Courseware

Indicate true (T) or false (F), or fill in the blank.

1. The existence of authoring systems has encouraged the generation of a much wider range of situation-specific courseware. _____

2. The authoring system takes over the role of the _____.

3. The creator of the courseware provides _____ instructions, which the authoring system converts into a program which allows the computer to function.

4. The authoring system should allow the use of other media, the use of color and graphics, and should support diagnostic and evaluative testing. _____

5. You need at least _____ to review an authoring system.

6. To help the trainer see the overall picture when using an authoring system to design CBL courseware, it is often useful to create a _____.

7. When creating frames, ensure that there are time limits on screens and that trainees cannot return to previous frames. _____

8. When creating CBL courseware, standardize and simplify the responses required of the trainee. _____

9. To ensure that a CBL implementation will be successful, you should check that the equipment is reliable, staff members are trained, _____ is accurate, users have been involved in the design, and there is _____ and _____ commitment.

■ **Checkpoint Answers**

1. T   2. programmer   3. plain English   4. T   5. half a day   6. storyboard   7. F
8. T   9. documentation, management, supervisor

SUMMARY

Computer-based learning can use a wide variety of (but not all) teaching/learning strategies and can handle many (but not all) types of content. Most CBL courseware is purchased off the shelf, so the evaluation of packaged courseware is an important skill for trainers. With the availability of authoring systems, many trainers now have the skills needed to create CBL courseware, but the time required to do this remains a problem. Finally, the implementation of a CBL system must be carefully planned to ensure that effective use is made of the system.

Chapter 16 Doublecheck

1. What is meant by hardware, software, and courseware?

_____

_____

_____

_____

2. What is the difference between a drill (or practice) and a tutorial program?

_____

_____

_____

_____

3. In computer-managed learning, a major activity is diagnosing. Explain what is meant by this term.

_____

_____

_____

_____

4. What are the advantages of CBL to the trainee?

_____

_____

_____

_____

5. What are the disadvantages of CBL to the trainer?

_____

_____

6. What basic questions should be asked when evaluating CBL courseware?

_____

_____

_____

_____

7. List the desirable characteristics of an authoring system.

_____

_____

_____

_____

8. List the steps for designing CBL courseware.

_____

_____

_____

_____

9. How can you make the course "user friendly"?

_____

_____

_____

10. What important factors should you consider to ensure that a CBL implementation will be successful?

_____

_____

■ Doublecheck Answers

1. Hardware is the actual equipment. Software is the computer program that controls and instructs the hardware. Courseware is the disk, booklets, and other materials which are the physical aspects of the training program itself.

2. A drill is based on the assumption that certain principles or procedures are known to the trainee (e.g., as in spelling or math). In a tutorial program additional information is given to the trainees when they show they can answer certain questions.

3. Based on the results of a pretest, the computer can diagnose which units of the program particular students can bypass because they already know the content of those units.

4. Reduced time to learn given material and to travel to a learning center; reduced dislocations to home life; control over the degree of boredom or stress experienced; entry levels and course content suited to individual; increased satisfaction and motivation; ability to become acquainted with computers in a structured and safe environment.

5. Difficult to integrate CBL with group learning activities; hardware incompatibilities; need complex and demanding skills; a threat to the employment security of some trainers.

6. Does the course achieve its own objectives effectively? Do the objectives of the CBL course dovetail well with the required learning objectives? Does the course use its chosen medium/media to best effect? Does the course use the most effective teaching/learning strategies?

7. The system must run on the hardware available; its cost per expected use must be reasonable; should be flexible, allow use of other media; should support color, graphics, and sound effects; should support diagnostic and evaluative testing; should maintain trainee records and provide reports to the trainer.

8. a. Identify training need.
   b. Develop objectives.
   c. Establish course content.
   d. Establish logic of content.
   e. Divide content into units.
   f. Develop objectives for each unit.
   g. Select strategies for units.
   h. Divide units into teaching frames.
   i. Write frames.
   j. Create testing frames.
   k. Create feedback frames.
   l. Create practice/application frames.
   m. Create remedial frames.
   n. Create review frames.
   o. Create pretests and posttests.
   p. Create introductory and concluding frames.
   q. Check logic of interconnections and overall course.

9. Clearly indicate how responses are to be given; use a consistent format for questioning; trainee responses should need only minimum input effort; use a consistent format for answers.

10. Equipment reliability; staff should be trained in the use of the CBL system; documentation should be logical and accurate; involve trainees in needs analysis, objectives setting, and course design; management and supervision must support CBL; have public evaluation of results.

17
LEARNING BASED ON WORK EXPERIENCE

Key Concepts

- *Advanced techniques.* Techniques that extend the repertoire of the trainer beyond the theory and skill sessions, the discussion, and the lecture.

- *Projects.* A trainee learns by performing a carefully selected and monitored project.

- *Action learning.* A particular use of projects in which a heterogeneous group of trainees assist each other to learn.

- *Mentoring.* Planning, organizing, and seeing through a developmental program for another person.

- *Structured diary analysis.* A trainee learns through structured analysis of on-the-job events.

Learning Objectives

After you have completed this chapter, you should be able to

- Describe four advanced training techniques which utilize on-the-job experiences.

- Explain when to use each of the techniques.

INTRODUCING OTHER TECHNIQUES

"What other training techniques can I use?" Quite a logical question for a trainer who wants to be as effective as possible. So far we have covered the theory and skill sessions, the discussion, and the lecture. These are basic techniques that every trainer should be able to use with confidence and skill. Unless a trainer has a thorough grounding in these basic techniques, he or she should not use more advanced techniques.

In Chapter 12, we described how to modify the skill-session model to suit on-the-job training. In this chapter, we will summarize four advanced techniques which are also well adapted to learning on the job. The techniques are

1. Projects

2. Action learning

3. Mentoring

4. Structured diary analysis

We are not aiming directly to develop your skills in using these techniques. Rather, this chapter is an overview to guide you in further study. We will explain what each technique is, outline when to use it, and give examples where appropriate.

Each of these techniques is either based directly on the day-to-day work experience of the trainee, or is based on activities which the trainee is asked to perform as part of the job. In every instance, the trainee is doing productive work for the organization at the same time that learning is occurring. Because of this, we regard them as on-the-job techniques. As would be expected, they generally suffer from the same problems and benefit from the same advantages as on-the-job training, which we have outlined in Chapter 12. Specific problems and benefits for each technique will be outlined in the following sections.

PROJECTS

Projects for learning purposes come in two types. While they are very similar to each other in terms of the finished product, the learning processes used are quite different.

Post-Course Project

The first type of project for learning purposes has already been described in Chapter 10, "Getting Training to Work," so we will examine it only briefly here. Basically, the project is "homework" at the end of a training program. This type of project, whether it is individual or group based, has two main purposes:

1. It allows trainees the opportunity (some say it forces trainees) to apply their recent learning to a real situation. This greatly promotes the development of skills in the area.

2. It prevents, or reduces, encapsulation of training. Problems of transferring learning from the training course to the job are minimized.

As a spin-off, these projects should also generate immediate benefits for the organization—an outcome that should not be underestimated with the present emphasis on cost-benefit.

An example of this type of follow-up project would be to give a supervisor *who has just finished a safety course* a three-week project involving the identification of all hazards in the factory and recommending appropriate methods of eliminating the hazards.

Whole-Course Project

The second type of project is a totally different proposition from a learning viewpoint. The idea is to provide a learning experience for the trainees by asking them to work on a task of organizational importance, usually in an area beyond their present expertise. To get the task done, the trainees must identify their learning needs in relation to the project, plan appropriate learning activities, and apply their learning to the immediate task. Truly mature learners may be able to do all this for themselves. In general, however, some form of guidance is required and provided, both to stop the trainees from floundering about unnecessarily and to ensure that the project actually achieves some organizationally useful outcomes.

This type of project is clearly qualitatively different from the post-course project. The post-course project is simply an application of on-course learning and is designed to encourage transfer of learning to the job. In comparison, the whole-course project is the total learning experience. The learning that occurs is clearly job- (or project-) related, and so transfer of learning is simply not a question. Note, however, that a whole-course project shares with the post-course project the distinct advantage of generating immediate benefits to the organization.

Let's compare a whole-course project to the post-course safety project described earlier. Instead of sending a supervisor to a safety training course, he or she is assigned a two-month project to identify all hazards in the factory and to recommend appropriate methods of eliminating the hazards. In this case, the trainee must first identify the information and skills he or she needs, then acquire the information/skills, and then apply them to the project. The result is a totally different learning experience from the equivalent post-course project. The whole-course project will almost certainly take longer, and the trainee will probably gather less material, but the trainee will have had the invaluable experience of controlling his or her own learning and gained the confidence and competence to apply the same process to future learning opportunities.

This process is often considered particularly useful in the further development of professionally qualified employees. In this instance, the trainees' existing qualifications give some (though not conclusive) evidence of pre-existing independent learning styles. In general, some degree of self-directed learning skills is needed if the trainee is to gain maximum benefit from the learning opportunities provided by the project.

When Should You Use A Project?

Use a post-course project when

- transfer of learning might be a problem.

- there is a need to show an immediate return on training investment.

- appropriate guidance (supervision) skills are available.

Use a whole-course project when

- you are dealing with mature (adult) learners who are willing and able to take responsibility for their own learning.

- a major learning objective is to develop and promote ongoing self-development skills.

- appropriate guidance (supervision) skills are available.

- the organization is willing to provide the necessary resources (especially time) for the trainee to learn.

- there is a need to show a direct return on training investment.

ACTION LEARNING

Action learning is not easy to describe, mainly because it is based on a particular experiential process, and each application of the process is unique. The originator of the concept, Reg Revans, has been somewhat concerned about the oversimplistic and mechanistic nature of some of the descriptions. We feel, however, that action learning is a significant recent development in the training field, so we will attempt to give a thumbnail sketch of the process while trying to avoid oversimplification.

Revans emphasizes the difference between programmed knowledge, which he calls P, and the questioning insight, which he refers to as Q. The essence of action learning is "doing then reviewing" rather than the acquisition of knowledge. It is therefore not sufficient to merely know, but necessary to be able to do.

In general, an action learning program requires a group of managers to come together in a learning set. This group becomes "comrades in adversity". Each manager is required to work on a defined and real project and at the end of a set time period (e.g., a week) is required to report to his or her peers on the problems encountered and how they were overcome. The emphasis is not on the content of the problem but on the process used or questions asked to overcome that problem.

David Brody has provided a visual presentation of the different types of action learning.

Environment

	Familiar	Unfamiliar
Familiar	1	3
Unfamiliar	2	4

(left axis label: **Problem**)

The dynamics of action learning can be seen most easily in Situation 4 where a trainee is faced with an unfamiliar problem in an unfamiliar environment. For example, a marketing manager in the coal industry may be given an accounting project in the tourist industry. The complete absence of any familiar content knowledge will force the manager to ask the important questions that will eventually lead to the solution of the problem. Throughout, the marketing manager will have the support of his or her learning set. In a similar fashion, projects can be set for situations 1, 2, and 3.

In some ways, projects and action learning are very similar. However, action learning emphasizes some aspects in a way which makes it qualitatively different from normal projects. First, there must be a group of learners, one of whom would normally have some knowledge or skill relevant to one of the other learner's projects. Second, the trainees use the group as the prime learning resource. And third, the emphasis is not on finding a solution to a problem, but always on identifying and refining the process used to attack the problem. The process is primary, the solution is secondary.

When Should You Use Action Learning?

Use action learning when

- Sufficient time is available.

- Trainees have good group and interaction skills.

- Trainees are willing to accept responsibility for their own learning and to contribute to others' learning.

- The trainer has good facilitation skills.

- Learning resources are available.

✔ Checkpoint: Projects and Action Learning

Indicate true (T) or false (F), or fill in the blank.

1. The post-course project is _____ at the end of a training program.

2. The post-course project encourages encapsulation of training. _____

3. A whole-course project provides a learning experience by asking the trainee to work on a task of organizational importance. _____

4. In general, some degree of _____ learning skills are needed for the trainee to gain maximum benefit from a whole-course project.

5. A whole-course project should only be used when the organization is willing to provide the necessary resources. _____

6. The essence of action learning is _____ then _____.

7. In action learning the emphasis is on the process or questions asked to overcome a problem. _____

8. Action learning can be used when the trainee prefers others to accept responsibility for his or her learning. _____

■ **Checkpoint Answers**

1. homework   2. F   3. T   4. self-directing   5. T   6. doing, reviewing   7. T   8. F

MENTORING

A mentor can be defined as a person who is given the responsibility of planning, organizing, and seeing through to completion a development program for a second individual. In effect, it becomes part of the mentor's job description to look after the appropriate development of a nominated person. In some ways, the task is analogous to that of a football coach, who, in addition to motivating and planning tactics for the whole team, must also identify and work on the individual strengths and weaknesses of each person on the team. The task of a mentor also has similarities to the role of a college faculty member who has responsibility for guiding and assisting post-graduate students through their individualized academic programs. In some respects, the mentor is also a public relations person, smoothing the path for the learner to follow, and a counselor who supports and encourages the learner through the difficult times.

Role of the Mentor

1. In consultation with the learner, the mentor identifies areas in need of development in the learner.

2. From this, learning objectives and action plans are agreed upon.

3. At agreed times, the mentor assesses the learner's progress, provides feedback to the learner, and modifies plans accordingly.

4. The mentor helps to identify appropriate learning activities from the wide range available and structures these activities into a coherent learning plan.

5. The mentor arranges for the learner to have ready access to selected learning activities.

6. The mentor may personally conduct some of the learning activities.

7. The mentor directs the learner to additional activities as the need arises.

8. The mentor attempts to encourage the development within the learner of an integrated perception of the job and the learnings from the activities.

9. The mentor acts as counselor and sounding board when required.

Many aspects of this role closely parallel career planning activities. In fact, many organizations which develop career plans for employees also appoint mentors to assist with the implementation of those plans. But mentoring can also exist in the absence of extensive career planning activities. The difference is really one of time scale. Mentoring in relation to the needs of the present job plus likely needs in the next twelve months hardly qualifies for the glorious title of career planning. However, when exactly the same activities are undertaken but aimed at a time scale of five to ten years, then clearly career planning is involved.

Organizational Requirements for Mentoring

As with all training activities, the organization must support, and be seen to support, the activities of the mentor. First, the organization must provide adequate time for the mentor to carry out the role effectively. Specifically, mentoring activities must be defined as a regular part of the activities of a job, and hence written into the job description. If they are simply added on to a standard job description, they will be seen as being add-ons and hence optional extras.

Personal Development Program
for Stuart Yasuto

Mentor Joan Richards

Date April 22, 1986

Needs	Learning Objectives	Actions	Evidence of Completion	Review Date
Present: Improved debriefing skills	Name & explain the stages of debriefing. Demonstrate stages in a training micro-session.	Find & read 5 articles on debriefing experiential learning. Observe Mary & John in debriefing sessions.	Write report outlining debriefing process. Run micro-session demonstrating stages.	June 20, 1986 July 5, 1986
Future: To be able to conduct a TNA.	Conduct a comprehensive TNA for the motor mechanics employed in the workshop.	Attend ASTD TNA workshop. Read Zenke & Kramlinger, Ulschak, & Turrell. Observe TNA for clerical supervisors. Participate in TNA for drivers as team member. Conduct motor mechanic TNA as team leader.	Written report containing summaries and analysis of reading. Attendance at team meetings & information gathering exercises. TNA report. TNA report.	May 15–19, 1986 August 25, 1986 May & June, 1986 November 5, 1986 February 20, 1987
To be aware of a wide variety of training methods and the situations to which they are suited.	Given a variety of learning situations, be able to choose a training method and justify the choice.	Read Huczynski. Produce a cross-referenced index based on Huczynski. Monitor training journals to incorporate relevant references in index. Attend relevant workshops & conferences as they occur. Visit organizations using unusual methods.	Completion of index. Completion of index. Brief reports on learning. Brief reports on visits.	August 30, 1987 August 30, 1987 Every 6 months. Every 6 months.

Secondly, mentoring activities must be perceived as valid means for achieving organizational goals, so that requests to organizational members to assist the learner are seen as valid requests, rather than impositions or favors.

Finally, the mentoring program must include an assessment and feedback system so that people who input time and effort to assist learners can be rewarded by the organization for their efforts.

Sample Personal Development Program

The program on page 241 has been jointly developed by a trainer and his or her mentor. It has a two-year time frame, and identifies needs, learning objectives, actions, evidence of completion, and review dates. It assumes a possible promotion from Trainer to Course Developer in about eighteen months.

When Should You Use Mentoring?

In general, mentoring can be used whenever there is a need to customize a learning program to the individual needs of a learner. In theory, every supervisor is a mentor for his immediate subordinates, and some organizations actually encourage more than just lip service to this goal. In practice, most organizations using a mentor system apply it in the arena of management development, or occasionally to the rapid development of an identified "star" employee.

Other components of the situation which should be closely examined before deciding on mentoring are:

1. Does the organization operate in a way which will encourage, support, and reward mentoring activities?

2. Are the learners willing to assist in identifying their own needs, planning their own programs, and evaluating their own efforts? That is, are they mature learners?

3. Are there people in the organization who already possess the wide range of training, counseling, and public relations skills which may be required for high-level performance of the mentor role?

STRUCTURED DIARY ANALYSIS

A cynic has defined experience as "that which allows us to recognize a mistake as soon as we make it—the second, third, or fourth time." This clearly suggests that our learning from experience is not 100 percent successful.

People can learn from experience. Having once burned our fingers, we know not to touch the stove. But equally, we often find ourselves thinking "I should have realized that after last time." In effect, we are saying "I had all the necessary experience, but I failed to learn from it." One method of helping to extract learning from experience is to keep a structured learning diary.

There are several critical components in the process of learning from experience. First, the learner must be able to accurately observe an experience. Second, the observations must be analyzed to extract general principles, which can be called anything from theories to learning points. Finally, the principles must be expressed in the form of guides to future action. If any of these components is not performed adequately, our learning from experience will become less than complete, or it will cease completely, or we will develop and learn invalid principles and guides to behavior.

To minimize problems with observation, analysis, and developing guides to action, a structured diary contains a standardized set of headings (or questions), which prompt the learner through the components of learning from experience and which maintain uniformity and hence comparability of reports of experiences. Our experience suggests that the following format is a useful guide:

1. Brief description of experience.
   In narrative form, describe the actual event(s) that occurred.
   Record who was present and what they did.

2. Detailed observations.
   Record, in point form,

   • what I observed about the experience (situation, other people).

   • what I observed about my own behavior and feelings.

   • what others observed about the experience (if they told me).

   • what others observed about me (if they told me).

3. What did I learn from this experience?
   Be specific. It is useful to state your learnings as deviations from your expectations (previously formed guides to action) or as confirmations of your expectations.

4. How do these learnings relate to theories or concepts I have read, heard about, or constructed myself?
   Compare your experiential learnings with theories and concepts you know. Are the theories supported? If there are discrepancies, how can they be explained?

5. What would I like to change?
   Again, be specific. Concentrate on your own behavior, and set objectives specifying behavior, standards, and conditions. Also note behavior changes you would like to see in others.

6. How will I change these behaviors?
   Outline specific procedures, including review dates.

When Can You Use A Structured Diary?

A structured diary can be used to promote any learning objective, including knowledge/skill acquisition and attitude/behavior change. The only prerequisite is that the diary keeper possess appropriate levels of skill to observe and analyze an experience, and to develop appropriate guides to action. Learning is then continually built up in a comprehensive and systematic way.

In the ultimate, it is possible to imagine an organization staffed by skilled diary keepers who, on the basis of their analysis of experience, can determine their own learning needs and organize for themselves new experiences appropriate to these needs. In effect, each person is planning and running his or her own unique training program. Many present training activities would become redundant, on-the-job learning would be the rule rather than the exception, and transfer of learning problems would virtually disappear. An organization peopled by self-teaching effective learners should be flexible, organic, and productive, all of which are desirable attributes for maximizing organizational effectiveness.

Sample of a Completed Structured Diary Sheet
Experiential Learning Diary

Brief Description of Experience: **Date:** April 22, 1986

Ran afternoon training session on assertion for two-day sales staff course. Session did not go well, with trainee dissatisfaction obvious both during and after session. This was the first "non-sales" training for these people, many of whom had simply been told to come to the course. Considerable "organization anger" was present, even after attempts to deal with it at the beginning of the course.

Important observations	Observed by me	Observed by other participants
1. About the experience	I observed dissatisfaction in several trainees. I assumed it was not because of content or process, which the trainees had OK'd that very morning. Organization anger still present.	Several trainees reported frustration at the time being wasted and their perception that content was pre-ordained. Other trainees later privately reported general satisfaction with session. Some recognition of apparent conflict between morning needs as stated in the morning and needs as evidenced in the afternoon.
2. About me (behavior, feelings)	I felt increasingly frustrated. I misinterpreted (or was unwilling to accept) clear signs of trainee dissatisfaction. Did my plans, (based on their stated needs that morning) become more important than their apparent present needs?	Comments on unnecessary detail and inflexibility.

What I learned (specifically) from this experience:

It might take more time than one session to defuse organizational anger.

Given certain perceptual predispositions, I can misinterpret the non-verbals of frustration and boredom to mean lack of understanding of content.

Trainee agreement to content at the beginning of the course may not hold true as course progresses.

How do these learnings relate to appropriate theories or concepts?

1. Non-verbals are fairly gross indicators, and can be misinterpreted.
2. Trainee approval of content at the beginning of a course is useful, but does not guarantee approval for the entire course. Renegotiation may be required at intervals.
3. Even when invited to participate in course and content planning (i.e., be adult learners), trainees may be unwilling to voice their requirement until they have built up a sufficient "head of steam," at which stage emotions may get in the way of problem solving.

What specific behaviors would I like to change? How?

1. I must be willing to use my confrontation skills earlier, so that dissatisfaction is dealt with before it blows up into a major problem. Objective: Make diary notes of each time I confront. Check at end of 1986 that confrontations occurred early enough in all appropriate situations.
2. I must be careful of misinterpreting non-verbals. Objective: Record all instances of misinterpretation of non-verbals that come to my attention. Check records monthly, and aim for decreasing monthly totals.

244

✔ Checkpoint: Mentoring and Structured Diaries

Indicate true (T) or false (F), or fill in the blank.

1. A mentor is a person who plans, organizes, and sees through to completion a development program for a second individual. _____

2. The mentor directs the learner to additional activities as the need arises. _____

3. The _____ must support, and be seen to support, the activities of the mentor.

4. The mentoring program does not necessarily include an assessment and feedback system. _____

5. In the process of learning from experience, the learner must be able to accurately observe, analyze these observations, and express the resultant principles in the form of _____ for the future.

6. A structured diary should include such questions as what did I learn from the experience and what would I like to change. _____

■ **Checkpoint Answers**

1. T   2. T   3. organization   4. F   5. guides   6. T

SUMMARY

On-the-job training can utilize a variety of techniques beyond the basic skill-session model. Projects, action learning, mentoring, and structured diary analysis can all be useful in specific circumstances.

Chapter 17 Doublecheck

1. Describe the two main purposes of the post-course project.

   _____

   _____

   _____

   _____

2. What is a whole-course project?

   _____

   _____

   _____

   _____

3. When should you use a whole-course project?

   _____

   _____

   _____

   _____

4. Describe the action learning process.

   _____

   _____

   _____

   _____

5. What is the role of the mentor?

   _____

   _____

_____

_____

6. What skills should the diary keeper have to use the structured diary analysis technique?

_____

_____

_____

_____

■ Doublecheck Answers

1. Allows trainees to apply their recent learning to a real situation; prevents or reduces encapsulation.

2. It is a project in which the trainee works on a task of organizational importance. The trainees must identify their learning needs, plan learning activities, and apply their learning to the immediate task.

3. When dealing with mature learners; when you wish to develop self-development skills; when guidance skills are available; when the organization will provide the necessary resources; when a direct return on training investment is required.

4. A group comes together in a learning set. Each person works on a defined project and reports back to the learning set on the problems encountered and how they were overcome. The emphasis is on the process used to overcome the problem, not on the content of the problem.

5. The mentor helps to identify learning needs, objectives, and action plans; provides feedback; helps to identify learning activities; arranges access to selected learning activities; may conduct some of the learning activities; directs the learner to additional activities; encourages an integrated perception of the learning; acts as counselor and sounding board.

6. Needs the skills to observe and analyze an experience and to develop appropriate guides to action.

18
OTHER ADVANCED TECHNIQUES

Key Concepts

- *Algorithm.* A form of logic (presented as a chart) which leads the trainee through a series of decisions and actions to diagnose a logical conclusion.

- *Programmed instruction (PI).* Packaged learning where the material is presented in small portions called frames. The learner controls the pace and path of learning through direct interaction with the programmed material.

- *Behavior modeling.* The learner copies a model performance and is given feedback, rewards, and further practice.

- *Contract learning.* Mature learners decide what, how, and how much they will learn, and prepare a contract specifying these details.

- *Self-teaching action group (STAG).* A small group (usually three members) that takes responsibility for its own learning.

- *Growth groups.* Groups designed to promote knowledge of self and to improve interaction with others.

- *Distance learning.* The specialized techniques used to promote learning when trainer and trainee are separated by distance.

Learning Objectives

After you have completed this chapter, you should be able to

- Describe seven advanced training techniques used in off-the-job training.

- Explain when to use each of the techniques.

Having examined advanced training techniques that are used on the job in the previous chapter, let's now look at some advanced techniques which are most likely to be used in off-the-job training. In this chapter, we will summarize seven techniques:

1. Algorithms

2. Programmed instruction (PI)

3. Behavior modeling

4. Contract learning

5. Self-teaching action groups (STAG)

6. Growth groups.

7. Distance learning

As in the previous chapter, we will give overviews of each of the techniques. We are not aiming at developing your skills, and recommend that you study the techniques further before attempting to use them. We have selected these techniques because of current usage (programmed instruction, behavior modeling, and growth groups), because we would like to see the techniques used more (algorithms and contract learning), or to give a taste of likely future developments (STAGs and distance learning). We have omitted many other techniques, but you can find readings about these by checking through the chapter bibliographies and the Career Development Review. In particular, the *Encyclopedia of Management Development Methods* by A. Huczynski (Gower, 1983) is an invaluable resource. In this overview, we will explain what each technique is, give examples if appropriate, and describe the conditions suited to the technique.

THE ALGORITHM

An algorithm is a form of logic that begins with the most general case and by the use of a series of decisions and actions leads the trainee to diagnose a path to a specific conclusion. The logic is represented as a chart, which is constructed so that the trainee follows no unnecessary paths. This saves time and avoids the risk of an overload of unnecessary information.

An algorithm is used mainly in diagnostic (or problem-solving) activities. It can serve directly as a job aid. For example, a technician might use an algorithm as a guide to isolate a fault in a complex electrical circuit. Alternatively, an algorithm may be used during training to explain the logic of a set of activities. Trainees may commit it to memory and use it as a task breakdown when they return to the job.

When Should You Use an Algorithm?

Use an algorithm

1. When an objective is to learn a skill involving diagnosis.

2. When the prose description of the skill is long or complicated.

3. When trainees are more familiar (and comfortable) with diagrams than prose descriptions.

Example of an Algorithm

This example involves the discounting policy of Luxury Limousines, Inc. The prose description is typical of documents that have been modified several times but have never had a thorough revision. It has no logical order, items overlap, and sentence structure and expression are inconsistent. In short, it is difficult to understand.

Discounting Policy—Luxury Limousines, Inc.

1. Discounts are calculated according to the type of customer, value of order, and method of payment.

2. If the customer is not a government department, a fleet buyer, or a private purchaser, refer customer to the sales manager.

3. Fleet buyers qualify for a discount of 10 percent irrespective of order value. Private purchasers qualify for the same discount if the total value of their order is $20,000 or over.

4. Private purchasers with an order value of $16,000–$19,999.99 qualify for a 6 percent discount.

5. 4 percent discount is available to private purchasers with an order value of $13,000–$15,999.99.

6. A private purchaser ordering in the range of $11,000–$12,999.99 receives a 2 percent discount.

7. An order below $10,999.99 receives no discount if the buyer is a private purchaser.

8. If the customer is a government department, it gets 12½ percent discount.

9. Sometimes approved specials will be offered. These are not available to government departments. Fleet buyers qualify for 15 percent discount on approved specials, as do private purchasers whose order value exceeds $15,000. All private purchasers of approved specials whose order value is $15,000 or less qualify for a 10 percent discount.

10. Government departments always pay cash. For non-government purchasers, discounts do not apply if payment will be made through a finance company.

Review the algorithm on page 254.

An algorithm is a much more effective way to express this information. By isolating the essential questions and presenting them as a series of yes or no decision points, the confusing prose version is converted into a decision aid that

- Is direct, saving time for the user.

- Requires no thinking activity beyond making yes or no decisions. In contrast to the prose version, the algorithm requires no memory or interpretation.

- Greatly reduces the possibility of error.

Checklist: The Algorithm

☐ Have I omitted all unnecessary information from the chart?

☐ Does the algorithm proceed from the most general to the most specific?

☐ Is wording brief and clear?

☐ Is the algorithm constructed so that the trainee follows no unnecessary paths?

Algorithm Discounting Policy—Luxury Limousines, Inc.

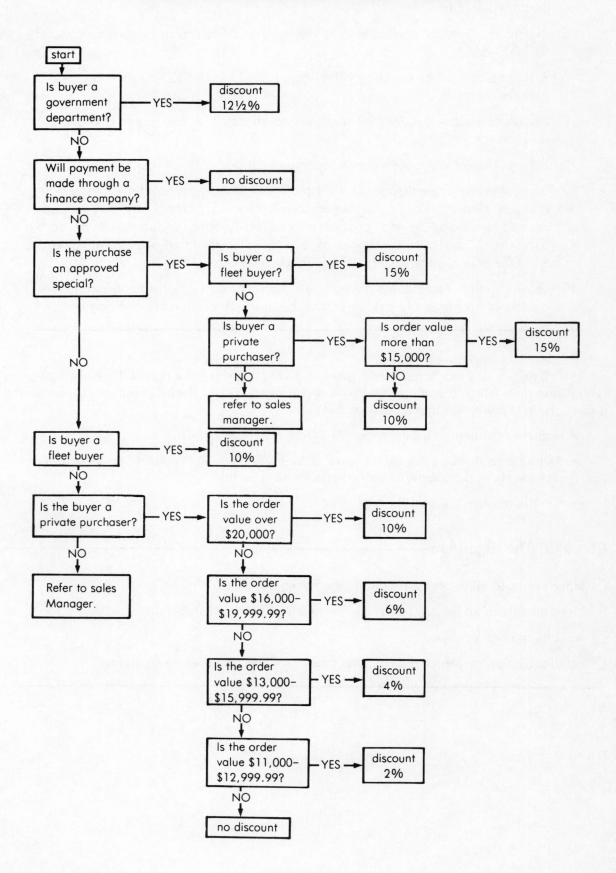

PROGRAMMED INSTRUCTION (PI)

Programmed instruction (PI) is an attempt to individualize learning by allowing each trainee to control his or her direct interaction with the program material. A PI package consists of carefully designed and pretested material presented in small units called *frames*. Each frame requires an overt response from the learner, who receives immediate feedback concerning that response. The learner progresses through the material at a pace that fits his or her ability and motivation.

Programmed instruction has two basic formats, a *linear* format, and a *branching* format.

Linear Format

A linear format uses frames that are very simple, contain limited and sharply focused information, and are often repetitive. This pattern ensures that the vast majority of trainees will answer each frame correctly and that correctness and repetition will make the need for remedial work unnecessary. Schematically, a linear program follows this pattern:

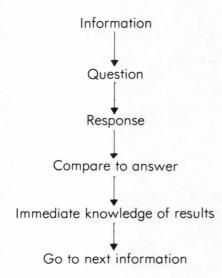

Information

↓

Question

↓

Response

↓

Compare to answer

↓

Immediate knowledge of results

↓

Go to next information

Branching Format

Linear programs demotivate some trainees because of their inflexibility, lack of challenge, and repetition. A branching format uses frames that have much more information content. The trainee answers a multiple-choice question at the end of the frame. The answer then determines whether the trainee proceeds straight on to new information or branches off to complete one or more remedial frames before returning to new information. Schematically, a branching program may follow the pattern on page 256.

Researchers currently have little information regarding the comparative effectiveness of the two formats.

When Should You Use Programmed Instruction?

Use programmed instruction

1. When the training objective is to convey information rather than to change attitudes or behavior.

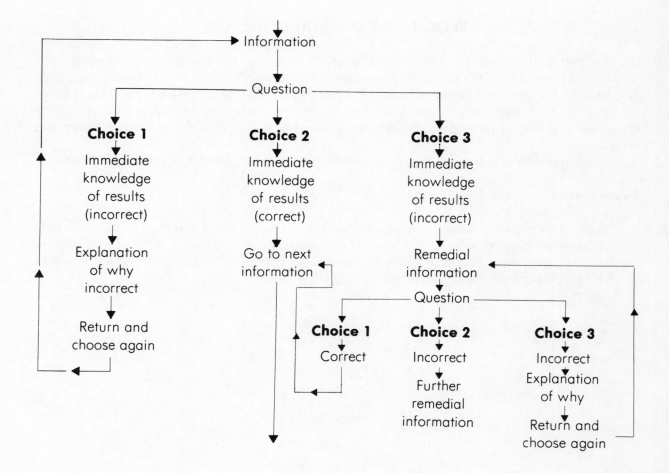

2. When the subject matter is stable and is required by many trainees. (This allows you to amortize heavy development costs.)

3. When you cannot conveniently gather trainees in one location.

4. When you have a critical requirement for standardized on-the-job performance.

5. When you have wide differences in trainee ability.

6. When you have sufficient time and resources to prepare the program (100 hours to prepare a program requiring 1 hour to learn is not uncommon).

Example of a Linear Program (Unvalidated)

This program would normally be presented one frame per page so that the trainee could neither see the answers in advance nor refer back to previous frames or answers as memory props.

BEHAVIOR MODELING

Although behavior modeling as a term has been in existence for only about twenty years and its conscious application for training purposes dates back only fifteen years, trainers have used the basic principles of the technique for centuries. In a nutshell, the request "Do as I do" delineates behavior modeling.

Example of a Linear Program (Unvalidated)

Frame	Content	Response	Correct Answer
1.	A training objective has three major characteristics. The first characteristic is: The objective contains a statement of terminal behavior.	GO TO FRAME 2	
2.	How many characteristics does a training objective have?		Three.
3.	What is the first characteristic?		Statement of terminal behavior.
4.	In addition to a statement of terminal behavior, an objective contains a statement of standards of performance.	GO TO FRAME 5	
5.	In addition to _____ the second characteristic of a training objective is _____		A statement of terminal behavior. A statement of standards.
6.	Standards are commonly expressed in terms of quality, quantity, and time.	GO TO FRAME 7	
7.	Quality, quantity, and time are used to specify _____.		A statement of terminal behavior. A statement of standards.
8.	Standards of performance may be specified by _____, _____, or _____.		Standards.

Frame	Content	Response	Correct Answer
9.	"To cut down a tree" is a statement of _____.		Quality, quantity, time.
10.	"To cut down a tree in five minutes" adds a _____ to the objective.		Terminal behavior.
11.	The third characteristic of a training objective is a statement of the conditions under which the behavior must occur.	GO TO FRAME 12	Standard of performance.
12.	What is the third characteristic of a training objective?		Statement of conditions of performance.
13.	If "Given a sharp axe" is added to the previous objective, it specifies a _____.		Statement of conditions of performance.
14.	The objective "Given a sharp axe, cut down a tree in five minutes" illustrates the three characteristics of a training objective. These three characteristics are _____.		Condition of performance.

END

1. Statement of terminal behavior
2. Statement of standards of performance.
3. Statement of conditions of performance.

From a theoretical point of view, behavior modeling combines aspects of Bandura's social learning theory and Skinner's operant conditioning. The general process is to show the trainees a skilled performance (a model), encourage the trainees to copy the performance (practice), and give detailed feedback on the practice (rewarding appropriately). The striking similarity of this process to the show, show and tell, and practice steps in the body of the skill session model is not accidental.

The detailed steps in developing and running a behavior modeling program are:

1. Perform a detailed TNA, so that the exact behavior to be modeled can be clearly specified.

2. Create the model to be copied. The model behavior is usually video-taped, so that it is available to trainees whenever and however often it is needed. Because the model is clearly based in a specific TNA, it will always be closely related to the work needs of the trainees, and transfer of learning problems will be minimized.

3. As an optional step, appropriate explanations (for example, the "why" of the behavior, or the theory behind it) can be given to the trainees.

4. Trainees view the model (or part thereof).

5. Trainees copy the model.

6. Trainees receive feedback on their performance and appropriate rewards.

7. Steps 5 and 6, or 4, 5, and 6, are repeated as necessary, until the desired behavior is established.

8. As the final optional step, trainees may be assisted to generalize the behaviors and/or the principles learned to different situations.

A major attraction of behavior modeling as a training method is that it is a virtually "pure" application of two of the major theories of human learning: social learning and operant conditioning. The major problem may be that it does not take sufficient account of the felt needs and previous experiences of the trainees. In other words, some trainees perceive behavior modeling to be too prescriptive and controlling.

When Should You Use Behavior Modeling?

1. Whenever there is only one correct and/or efficient way of doing something (e.g., operating a lathe).

2. When the learning objective is to develop a behavior.

3. When there is a critical requirement for standardized performance (e.g., preparing input for a computer).

4. When trainees will accept the prescriptive nature of the training.

5. When the trainer has adequate observation, feedback, and rewarding skills.

Comment

The process just described is carefully planned behavior modeling as used in formal training programs. Note, however, that much informal behavior modeling occurs in the workplace, with workers copying supervisors and new workers copying skilled workers (see Chapter 12). Trainers must be continually aware of the possibilities of modeling, planning their own behavior accordingly and bringing the concept to the attention of significant others (e.g., supervisors).

✔ Checkpoint: Algorithms, Programmed Instruction, and Behavior Modeling

Indicate true (T) or false (F), or fill in the blanks.

1. An algorithm leads the trainee to diagnose a path to a specific conclusion. _____

2. An algorithm is used when the prose description of the skill is long or complicated. _____

3. A programmed instruction package consists of carefully designed and pretested material presented in small units called _____.

4. Programmed instruction should be used when the training objective is to change attitudes. _____

5. The request "Do as I do" delineates _____.

6. Behavior modeling is an application of social learning theory and operant conditioning. _____

■ **Checkpoint Answers**

1. T   2. T   3. frames   4. F   5 . behavior modeling   6: T

CONTRACT LEARNING

Contract learning, as its name suggests, is based on an agreed contract between the trainer and trainee. During the first stage of the learning contract, the parties agree on:

1. *The objectives* that are to be achieved by the trainee. These are written in the usual form of terminal behavior, standards, and conditions. These objectives then define the parameters for the learning experience. If the trainee is to take total responsibility for the learning experience, then he or she formulates all the objectives. This ensures that all individual needs can be fulfilled. However, if the trainer has to ensure that the learning is also congruent with organizational needs, then some non-negotiable objectives can be formulated. Non-negotiable objectives are those minimum requirements that the trainee must achieve.

2. *What* is to be learned by the trainee. This covers all the knowledge and skills that are needed so that the objectives can be achieved.

3. *How* the skills and knowledge are to be achieved. Typically, a list of resources such as textbooks, practitioners, experts in the field, peers, subordinates, and customers is created. This is quite a significant role for the trainer, who is acting as bibliography and resource broker.

4. *The evidence* that the trainee is to present to show that the objectives have been achieved. This step is very much the responsibility of the trainee who should be encouraged to use his or her imagination. Although trainees readily use the business report or assignment, the more creative tend to use oral and video reports.

Advantages

The advantages of the approach include:

1. It can be flexibly adapted to suit a wide variety of situations.

2. The learning appears to be deeper and more permanent.

3. The trainees begin to learn the basic process that they can use in their own continued self-development.

4. It allows adults to utilize their past experience in learning.

5. As trainees are pursuing their own goals, a higher level of energy is often created.

Disadvantages

Although its proponents appear to claim that contract learning has universal application, it does have some problems, including:

1. Some people prefer a structured approach to learning and often feel insecure when left to their own devices.

2. Social and organizational cultures do not always nurture or reward the abilities required for self-directed learning. A trainer going against these norms will often meet considerable resistance from upper management and trainees.

3. The trainer is often faced with considerable demands on his or her time, knowledge, and energy as trainees enthusiastically pursue their individual goals.

When Can You Use Contract Learning?

One of the major characteristics of adult learning is that it is almost infinitely adaptable. Consequently, there are really only two conditions required before contract learning can be implemented. These are

- The trainer must have adequate skills and sufficient resources (especially time) available.

- Trainees must have appropriate levels of maturity and self-directed learning skills.

Example Of A Learning Contract

<table>
<tr><td></td><td colspan="2" align="center">**Learning Contract**</td></tr>
<tr><td>**Objectives**</td><td>1.</td><td>Discuss the concepts of unassertiveness, aggressiveness, and assertiveness, and identify the differences between the three behaviors.</td></tr>
<tr><td></td><td>2.</td><td>To act assertively in relatively threatening situations.</td></tr>
<tr><td>**What**</td><td>1.</td><td>The theoretical definitions of unassertiveness, aggressiveness, and assertiveness.</td></tr>
<tr><td></td><td>2.</td><td>The observable verbal and non-verbal behaviors of each.</td></tr>
<tr><td></td><td>3.</td><td>The verbal and non-verbal skills of being assertive.</td></tr>
<tr><td>**How**</td><td>1.</td><td>Attending an assertiveness training course of at least three days duration.</td></tr>
<tr><td></td><td>2.</td><td>Read three contemporary textbooks on assertiveness.</td></tr>
<tr><td></td><td>3.</td><td>Speak with some counselors.</td></tr>
<tr><td></td><td>4.</td><td>Observe, in my everyday interactions, how people act assertively, unassertively, and aggressively. List ways I would respond assertively to those behaviors.</td></tr>
<tr><td>**Evidence**</td><td>1.</td><td>A 2,000 word report describing the three concepts and the differences between them.</td></tr>
<tr><td></td><td>2.</td><td>A list of the assertive, unassertive, and aggressive behaviors I have observed and a brief description of how I would have responded assertively.</td></tr>
<tr><td></td><td>3.</td><td>Be involved in three situations where I use my assertive behavior. Two of these situations will be role plays under the guidance of an experienced trainer or counselor and the third will be a "real-life" situation. I will record this "real-life" interaction on a tape recorder and also present a 500-word analysis of it.</td></tr>
</table>

SELF-TEACHING ACTION GROUP (STAG)

Another technique which is learner controlled is the self-teaching action group (STAG). In contrast to contract learning, it is based on small groups. In some respects, a STAG is action learning moved off the job and given more structure.

The procedure is to form STAGs of three trainees, selected so that the trainees in the group have different levels of ability. No leader is appointed. Each STAG is provided with a suitable work area and a statement of its learning objective. This objective is subdivided into a series of sub-goals that create a goal-path for the group's activities. Each STAG is also given a complete set of resource materials (relevant books, articles, audio-visuals, etc.), which are indexed for ease of reference.

Next, the trainer must brief trainees on the objective, the learning method, and the resources. This is crucial. As a final part of the briefing, each trainee accepts a contract in which he or she takes responsibility for making sure that the others in the group have attained the learning objective. After this, the STAG proceeds with its learning experience, calling on the trainer for help if needed. The STAG concludes when each trainee can demonstrate to the trainer that he or she has attained the learning objective. The trainer acts as a guide and resource, and the trainees are fully responsible for their own learning.

When Should You Use A STAG?

You can use a STAG

1. When trainees are mature and willing to accept responsibility.

2. When trainees have adequate communication and interpersonal skills.

3. When the objective is information analysis and integration.

4. When sufficient resources and time are available.

GROWTH GROUPS

Growth groups can be likened to Heinz products—they come in at least fifty-seven varieties. From their infancy in the late 1940s, they are now widely used in many forms and under many titles. They range from relatively structured, impersonal, and short-term training exercises used to develop social skills through to the intense, freewheeling, and highly personal activities that occur in encounter, sensitivity, and T groups. Whatever the specific mode of operation of the group, we will use the generic term growth group to describe any group activity which has the following characteristics:

- A face-to-face, relatively unstructured group format is used for the learning experience.

- The key group activity is interaction among members.

- Members develop sufficient trust in each other to communicate about matters which would usually be classified as unacceptable or too risky.

- There is frequent feedback and analysis of the content and process of the interaction.

- There is an emphasis on dealing with problems that cannot be solved by old forms of behavior.

- There is an incentive to experiment with new behaviors in a supportive environment.

Because of their variety, it is difficult to describe what happens in growth groups. Some ideas can be obtained by watching the first ten minutes of the movie *Bob and Carol and Ted and Alice* at one extreme, and by glancing through the exercises provided in *A Handbook of tructured Experiences for Human Relations Training* by Pfeiffer and Jones at the other. Another option is to join a local group yourself, and see the process firsthand.

When Should You Use a Growth Group?

1. When a skilled leader is available. Growth groups, particularly the more intense versions, are no place for the enthusiastic amateur. Both research and experience suggest that the skill of the leader is a crucial factor in determining the effectiveness of the group.

2. When the learning objectives include at least one of the following:

   - to inform trainees of how they are perceived by others and how their behavior affects others.

   - to acquire insights into why people behave the way they do.

   - to foster increased tolerance and acceptance of the behavior of others.

   - to develop new ways of interacting with others, and to receive feedback on and support for the attempt.

   - to develop understanding of how groups operate.

Are Growth Groups Effective?

Growth groups, perhaps because of their highly personal nature, seem to produce rabid supporters and equally irrational non-believers. As with most training methods, the research indicates that sometimes growth groups work and sometimes they don't. Peter B. Smith (in *Small Groups and Personal Change*, Methuen, 1980) indicates that 91 studies reported 177 tests of immediate effects of training (ranging from measures of self-concept, through degrees of prejudice, to participation with and perception of others) and detected significant effects in 96 instances. Of the 28 studies which included follow-up measures some time after training, only 17 out of 52 tests showed positive effects. In short, a good deal of measurable (though not necessarily behavioral) change does occur after growth groups but there is a substantial fade-out of these effects over time.

A Concern!

Growth groups may place considerable stress on individuals, damaging their "psychological safety." Some participants grow through the stress to their own advantage, but other participants may suffer serious psychological damage. Hence, there is a major need to carefully select both the participants and the leader for such training activities. This applies particularly to participants who have an ongoing relationship outside the group (for example, co-workers in an organization).

✔ Checkpoint: Contract Learning, STAG, and Growth Groups

Indicate true (T) or false (F), or fill in the blank.

1. In contract learning, the parties agree on the objectives, what is to be learned, how the skills and knowledge are to be learned, and the _____ to show how the objectives are to be achieved.

2. Contract learning allows adults to utilize their past experience in learning. _____

3. You can use a STAG when, among other requirements, trainees have adequate communication and interpersonal skills. _____

4. Growth groups use individualized highly structured formats. _____

5. In growth groups there is an incentive to experiment with new behaviors in a supportive environment. _____

■ **Checkpoint Answers**

1. evidence   2. T   3. T   4. F   5. T

DISTANCE LEARNING

How does a trainer get a trainee to learn when they are separated by a significant geographical distance? The techniques that are used have been grouped under the heading of distance learning. The concept has recently received a significant impetus from two almost contradictory directions. The first is the drive for cost-effectiveness in economic hard times, resulting in trainers finding it more difficult to arrange for trainees to be released from their jobs, and to justify high travel and accommodation costs. The second impetus is the comparative availability of hi-tech (and high cost) media which effectively reduce the tyranny of distance. Video, micro computers, computer networks, and teleconferencing are the more common of these. Many trainers have found that, once their organization has micro computers or videorecorders for customer or administration activities, time for distance learning by staff can also be built into the equipment usage schedule. This allows the former costs of travel and accommodation to be devoted to the development of computer and video learning packages. Although the printed word still plays an important role in distance learning, it is being increasingly supplemented by hi-tech packages which are interesting, informative, and even exciting.

Distance learning reflects all the advantages and disadvantages of the different training techniques the course designer might decide to use. In addition, it has to deal with the additional factor of distance separating the trainer from the learner, which (except in the case of computer networks and teleconferencing) means limited communication and delayed feedback for both parties. In these circumstances, it is critically important that course design and presentation of material are as effective as possible, and great attention should be given to these matters.

Some of the present applications of technology to distance learning are

- The availability of off-campus courses where all material is transferred in both directions via floppy disks.

- The preparation of staff prior to the installation of new equipment via video and computer packages.

- The use by banks and financial institutions of video-recorders which deliver product information to customers some of the time and run training packages for staff at other times.

- Regular updating of the product knowledge of geographically dispersed salespersons, either by video or computer program.

- The production in some organizations of a regular news magazine video program, keeping all staff up to date on events in the organization, and putting human faces on information sources instead of impersonal titles and signatures.

- Computer bulletin boards are being harnessed to provide organized, rather than haphazard, learning experiences.

- Several major computer networks (e.g., PLATO) are providing efficient distance learning in some applications.

A Warning!

The hi-tech bandwagon is rolling irresistibly at present. But take care when jumping aboard! Carefully investigate the present and future needs of your organization, acquaint yourself with present hardware and courseware and with likely future developments, and choose very carefully before committing yourself (and your organization) to what will almost certainly turn out to be a significant expenditure.

Comment on Advanced Training Techniques

While, in theory, the newer training techniques based on individualized learning have much to recommend them, the actual utilization of these techniques is an art still in its infancy. Very little research has been done on their costs and benefits, so that there is a scarcity of hard data on which to make comparisons between these and other techniques. So, to a certain extent, using these newer techniques is an act of faith by the trainer, who might find his or her faith hard to justify in terms of cost benefits.

SUMMARY

Advanced training techniques combine elements of basic training techniques with some specialized skills to extend the repertoire of the trainer. In this unit, we have examined the case study, the role play, and computer-based learning in detail. In addition, we have summarized four on-the-job techniques (projects, action learning, mentoring, and structured diary analysis) and seven techniques used mainly off the job (algorithms, programmed instruction, behavior modeling, contract learning, self-teaching action groups, growth groups, and distance learning).

Chapter 18 Doublecheck

1. When should you use an algorithm?

2. What is the difference between the linear and branching formats of programmed instruction?

3. What are the steps in developing and running a behavior modeling program?

4. List the advantages of contract learning.

5. When should you use a STAG?

6. What are the characteristics of growth groups?

_____

_____

_____

_____

7. What is a significant concern with growth groups?

_____

_____

_____

_____

8. Discuss how distance learning has recently received a significant impetus from two almost contradictory directions.

_____

_____

_____

_____

■ Doublecheck Answers

1. When an objective is to learn a skill involving diagnosis; the prose description of the skill is long or complicated; trainees are more familiar (and comfortable) with diagrams than prose descriptions.

2. A linear format uses frames that are very simple, contain limited and sharply focused information, and are often repetitive. A branching format uses frames that have much more information content, and the trainee answers multiple-choice questions at the end of the frame. The answer determines whether the trainee proceeds straight on or branches off to remedial frames.

3. Perform a detailed TNA; create the model; trainees view the model; trainees copy the model and receive feedback; trainees generalize behavior and principles to different situations.

4. Adapted to suit a wide variety of situations; learning appears to be deeper and more permanent; lets one learn a process to use in own continued self-development; allows adults to use past experience; often creates a higher level of energy.

5. When trainees are mature and willing to accept responsibility; when trainees have adequate communication and interpersonal skills; when the objective is information analysis and integration; when sufficient resources and time are available.

6. A face-to-face, relatively unstructured format is used; the key group activity is interaction among members; members develop trust in each other; members give frequent feedback and analysis of content and process; emphasis is on dealing with problems that cannot be solved by old behaviors; provides incentive to experiment with new behaviors.

7. Growth groups may place considerable stress on individuals, damaging their "psychological safety." Therefore, you need to carefully select both the participants and the leader for such training activities.

8. The first is the drive for cost-effectiveness in economic hard times, resulting in trainers finding it more difficult to have trainees released from their jobs. The second is the comparative availability of hi-tech (and high cost) media which effectively reduce the tyranny of distance.

V. TRAINING AIDS

19
USING BOARDS AND CHARTS

Key Concepts

- *Visual aids.* Training tools that supplement or enhance the training session by encouraging multiple-sense learning.

- *Boards.* Blank displayed surfaces upon which the trainer can write or display information that parallels or exemplifies the presentation. Boards include the chalkboard, whiteboard, paperboard.

- *Board and chart aesthetics.* Trainer must balance readability against quantity; freehand lettering against professional lettering; color for emphasis against color for decoration.

- *Prepared chart.* A large piece (or several large pieces) of paper (prepared before and not during a session) on which you present some information or important points.

- *Magnetic displays.* Use small magnets to attach displays to a metal board.

Learning Objectives

After you have completed this chapter, you should be able to

- List and describe the three types of boards.

- Explain the problems in planning boardwork.

- List the checks you should make regarding boardwork *before* you begin the training session.

- List the do's and don'ts of boardwork.

- Describe magnetic displays.

- List the advantages and disadvantages of the prepared chart.

- Write a board plan.

INTRODUCTION

Using visual aids to achieve multiple-sense learning should be as natural to a trainer as swimming is to a fish. Of all the aids available, boards are undoubtedly the best and easiest to use. They are simple to handle, allow a "buildup" of ideas during a presentation, and have a strong visual impact when properly used.

Unfortunately, these very advantages can lead to the misuse of these aids. The board that a trainer uses during a session as a "scribbling pad" on which to jot thoughts as they pop into his or her head ends up looking like a confused jumble (and possibly does more harm than good). You must plan the boardwork and carefully present it to utilize its full potential as a learning aid.

In this chapter, we will discuss boards and boardwork and then go on to two special visual aids, the magnetic display and the prepared chart.

BOARDS AND BOARDWORK

There are three types of boards.

The chalkboard. This has a green or black matt finish. It is the familiar "blackboard" from school days. Its average size is 8 ft × 3 ft (2400 mm × 900 mm), and it is usually prominently placed in the visual area (the area that all trainees can comfortably see).

The whiteboard. This is an alternative to the chalkboard. It has a glossy white surface on which you write with special whiteboard pens. The main advantage of the whiteboard is the lack of chalkdust, which makes it particularly suitable for use in rooms containing electronic equipment or in areas where someone is allergic to chalkdust. The main disadvantage of the whiteboard is the tendency for some (particularly plastic ones) to retain permanently an image of any writing left on them for more than a few hours.

The paperboard. A number of sheets of blank paper (3 ft × 4 ft or 900 mm × 1200 mm) are clipped to a board or stand so that the trainer can write on it with felt-tip pens. Its main advantage is that you can transport it from room to room or even take it outside. Its main disadvantage is that once you use a sheet, you must flip it over the back of the stand, out of sight of the trainees. You can overcome this to a certain extent by sticking the used sheets on the walls of the room. This can be time consuming, however, and there is usually only a limited amount of space on the front wall.

Another ploy is to use several paperboards, which can provide a writing area as big as any chalkboard or whiteboard.

The Board Plan

Yes, you even need to plan your boardwork. Good boardwork does not just happen; it is the result of planning. First of all, remember never to use the board as you would a notebook. As you conduct the session, the board display should grow in a logical manner that parallels your session.

Once you have decided on the session topic and key points, visit the training room for a good look at the board. First, how large is the board? Can you divide the board into areas? Usually, you can divide the board into three or four areas. Then, for example, you can use one area to display each explanation step in the session. You will probably need about 3 feet (1 meter) for each area.

After you have checked the board, you can plan the entire session. You can also sketch the board layout on paper. This sketch becomes your board plan. For a session on "Training Objectives," for example, you can use a board plan that looks like this:

Training Objectives

1. Behavior
   a. Action verb
   b. Abstract
      vs.
      Concrete
   c. See-Do

2. Standards
   a. How well
      – Error
        rate
      – Time
   b. Time
      invested

3. Conditions
   a. Resources
      – Provided
      – Withheld
   b. Pedantic?

In this board plan, the trainer has divided the board into three areas, and each outlines an explanation step. As the session progresses, the trainer writes the information on the board. It unfolds in a natural fashion from left to right, with previous information before the trainees for the whole session. Note also how the session title "Training Objectives" appears at the top so that it, too, appears before the trainees for the whole session.

The board plan for a paperboard would be a little different because the paperboard has a smaller area. In fact, you would need three board plans for a session on "Training Objectives."

These three board plans may be sketched on one piece of paper or three pieces of paper, depending on your preference. Note, however, that the trainer has to either flip the used sheets over the back of the stand or take them off the stand and stick them on the walls if they are to be kept in front of the trainees. Also note that the session title "Training Objectives" does not appear. There is no space for it.

The board plan, then, becomes the blueprint for what you will write on the board. When planning, of course, you must consider

1. The size of the board.

2. How you can most effectively divide the board.

3. The amount of information you want to put on the board. Your board plan ensures that the information will fit on the board and that it will be presented in a logical and understandable manner.

Two Problems

In planning boardwork, you will come across two problems.

Readability vs. quantity of information. The more information you display on the board, the smaller you must make the lettering. Conversely, the less information you display, the larger you can make the lettering. As a rule of thumb, for the lettering to be easily readable at 20 feet (about 6 meters), make the lettering 2 inches (about 50 mm) high and increase the size of the letters one-half inch (about 13 mm) in height for every 10 feet (about 3 meters) of additional distance.

Variety of color. Color breaks the visual monotony, but use it judiciously to differentiate between items and to emphasize particular points. Beware of the tendency to use too much color. A "Joseph's coat-of-many-colors" approach will not enhance your presentation.

Board Check

Some of the following checks may seem obvious, but you can become very embarrassed if you forget them. Run through these checks *before* you begin the session.

1. Have a duster or eraser handy.

2. Be sure that you have a sufficient quantity of chalk or pens (and the colors you need).

3. Clean the board. (Nothing is more distracting than old lettering.)

4. If you have trouble writing horizontally on a chalkboard, use parallel cleaning. First, clean everything off the board. Then "clean" the board again, using strokes that are parallel to the ground and that run the full horizontal length of the board. The strokes will leave faint parallel lines that you can use as a rough guide for writing.

5. Be sure that you display your board plan, for your use, near the board.

Do's

1. Write legibly. You may find that printing is best.

2. Write quickly. Use abbreviations that the trainees will recognize, and only put key words on the board.

3. Allow trainees time to copy down what you have put on the board. As a general guide:

   Write on the board.
   Walk to one side.
   When you can see that everyone has stopped writing, explain your point.
   This mobility adds variety in your presentation.

4. Use signposts. Look back to the example of the "Training Objectives" board plan. Numbers, letters, or dashes are good signposts that will reinforce the relative importance of a point and the section to which it belongs.

5. Use color to differentiate sections and points, but don't overdo it! Use color to enhance the logical flow. For example, in the "Training Objectives" board plan, you could use a different color for each section.

6. Periodically, or at the conclusion of a session, walk to the back of the room and check your boardwork for visibility, clarity, layout, and color.

Don'ts

1. Don't talk to the board. Your voice will sound muffled to the trainees, and you will lose contact with them. If you find that you occasionally have to talk to the board, talk *directly* to the board; it will act as a sounding board, bouncing your voice back to the trainees behind you. Note, however, that this is simply a technique to make the best of a bad situation. With adequate planning, you can avoid the situation entirely.

2. Don't stand in front of the board after you have written on it (for obvious reasons).

3. Don't use "invisible" colors. Some colors are very difficult to see from the back of the classroom. Check all colors before your session, and remove all "invisible" colors from the vicinity of the board so that you don't inadvertently use one of them. Check particularly for dark blue and dark red chalks on the chalkboard and light yellow on the whiteboard.

✔ Checkpoint: Boards and Boardwork

Indicate true (T) or false (F), or fill in the blank.

1. There are three types of boards: the chalkboard, the _____, and the paper-board.

2. The board can be effectively used as a "scribbling" pad. _____

3. You begin a board plan by inspecting the board in the training room. _____

4. Next you commit a sketch to paper. _____

5. The problems in planning boardwork are _____ vs. quantity of information as well as variety of color.

6. To allow trainees time to copy down what you have put on the board, you

   a. Write on the board.

   b. _____

   c. Explain your point when you see that everyone has stopped writing.

7. Signposts clutter your display, so avoid them. _____

8. Make color highly decorative, for we need to entertain the eye. _____

9. One advantage of the whiteboard is the lack of chalkdust. _____

10. You should generally avoid talking to the board. _____

■ **Checkpoint Answers**

1. whiteboard   2. F   3. T   4. T   5. readability   6. Walk to one side.   7. F   8. F
9. T   10. T

MAGNETIC DISPLAYS

It is a big advantage if the chalkboard or whiteboard is "magnetic." (Actually the board is not magnetic, it simply has a metal base.) You can buy plastic strips impregnated with magnetic powder in most training equipment supply shops. You cut these strips and place them on the back of the prepared pieces of cardboard. On the front of the cardboard you may have key words, diagrams, or pictures. Rather than wasting time writing or drawing on the chalkboard or whiteboard, you can stick on the cardboard signs as you talk.

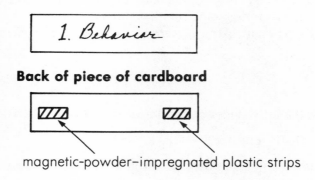

Back of piece of cardboard

magnetic-powder-impregnated plastic strips

The information on the board can then be "built up" to a full display as follows:

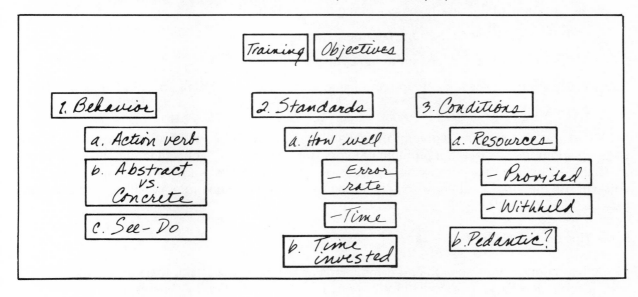

Magnetic displays have two other advantages. First, they allow you to incorporate some simple movement into the presentation (such as a car moving down a street). Second, in training situations such as on-the-job, where no other type of board is available, you can use any convenient metal surface, such as the side of a truck or a bulldozer blade.

THE PREPARED CHART

The prepared chart is a visual aid that is often overlooked by the trainer. The chart is usually a large piece of paper on which you visually present some information or important points. Several charts, when hung from a stand, can be flipped over as each point is introduced. Thus you can use the prepared chart like a paperboard, but you don't write out the text during the session.

Advantages

Here are some of the advantages of the prepared chart:

1. You can use charts repeatedly.

2. You can prepare charts in advance and thus save session time. But remember that you must allow trainees sufficient time to copy the chart.

3. Charts can provide an effective display of selected information.

4. Using a chart can widen the "visual area" available to the trainer. The "visual area" can consist of a screen for the overhead projector, a board in the middle, and a chart (See Chapter 24, "The Training Room.")

If you elect to make the chart yourself, there are alphabetic-numeric stencils available on the market. Although they are limited in printing style, the appearance they create is quite neat. A problem with stencils is that the normal chart pens will smudge. A useful technique is to use overhead transparency pens with the stencils and produce only the outline of the letters. Then you can fill in these letter outlines.

Disadvantages

Here are some of the disadvantages of the prepared chart:

1. They require special storage facilities.

2. They're bulky and awkward to transport.

3. They require special care in handling to avoid creasing, ripping, or smudging.

4. They take time to prepare.

Here you also face the problems of readability vs. quantity of information and of variety of color. In addition, you face the problem of either printing the chart yourself (and perhaps having to accept a mediocre job) or paying a professional sign-writer so as to ensure a high impact. If you will use the chart frequently and for a long period of time, the professionally made product may be your best option.

Some Tips on Using Charts

When conducting a session and using charts as the main visual aid, you can write information or reminders or key points lightly in pencil on the chart. During the session, you will be able to read these, but they will not be visible to the trainees.

If you are using a series of charts, then you will need to flip each page over as the session progresses. By far the easiest way to do this is to use a long pointer. Insert this about halfway up behind the page you want to flip over. Lift the pointer (and the page) and move them over the back of the chart holder. The paper will not crease or crinkle.

Finally, remember that the chart is very useful for displaying your training objective for the session. You can place it on a chart holder to one side of the room where it will remain in sight for the full session but will not distract trainees.

✔ Checkpoint: Magnetic Displays and Prepared Charts

Indicate true (T) or false (F), or fill in the blank.

1. A "magnetic" board is not magnetic; it simply has a metal base. _____

2. You stick magnetic plastic strips on the back of a piece of cardboard. _____

3. On the front of the piece of cardboard you write key words, _____, or pictures.

4. In training situations where there is no other type of board available, such as on-the-job, you can stick the magnetic signs on any convenient _____.

5. The prepared chart is planned and prepared _____ the session.

6. Prepared charts are generally used only once. _____

7. When charts are prepared, professional hand lettering is always preferred to freehand work. _____

8. Preparing charts in advance does save _____.

9. You can use a _____ to flip each page over as the session progresses.

10. The prepared chart is very useful for displaying your training objective(s). _____

■ **Checkpoint Answers**

1. T   2. T   3. diagrams   4. metal surface   5. before   6. F   7. F   8. session time
9. long pointer   10. T

PROCEDURE: PREPARING AND USING BOARDS

Visit the Training Site

1. Examine the board.

2. Decide where to place the stand (if boards are movable) and/or decide where on the wall to hang sheets.

The Plan

1. Take into account the constraints of the board dimensions.

2. Divide the plan into sections (reflecting the sections of the session).

3. Write the key points under section headings.

4. Use logical (developmental) order.

Room Preparation

1. Are all necessary materials available (chalk and duster, pens and cleaner, sheets and pens)?

2. Are there sufficient colors?

3. Are any colors "invisible"? (If so, remove them.)

4. Clean board (using parallel cleaning).

5. Choose a site to place the board plan for reference during the session.

During the Session

1. Write legibly. (Print?)

2. Write quickly.

3. Allow time for trainees to copy boardwork.

4. Use signposts.

5. Use color as a signpost and to enhance meaning.

6. Don't talk to the board.

7. Don't obscure the board.

8. Don't use invisible colors.

PROCEDURE: THE PREPARED CHART

1. Decide on the general information that is to be covered, using a chart as the visual aid.

2. Cut this information to its most succinct points.

3. Print these key points on an ordinary sheet of paper that has the same proportions as the chart. Experiment with layout, designs, colors.

4. Rule up the chart paper (using faint pencil lines).

5. Check the planned layout. Are there too many words to go on the chart? If so, go back to Step 2.

6. Either freehand or using stencils, print the final layout/color emphasis that you have decided upon.

7. Periodically during construction, check the size and legibility of printing from the back of the room.

SUMMARY

Using visual aids to achieve multiple-sense learning should be as natural to a trainer as swimming is to a fish. Boards and charts are the basis of the trainer's collection of visual aids. The trainer must learn the essentials of good aesthetics when preparing boards and must also understand the principles of using each kind of board.

Chapter 19 Doublecheck

1. Describe the three types of boards.

   _____

   _____

   _____

   _____

2. What problems do you face when planning boardwork?

   _____

   _____

   _____

   _____

3. What checks of the board should you make before you begin the training session?

   _____

   _____

   _____

   _____

4. List the do's and don'ts of boardwork.

   _____

   _____

   _____

   _____

_____

_____

_____

_____

5. List the advantages and disadvantages of the prepared chart.

_____

_____

_____

_____

_____

_____

Application Exercise

Given the following information, write a board plan for a session on the "Control Function." Assume a board size of 10 ft × 3 ft (about 3000 mm × 900 mm). Also, design a chart for the training objective(s) of the session.

Summary of content for session on "Control Function." The functions of management are to plan, organize, lead, and control. In this session, we will discuss the control function. This discussion will cover the components of control systems, the characteristics of good control systems, and human reactions to control.

The components of a control system are:

1. A predetermined standard.

2. A sensor.

3. A comparator.

4. Corrective action.

A predetermined standard establishes a base measurement against which future results can be judged. This in fact shows the overlap of the planning function and the control function, as these predetermined standards are the objectives established in the planning process. The ways of establishing standards are

1. Historical standards—based on an analysis of past performance.
2. Engineered standards—based on an objective quantitative analysis of a specific work situation.
3. External standards—derived from other organizations.
4. Manager's standards—based on the manager's experience and judgment.

The sensor measures the current performance in the workplace. In establishing the sensor, the manager must take into account the cost and the degree of accuracy needed and must ensure that the method of measuring is congruent with the predetermined standard.

The comparator. In many ways this is the easiest step. The information gathered by the sensor is compared with the predetermined standard. This may be done by ratios, graphs, trends, mathematical equations, or any other way that is appropriate to the situation.

Corrective action. If it is apparent that the predetermined standard is not being achieved, then action must be taken to correct the situation. This is a problem-solving activity and may involve a reassessment of priorities, alternative courses of action, or even changing the standards themselves.

There are several characteristics of a good control system. They include:

Timeliness. To be of greatest use, control information must mirror the current situation. Control systems should allow managers to take the pulse of the organization, not conduct a postmortem.

Reliability. This means that the information must be accurate.

Economics. A control system costs money. To be an economical investment, therefore, the control system must save more than it costs to establish and maintain. This economical characteristic may have to be compromised with the needs for timeliness and reliability.

Stressing the exception. A control system should identify genuine exceptions; otherwise, the manager will be swamped with information.

The human element in control systems should always be considered. There are a number of problems that can arise.

Looking good. This problem is supposedly quite common in some government agencies. A department is given a budget with the stipulation that any funds not spent at the end of the year must be returned. What often happens is that, at the end of the year, there is a rush to spend—quite often on frivolous purchases. In other words, the purpose of the control system is exaggerated.

Contamination. People are observant, and employees soon realize what is being measured and what is not. They will concentrate their efforts where results are being measured, regardless of whether this effort is productive. The manager should therefore set the predetermined standard with this in mind.

Easily measured factors. Some activities are easy to measure, others are more difficult. However, the easily measured activities may not be the valid ones for the control system.

Intergroup conflicts. When performance is measured, it becomes visible. This can lead to conflict between groups, especially when resources are scarce.

The control function is the last of the management functions, but in many ways it is the most important. The components of a control system, the characteristics of a good control system, and the human reaction to control should all be considered when discussing the control function.

■ Doublecheck Answers

1. *The chalkboard* is the familiar "blackboard" from school days. It has a green or black matt finish and is usually prominently displayed in the "visual area." *The whiteboard* is an alternative to the chalkboard. It has a glossy, white finish on which you write with special whiteboard pens. *The paperboard* has a number of sheets of blank paper (3 ft × 4 ft or 900 mm × 1200 mm) clipped to a board or a stand so that you can write on the paper with felt-tip pens.

2. *Readability vs. quantity of information.* The more information you display on the board, the smaller you must make the lettering. Conversely, the less information you display, the larger you can make the lettering.
   Variety of color. Color is needed because it breaks the visual monotony. However, beware of a "Joseph's coat-of-many-colors" approach. Use color judiciously to differentiate between items and to emphasize particular points.

3. Have a duster or eraser handy. Have available a sufficient quantity of chalk or pens. Clean the chalkboard (using parallel strokes). Have the board plan ready for your use near the board.

4. DO's: Write legibly. Write quickly. Allow trainees time to copy. Use signposts. Use color to differentiate. Periodically check your boardwork for visibility and clarity.
   DON'Ts: Don't talk to the board. Don't stand in front of the board. Don't use "invisible" colors.

5. ADVANTAGES: Can be used repeatedly. Can be prepared in advance and thus save session time. Can produce an effective display of selected information. Can widen the "visual area."
   DISADVANTAGES: Requires special storage facilities. Is bulky and awkward to transport. Requires special care in handling. Takes time to prepare.

■ Application Exercise Notes

Board Plan

CONTROL FUNCTION

1. COMPONENTS
   a. Pre-determined Standard
   b. Sensor
   c. Comparator
   d. Corrective action

2. CHARACTERISTICS
   a. Timeliness
   b. Reliability
   c. Economics
   d. The exception

3. HUMAN ELEMENT
   a. Looking good
   b. Contamination
   c. Easily measured
   d. Intergroup conflicts

CONTROL FUNCTION

a. Explain the 4 components.
b. Explain the 4 characteristics of good control system.
c. Explain the 4 human elements.

Note that the statement of standards and conditions has been left out. Including them would be pedantic.

20
USING THE OVERHEAD PROJECTOR

Key Concepts

- *Importance of projectors.* Stress and enhance the spoken word and allow highly imaginative application.

- *Transparency.* Of three types. The first is an untreated acetate sheet that can be written on with special pens. The second is a treated heat-sensitive acetate sheet that when put through a heating machine accepts an image transferred from a master. The third is a treated acetate sheet which, when fed through a plain paper photocopier, produces an image of the master.

- *Master.* The original image for the treated transparency. Must have a high carbon content for use with the heat-transfer process.

Learning Objectives

After you have completed this chapter, you should be able to

- Explain the value of using an overhead projector.

- Label the components of an overhead projector.

- Describe how to use the adjustments on the overhead projector.

- Explain how to combine the use of the board and the overhead projector.

- Design transparencies.

- List the do's and don'ts of using transparencies.

THE OVERHEAD PROJECTOR

You probably know the saying "A picture is worth a thousand words." It sums up the advantages of using the overhead projector. Even "pictured" words add considerably to the worth of the spoken word. The overhead projector

1. Has a very high visual impact.

2. Saves session time (since transparencies are usually made before the session).

3. Gives a high degree of control over what trainees will see and when they will see it.

4. Allows a high degree of freedom for the trainer's imagination.

The only practical disadvantages of using the overhead projector are that you cannot keep information on overhead transparencies in front of the trainees for the whole session, and some trainees find the bright light on the white screen a little tiring.

Construction

Here's a diagram of the projector.

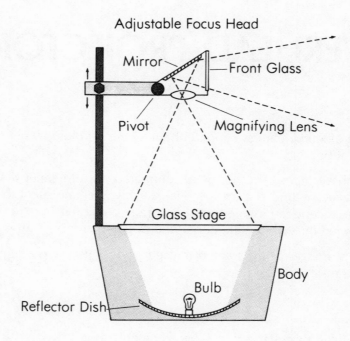

The "bulb" and "reflector dish" send a strong beam of light up through the "glass stage" on which you place the transparency. The image of the transparency is then projected into the "adjustable focus head" where, by means of a magnifying lens, a mirror, and a front glass, the image is projected onto the screen.

Adjusting the Overhead Projector

There are four basic adjustments.

1. *Size of image.* You can make the size of the image on the screen larger by moving the projector away from the screen. (A word of caution: Don't move the projector while it is turned on. The bulb can "blow" quite easily while it is hot.)

2. *Focus.* You adjust the image on the screen by moving the focus head and the horizontal arm up or down the vertical shaft. This brings a blurred image into sharp focus.

3. *Position of image on screen.* You can alter the position in the vertical plane by rotating the adjustable focus head up and down on the pivot. Have the top of the image exactly level with the top of the screen. You can adjust the horizontal position by turning or moving the projector sideways.

4. *Brown/blue coloring.* Sometimes you may see a brown or blue coloring on the screen when you turn the projector on. This indicates that the bulb is either too close to or too far from the glass stage. You will usually find an adjusting wheel either at the back of or underneath the projector that moves the bulb up or down.

The Screen

The screen is usually of white material and can be either wall-mounted or portable. If the screen is perfectly vertical and above the level of the projector head, then the projected image will not appear square.

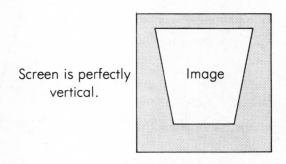

Screen is perfectly vertical.

Image

This distorting is called *keystoning* because of the keystone shape. The keystoning is caused by differences between the distances that bottom and top rays of light have to travel between the focus head and the screen. The further the ray of light has to travel, the wider the image.

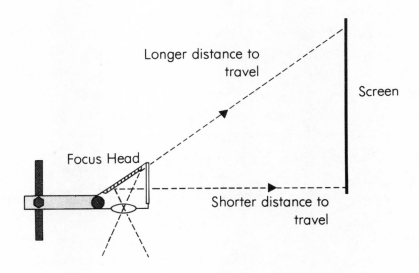

Longer distance to travel

Screen

Focus Head

Shorter distance to travel

To correct this distortion, simply tilt the screen so that the distances traveled by the various rays of light are about the same at the top and bottom. Rotating the focus head does not remove keystoning. It simply moves the image up or down the screen.

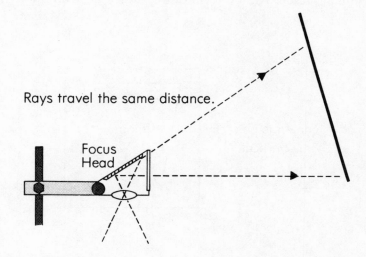

Rays travel the same distance.

Focus
Head

In addition to adjusting the screen so as to prevent keystoning, take care in the placement of the screen and the overhead projector in the training room. (See Chapter 24, "The Training Room.")

1. Place the screen so that every trainee in the room can comfortably see it.

2. Set the projector low (probably with the glass stage at the same height as the table in the front of the room) to minimize obstruction of the screen.

3. Place the projector so that the trainer can operate it with a minimum of fuss.

✔ Checkpoint: The Projector

In the blank, give the letter of the projector part.

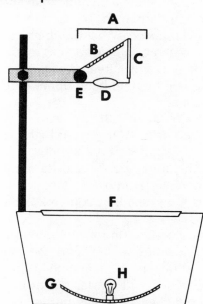

1. Pivot _____

2. Mirror _____

3. Focus head _____

4. Glass stage _____

5. Reflector dish _____

6. Bulb _____

7. Front glass _____

8. Magnifying lens _____

Indicate true (T) or false (F).

9. You can make the image on the screen larger by moving the projector toward the screen. _____

10. You can alter the focus of the image on the screen simply by moving the focus head up or down the vertical shaft. _____

11. A brown or blue color on the screen when you turn the projector on probably means that the bulb is too close to or far away from the glass stage. _____

12. Keystoning is a distortion on the screen image caused by differences between the distances that the bottom and top rays of light have to travel between the focus head and the screen. _____

13. You can correct keystoning by tilting the screen. _____

■ **Checkpoint Answers**

1. E   2. B   3. A   4. F   5. G   6. H   7. C   8. D   9. F   10. T   11. T
12. T   13. T

TRANSPARENCIES

There are three basic types of transparencies, write-on, burn-on, and photocopy.

The *write-on* transparency is a clear acetate sheet on which you use special colored pens. The pens have either non-permanent or permanent ink. You can erase the non-permanent ink with a damp rag (or even a sweaty hand, which can prove a disadvantage). You can erase the permanent ink with an organic solvent such as methylated spirits or mineral turpentine.

The *burn-on* transparency is a treated acetate sheet that is sensitive to heat. It is readily recognized because the tip of the right-hand upper corner of each sheet is cut off. You do not write on this heat-sensitive sheet.

First, you need an original (called a *master*) with a high carbon content. You can either make the master yourself using a 2B or soft high-carbon pencil, or you can cut a master image out of a magazine or newspaper. There are now even typewriter-like machines that create very professional masters, including graphs and bar charts as well as various sizes of printing. You can covert almost any material into a suitable transparency by photocopying it and using the photocopy (which has a high carbon content) as the master. The main criterion is high carbon content.

You place the transparency on top of the master, with the cut corner to the top right-hand side. You pass both the transparency and the master through a transparency maker ("heat machine"). The infrared rays in the machine "burn" the master's image onto the transparency. The slower the transparency and master go through the machine, the hotter the transparency and master get and the darker the image burned onto the transparency. Of course, if the image is burned too much, then the transparency becomes a series of black "blobs" and you cannot use it. Different types of transparencies require different heat settings; so be sure to consult the manufacturer's instructions. You may also need to experiment a little to get the correct heat level.

There are five basic types of burn-on transparencies. The categories are based on the colors of the transparency after it has been through the "heat machine."

1. Black on clear.

2. Black on color.

3. Color on clear.

4. Color on black.

5. Clear on color.

The *photocopy* transparency is a relatively recent arrival. To make a transparency, you simply pass the specially treated acetate sheet through a plain paper photocopier which you have "loaded" with the master in the usual way. The process is simple and inexpensive when compared to burn-on transparencies. It is also very flexible when utilizing the reduction and enlargement capability of modern photocopiers. Specifically, it allows the easy enlargement of any printing (including typing) to a size suitable for an overhead transparency. However, avoid the temptation to simply copy large chunks of prose which will inevitably breach most of the rules listed in the next section.

Making Transparencies

Here are general rules for making transparencies.

1. Use one transparency for one idea.

2. Use print that is about ¼ inch (6 mm) high. As a rule, do not use "ordinary" typeset copy, because the print is much too small.

3. Use about four words per line.

4. Use about size lines per transparency.

5. Use graphs, diagrams, or cartoons, if you like, with or without accompanying words.

6. Use color if appropriate. (The overhead projector is ideal and can have great impact.)

Do's

1. Use colored background transparencies as much as possible to cut down on the glare. For the same reason, cover any unused (clear) portion of the transparency with paper. The only exception is an audience with vision problems (e.g., aged persons) who may need maximum possible brightness.

2. Attach each transparency to a cardboard frame (or mount). This makes the transparency easier to handle and prevents the transparency from buckling due to the heat from the glass stage.

3. When you wish to point to a particular word or item, lay a pencil or similar pointer on the transparency. This will create a shadow pointing to the word. Don't hold on to the pointer, since you may not hold it steady. *Lay* the pointer on the transparency.

4. Mask areas and then progressively uncover them to emphasize the particular words or part of the diagram that you are talking about. Use a sheet of paper between the transparency and the glass stage for the mask. Gradually pull the sheet of paper down as you talk about the next points. (Note: Having the mask under the transparency keeps the still heat-sensitive transparency from overheating and also prevents the masking sheet from slipping out when you are discussing material near the bottom of the transparency.)

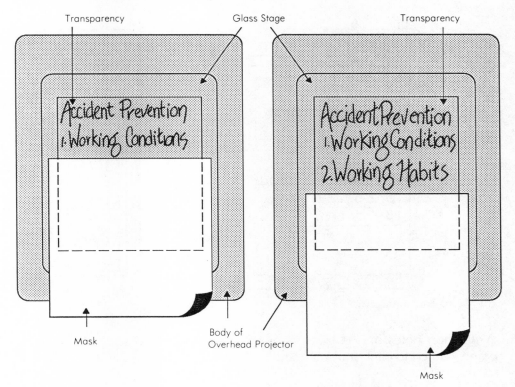

5. Use overlays for complicated images. Put a small part (or basic piece) of the image or message you wish to project on the first transparency. Attach this transparency to a mount. Put another part of the image or message on another transparency, and hinge it to the mount with two pieces of tape so that it flips over onto the first transparency. Continue this and gradually build up to the full, complicated image.

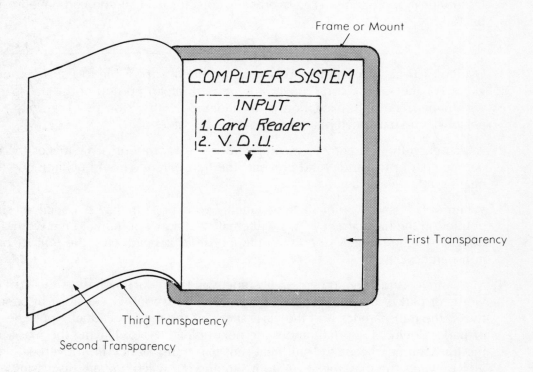

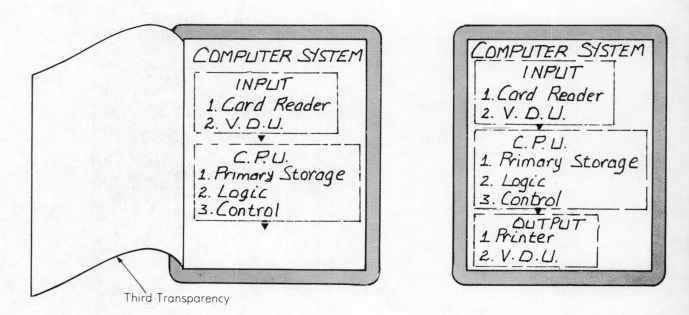

6. Write short notes on the transparency mounts to remind yourself of the learning points related to each transparency.

Don'ts

1. Don't talk to the screen. One of the benefits of the overhead projector is that it allows you to see (on the glass stage) exactly what your audience is seeing (on the screen) while you maintain the important visual link with the audience by facing them. If you wish to reinforce the message on the screen by reading it out, you can read it from the transparency on the stage of the projector rather than reading from the screen.

2. Don't walk between the projector and the screen. First, the intense light will blind you for several seconds. Second, a distracting silhouette of your head will appear on the screen.

3. Don't stand between the projected image and the trainees. The screen is usually placed at one side of the room, and it is quite easy to inadvertently block the view of some trainees. If possible, sit down at the overhead projector. This will assist you in reading off and pointing to the transparency on the overhead projector stage—and it will also give you a chance to rest your feet!

4. Don't leave the overhead projector light switched on. The glare of the direct light on the white screen can be quite distracting and tiring. So switch off the light after viewing each transparency.

Two Additional Tips

Build up a resource file of cuttings from newspapers and magazines. Collect drawings, cartoons, headlines—anything that is suitable for a transparency and that takes your fancy. You never know when you may need some odd shape or picture to emphasize a point.

Also, you can use the screen just like a board by writing on a blank transparency sheet on the overhead projector stage. Some overhead projectors are equipped with two rollers and a long length of transparency sheet just for this purpose.

As you can now see, the uses of the overhead projector are limited only by your imagination.

Using the Overhead Projector in Conjunction With the Board

How you present your session, of course, depends on the subject matter, the trainees, and your own preference. As a general rule, we have found it best to write the main points on the board progressively, expanding each point either verbally or on the overhead projector as you proceed. In this way, you keep the most important facts in front of the group for the whole session. Therefore the steps in presenting information to trainees are

1. Write the key word on the board.

2. Walk to one side.

3. Wait until trainees finish writing.

4. Explain or illustrate the key word either verbally or (preferably) by using overhead transparencies.

One of the best tests of how well you have designed the visual aids for the session is whether or not you can present the session without talking. (Of course, you would not do this in a live session.)

✔ Checkpoint: Transparencies

Indicate true (T) or false (F), or fill in the blank.

1. Special colored pens are used on the write-on transparency. _____

2. Any master can be used with the burn-on transparency. _____

3. The five types of burn-on transparencies are

   a. _____.
   b. Black on color.
   c. Color on clear.
   d. Color on black.
   e. Clear on color.

4. "Ordinary" typeset copy can be used as a master for burn-on transparencies. _____

5. Use colored background transparencies as much as possible to cut down on the total amount of glare. _____

6. When you wish to point to a particular item, hold a pencil in your hand and point to the transparency on the stage of the overhead projector. _____

7. Write short notes on the transparency mounts to remind yourself of learning points related to each transparency. _____

8. When reading off an overhead transparency, sit down. _____

9. Don't walk between the projector and the screen. _____

10. You can use the screen as a board by writing on a blank transparency sheet on the overhead projector stage. _____

11. Photocopy transparencies are especially useful when you wish to enlarge the image. _____

■ **Checkpoint Answers**

1. T   2. F   3. Black on clear.   4. F   5. T   6. F   7. T   8. T   9. T   10. T   11. T

Checklist: The Overhead Projector and Transparencies

THE OVERHEAD PROJECTOR

Have I

☐ Placed the screen so that everyone can see it?

☐ Tilted the screen to overcome keystoning?

☐ Placed the projector far enough away from the screen to have a large-sized image?

☐ Set the projector low to minimize obstruction of the screen?

☐ Placed the projector so that I can operate it with a minimum of fuss?

☐ Adjusted the focus head and horizontal arm on the vertical shaft to give a clear image on the screen?

☐ Made adjustments so that there is no blue/brown coloring on the screen?

TRANSPARENCIES

Making Transparencies

Have I

☐ Used one transparency for one idea?

☐ Printed about ¼ inch (6 mm) high?

☐ Used no more than four words per line?

☐ Used no more than six lines per transparency?

☐ Used color effectively?

☐ Used colored background transparencies as much as possible to cut down on the total amount of glare?

☐ Attached each transparency to a cardboard frame or mount?

☐ Written short notes on the transparency mount to remind myself of the learning points?

Using Transparencies

Did I

☐ Lay a pointer on top of the transparency when pointing to a particular word or item?

☐ Use masking to progressively uncover each line on the transparency?

☐ Use overlays for complicated images?

☐ Sit down to read off the transparency on the stage?

Did I avoid

☐ Talking to the screen?

☐ Walking between the projector and screen?

☐ Leaving the projector light on between transparencies?

SUMMARY

"A picture is worth a thousand words" sums up the advantages of overhead projection. Therefore, the trainer must understand how to work with the projector and with transparencies. The three types of transparencies are the untreated acetate sheet, which you can write on with special pens; the treated heat sensitive acetate sheet, which can be made to accept an image transferred from a master; and the treated acetate sheet, which accepts an image from the master when passed through a plain paper photocopier.

Chapter 20 Doublecheck

1. List the advantages of using an overhead projector.

_____

_____

_____

_____

_____

2. Explain the four basic adjustments of the overhead projector.

_____

_____

_____

_____

_____

_____

_____

_____

_____

_____

3. Describe the three basic types of transparencies and how they are made.

_____

_____

_____

_____

_____

4. List the do's and don'ts of using transparencies.

_____

_____

_____

_____

_____

_____

_____

_____

_____

5. Describe how you can use the overhead projector and the board in combination.

_____

_____

_____

_____

_____

■ Doublecheck Answers

1. Has a very high visual impact. Saves time (since transparencies are usually made before the session). Gives a high degree of control over what the trainee will see and when. Allows a high degree of freedom for the trainer's imagination.

2. a. You can make the *size of the image* on the screen larger by moving the whole projector away from the screen.
   b. You can bring a blurred image on the screen into sharp *focus* by moving the focus head and the horizontal arm up or down the vertical shaft.
   c. You can alter the *position* on the screen (1) in the vertical plane by rotating the adjustable focus head up and down on the pivot and (2) in the horizontal plane by turning or moving the projector sideways.
   d. A blue/brown coloring on the screen when you turn on the projector indicates that the bulb is too close to or too far from the stage. An adjusting wheel either at the back of or underneath the projector moves the bulb up or down.

3. The *write-on* transparency is a clear acetate sheet on which you can use special colored pens that have either non-permanent or permanent ink. The *burn-on* transparency is a treated, heat-sensitive acetate sheet. The tip of the right-hand upper corner is cut off. This transparency is made by putting the transparency and a high-carbon master through a "heat machine." The image of the master is then burned onto the transparency. The *photocopy* transparency is made when a treated acetate sheet is passed through a plain paper photocopier.

4. **Do's:**

   Use colored background transparencies to cut down glare. Attach each transparency to cardboard frames or mounts. Lay the pointer on top of the transparency when pointing to a particular word or item. Mask areas and then progressively uncover them to emphasize the particular words or part of the diagram. Use overlays for complicated images. Write short notes on the transparency mounts as reminders.

   Dont's:

   Don't talk to the screen. Don't walk between the projector and the screen. Don't stand between the projected image and the trainees. Don't leave the overhead projector light switched on between transparencies.

5. Write the main points on the board progressively, and expand each point using the overhead projector as you proceed. The steps are (a) Write the key word on the board. (b) Walk to one side. (c) Wait until the trainees finish writing. (d) Illustrate the key word with a transparency on the overhead projector.

21
AUDIO-VISUAL TIPS

Key Concepts

- *Importance of audio-visual media.* Essential to dramatizing presentations, developing ideas, and increasing motivation.

- *Slides.* Available in various sizes. Good for "real" scenes.

- *Audio-tapes.* Cassette form especially easy to handle. Useful for "importing" an authority into the session.

- *Slide-tapes.* Most common format is 35-mm slides with standard audio cassettes. Easily produced.

- *Filmstrip-tapes.* Easy to handle (and impossible to get out of order) but inflexible.

- *Motion pictures.* Most common format is 16 mm with optical sound track. Gives very lifelike representation and is suitable for large audiences.

- *Video.* Variety of formats. Same advantages as motion pictures. Relatively easy to make yourself.

- *Using audio-visuals.* Use either as adjuncts to a session or as a substitute for the trainer. Select and use the audio-visual with care. Know your equipment.

Learning Objectives

After you have completed this chapter, you should be able to

- Explain the importance of the audio-visual media.

- Describe the different types of audio-visual aids available.

- List the steps for presenting an audio-visual.

INTRODUCTION

The presence of television in almost every home in the country has greatly changed our attitudes toward media. Whereas Grandfather was content to read a description of an event in the newspaper, nowadays we expect to see it for ourselves on television. Our attitude has spilled over into the training situation, where trainees now expect much greater use to be made of audio-visual technology to dramatize a presentation. We generally applaud this approach, for it often leads to improved motivation and learning and always adds variety to the training activities. It does mean, however, that trainers must develop skills in the selection and use of the media. In this chapter, we will look at these skills.

TYPES OF AUDIO-VISUALS

We have already discussed the board and the overhead projector, the two most frequently used visual media. We will now look at slides (a visual medium), audio-tapes (an audio medium), and then the four major types of audio-visuals:

1. Slide-tapes

2. Filmstrip-tapes

3. Motion pictures

4. Video

Slides

You can purchase slides in a variety of sizes. The most common is 35 mm. Slides are better than the overhead projector for presenting "real" scenes (rather than *drawings* of scenes). They are also better in some aspects of microscopic and technical areas where a camera can photograph what the unaided eye cannot see. The major disadvantage of slides is that you must darken the room to see the projected image clearly. Another is that compared to an overhead transparency, the production of a slide may be a rather complex procedure, with special lenses, film types and lighting.

Audio-Tapes

Audio-tapes in cassette form are easy to handle and can have significant impact if used to "import" into a session a recognized authority on a particular topic. Use such audio material in short bursts to prevent boredom. Make sure they have a reasonable quality of sound reproduction so that trainees can understand the speaker without difficulty. The major problem for the trainer is to minimize visual distractions.

Slide-Tapes

The most common format is 35-mm slides with standard audio-cassettes, but several other formats are available. The major advantage of slide-tapes over other types of audio-visuals is the comparative ease with which they can be produced by any trainer. They are somewhat limited, however, by the "still" nature of the visual image.

Filmstrip-Tapes

Compared to slides, filmstrips lack the flexibility necessary to allow minor modifications to the content and/or order of the visuals. They are, on the other hand, easier to handle and impossible to get out of sequence.

With both slide-tapes and filmstrip-tapes, you must be sure that audio and visuals are synchronized. "Out of sync" audio-visuals produce a negative learning experience.

Motion Pictures

We have several formats, but 16 mm with an optical rather than magnetic sound track is virtually universal in industrial and educational situations. The major advantages of this type of audio-visual are its lifelike representation (using color, motion, and integrated sound) and its suitability for presentation to large audiences.

Video (or Closed-Circuit Television)

Video has the same advantages as motion pictures, including suitability for relatively large audiences when using a 5-foot (1500 mm) screen that is now available. It has the additional great advantage that you can "make your own," which is particularly important in providing detailed feed-back to trainees learning behavioral skills.

At present, the technology of video is not standardized, so we suggest consultation with an expert before making any purchases of equipment. Also, when borrowing or buying video-tapes, you must be absolutely certain of the format of your system. Video-tapes may use 1-inch, U-matic (3/4 inch), VHS (1/2 inch), Beta (1/2 inch), or 8-mm formats; and they may be recorded using PAL (European and Australian), NTSC (American), or one of several other systems. A clear initial specification of the format required for your equipment will save many conversion and/or exchange problems later.

Video can be used in several different ways, each of which has different requirements.

- Pre-recorded video. This is basically a motion picture translated to the electronic medium. It has the same advantages and disadvantages and is used in the same way as a motion picture.

- Video for feedback. This requires a very basic "make your own" capacity. A small camera and microphone to plug into the video-tape recorder are usually sufficient, and no high-level photography or production skills are required. The usual procedure is to simply point the stationary (and unattended) video-camera at trainees learning behavioral skills, and then replay the tape (either publicly or privately) to allow the trainee to see his or her performance from an outsider's viewpoint. This can be a powerful (if sometimes traumatic) learning tool, especially if accompanied by a structured analysis process, which usually takes the form of a questionnaire. The feedback sheets on the theory, skill, and discussion sessions which are included in this book are examples of structured analysis processes suitable for use with video feedback.

- Homemade video programs. Homemade video programs can utilize the full range of equipment, from one person carrying a "port-a-pack" to a multi-camera studio, editing suite, and six-person production crew. No matter how grand the production, "making your own" has the distinct advantage of showing "real" people in real situations, which reduces the problem of transfer of training. The major difficulties include quality comparisons with network television and the need to work with amateur talent.

Making your own programs requires a wide range of skills which are beyond the scope of this book. However, any skilled trainer should be able to use existing skills to create a basic video script. In many ways, the process is the same as creating a training session. The major steps are:

1. Analyze the audience (compare to training needs analysis).

2. Write program objectives (compare to writing training objectives).

3. Decide main points of content (compare to task breakdown).

4. Visualize the pictures that will get the message across. A storyboard (cartoon-like layout of the main pictures) is very useful here (compare to planning visual aids).

5. Write the dialogue/narration to be used (compare to filling in the details on the session plan).

The critical point to remember is that video is a visual medium, so you should always be thinking in pictures. The ultimate test of an educational or training video is to turn off the audio and check that the intended audience can extract the major learning points by watching the pictures only.

USING AUDIO-VISUALS

You can use audio-visuals in two very distinct ways. You can use them as adjuncts to a session in order to illustrate particular points. Audio-visuals used in this way will be brief. They are often "homemade" by the trainer to serve his or her specific purpose. The more common use of audio-visuals, however, is as a substitute for the trainer. The audio-visual presentation itself almost becomes the session. Here, the trainer's primary responsibility is to establish that *the goals* for *this* group of trainees are likely to be achieved by using a particular audio-visual. The goals of the present session must coincide with the goals of the originators of the audio-visual. If the trainer does not take great care regarding this point, trainees will not see the relevance of the audio-visual and will quickly assume that audio-visuals are for "rest and recreation." We have no objection whatever to audio-visuals being entertaining, but they must also (and much more importantly) promote learning and be seen to promote learning.

The prerequisite to using audio-visuals is to be thoroughly familiar with the operation of your equipment. At a basic level, know how to set up and use each projector, player, recorder, camera, and so on that you may use as a training aid. When you have done this, we suggest that you also learn how to diagnose problems in the equipment, perform basic repairs (such as replacing bulbs in projectors), and carry out routine maintenance (such as lens and head cleaning, and oiling). You will then be both competent and confident in the use of your equipment.

Having mastered the equipment, how do you use an audio-visual aid in a training session?

Prior to Session

The session objectives. Yes, again we must start with the objectives. Once you have set these, you can identify—quite specifically—the contribution that an audio-visual may make to the session.

Gathering material. Most audio-visual suppliers provide catalogues, and the better catalogues provide the title, running time, and a brief synopsis of the content. For other material, you may be able to gather information from acquaintances and contacts who are involved in training. Select and obtain all the material that appears appropriate to your identified objectives.

The preview. View the audio-visuals you have chosen. The aim is to select the aid most suited to your needs and to note anything about the program that may influence the way you will use it in the training session. Basic questions to ask yourself include:

- Does the audio-visual help to achieve my objective?

- Does the audio-visual have a clear message that it puts across convincingly?

- Are there aspects of the audio-visual that could be dysfunctional or distracting? For example, look for accent of the speakers; cultural differences; life-value differences; out-of-date clothes, buildings, or cars; inappropriate gimmicks; and actors who are distractingly recognizable.

Selection. Choose the audio-visual that best meets your need. Record in your audio-visual file the title, source, cost, and any other useful information. Take steps to ensure that the audio-visual is available for your session.

View the selected aid again (or even several times, if necessary). Check that you can briefly describe the content of the audio-visual, and note any key concepts or illustrations that you want trainees to particularly observe. If you want the trainees to note any rules or lists of steps contained in the audio-visual, decide what action you should take in relation to the rules or lists. You might make an overhead transparency or a poster for each. You might even wish to provide a copy for each trainee. Alternatively, you may decide that the trainees would benefit from some activity, so take note of where to stop the audio-visual so that trainees may take notes without having to absorb additional audio-visual material at the same time.

Check that the *equipment* you need for showing the audio-visual is available and that you are able to operate it.

If necessary, *adjust your session plan* to optimize learning from the audio-visual that you have chosen.

Presenting the Audio-Visual

Have the audio-visual set up and ready to run before the session begins. A little time spent on this can save you from disruptive and embarrassing equipment failures later.

Introduce the audio-visual. Briefly describe what will happen. Next, explain why you have selected this particular audio-visual. Then list (preferably using visual aids) the key points you would like the trainees to particularly note. Finally, briefly mention any aspect of the audio-visual that could distract the trainees' attention from the basic message (for example, the familiar face of a TV star).

Then show the audio-visual.

At the End of the Audio-Visual

Hold a "debriefing" at the end of the audio-visual. Follow these steps:

1. Use a preplanned strategy to regain the active attention of the trainees. Some audio-visuals promote a somewhat passive learning environment, and trainees may need something to get them active again.

2. Through questioning, draw from the trainees the pertinent points made by the audio-visual, and list these on a board or other visual aid. Alternatively, ask trainees to write down the key points, so that every trainee becomes active.

3. From these points, develop a statement of the main theme of the audio-visual.

4. Show how this theme helps to achieve the objective of the session.

After the Session

1. Complete any report forms required on the condition of the audio-visual.

2. Collect all your notes about the audio-visual. Make additional notes on its apparent usefulness, the trainees' reactions, and how to use it next time. File all notes for possible future reference.

3. Return the audio-visual to the place it came from.

4. Arrange for payment of any charges.

Comment

Although they may be powerful learning devices, audio-visuals are by no means foolproof. By following the procedures outlined in this chapter, you can maximize the benefits of using audio-visuals and at the same time avoid their pitfalls. Remember that the original, and often still the best, audio-visual aid to learning is the face-to-face trainer. Consequently, the critical question a trainer should ask about any audio-visual is, "Does the audio-visual promote the learning of the material better than I could promote it myself?"

✔ Checkpoint: Audio-Visuals

Match each item in the left-hand column with the appropriate item in the right-hand column.

1. audio-tape _____

2. slide-tape _____

3. Filmstrip-tape _____

4. Motion picture _____

5. Video _____

a. Flexible enough to allow you to change the order.

b. Has to be used in short bursts to prevent boredom.

c. Most common format is 16 mm.

d. Gives still pictures that are impossible to get out of order.

e. Invites audience participation.

f. Allows you to make your own moving images.

Indicate true (T) or false (F), or fill in the blank.

6. Audio-visuals can be used either as adjuncts to the session or as a _____ for the trainer.

7. You must be thoroughly familiar with the _____ of your equipment.

8. If another trainer recommends an audio-visual, it is not necessary to preview it. _____

9. Introduce the audio-visual so that the trainees know what will happen. _____

10. Debriefing at the end of a film is not necessary. _____

11. The major uses of video are _____ video, video for _____, and _____ video.

12. When writing your own video scripts, the critical thing is to _____.

■ **Checkpoint Answers**

1. b   2. a   3. d   4. c   5. f   6. substitute (or replacement)   7. operation   8. F   9. T
10. F   11. Prerecorded, feedback, make-your-own   12. think in pictures.

PROCEDURE: SETTING UP THE MOVIE PROJECTOR

We have already mentioned the need to be thoroughly familiar with the operation of your equipment. To achieve this, creating an operating procedure is invaluable. As an illustration, here is a procedure for setting up a movie projector. The procedure also illustrates several points important in the setting up of any audio-visual aids. It is also a good example of a task breakdown.

1. Set up a portable stand or another firm base to place the projector on.

2. Place the projector on the stand. Unclip the speaker if it is part of the projector's protective casing.

3. If possible, place the speaker under the screen. As a result, the voice will appear to come from the image on the screen.

4. Ensure that the speaker lead is plugged into both the speaker and the projector. (It is usual to lay the speaker lead around the walls for safety reasons. The lead can also be taped to the floor for additional safety.)

5. Set up the "film spool" and "take-up spool" arms on the projector.

6. Place the take-up spool on the rear arm.

7. Plug the projector lead into the power socket and turn on.

8. Turn on the "power on" switch on the projector.

9. Turn on the projector lamp so that the light falls on the screen. Adjust the lens so that the perimeter of the light becomes quite sharp.

10. Raise the front of the projector so that the top of the rectangle of light falls just under the top of the screen.

11. Move the projector and stand forward or backward so that the two sides of the square of light touch the two sides of the screen. Re-adjust as in 9 and 10.

12. Load the film. (Follow the instruction manual for your particular make and model of projector for this operation.)

13. Run the film through, noting when the starting point is reached. Usually this starting point is the name of the film, but there is no reason why you cannot start half-way through the film if the first half does not help you attain the objectives of the session.

14. Check the focus and adjust the framer if necessary.

15. Adjust the volume to a satisfactory level.

16. Check the viewing and hearing quality of the film from the most distant seats in the room.

17. Adjust the room and/or equipment until viewing and hearing are satisfactory.

18. Reverse the film until the starting point is again reached.

19. Switch off the projector and unplug the lead at the power socket (For safety).

SUMMARY

Trainees expect audio-visuals to be used in training sessions. Select the type of audio-visual that suits the situation. Know your equipment thoroughly. Assess the audio-visual program before the session. Present it in a way that assists in achieving the learning objective(s). Debrief after the audio-visual. Keep administrative and evaluative notes about the audio-visual.

Chapter 21 Doublecheck

1. Why is it important to use audio-visual media?

   _____

   _____

   _____

   _____

2. List the one visual, one audio, and four audio-visual media discussed in this chapter.

   _____

   _____

   _____

   _____

3. What questions should you ask when previewing an audio-visual program?

   _____

   _____

   _____

   _____

4. How should you introduce an audio-visual to trainees?

   _____

   _____

   _____

Application Exercise

Analyze the film projection procedure on page 314 to identify factors that must be considered whenever you set up any piece of audio-visual equipment. Construct a general checklist for all audio-visual equipment.

■ Doublecheck Answers

1. Involves the principle of multi-sense learning. About 80 percent of our information comes from sight. (One picture is worth a thousand words.) Because of daily exposure to media, trainees expect trainers to use audio-visuals.

2. Slide, audio-tape, slide-tape, filmstrip-tape, motion pictures, video.

3. Does it help to achieve my objective(s)? Does it have a clear message that it puts across convincingly? Does it have aspects that are dysfunctional or distracting (such as accents, cultural or value differences, out-of-date props, inappropriate gimmicks, and recognizable actors)?

4. Explain briefly what will happen. Explain why you are showing the audio-visual. List the key points you would like the trainees to note. Warn of any distracting factors.

■ Application Exercise Notes

☐ Is the equipment on a firm, stable base?

☐ Are various items of equipment connected as necessary?

☐ Is the sound source close to the visual image?

☐ Are all cords placed safely?

☐ Does the visual image use the whole screen?

☐ Is the visual image clear?

☐ Is the audio volume satisfactory?

☐ Have I checked that everyone in the room can see and hear?

☐ Is everything left ready to start?

VI. MANAGING THE LEARNING EXPERIENCE

22
DESIGNING A PROGRAM

Key Concepts

- *Concluding objectives*. The training objectives for the whole training program.

- *Enabling objectives*. The objectives that enable the concluding objectives to be achieved.

- *Session objectives*. The enabling objectives are divided into session objectives, which become the objectives for each session conducted during the program.

- *Program structure*. The program is divided into an introduction, a body, and a conclusion.

- *The written training schedule*. The final product of program design. A day-by-day description of what happens in the training program.

- *The matrix program*. Allows the entire program to be seen at one glance. Has the days of the week on one axis and the time of the day on the other.

Learning Objectives

After you have completed this chapter, you should be able to

- Explain the hierarchy of objectives.

- Diagram the hierarchy of objectives for a training program.

- Discuss the structure of a program.

- List and discuss five other considerations when designing a training program.

- Diagram a matrix schedule.

DECISION TIME

Now comes decision time. You have been given the objectives of a training program from the training needs analysis, and now you have to decide what to include, emphasize, and exclude. Would it be more beneficial to cover one particular aspect before another? What guidelines are needed on how the skills and information should be presented, practiced, and tested? What about the preferences of the trainees? Indeed, do they have any preferences? How can we best make the program appear worthwhile—to the trainees, their supervisors, and management? Will achieving this interfere with the training process?

When designing a training program, questions such as these must be examined closely. The questions must be answered; so let's look at the problem in an organized manner to see if we can create order out of the chaos. We will look first at the hierarchy of objectives and then, using an extended example, detail how you can design and structure a program. This example will result in a matrix schedule for a fully developed training program.

PROGRAM STRUCTURE: HIERARCHY OF OBJECTIVES

In Chapter 7 of this book, we discussed the writing of training objectives and stated that each training objective should contain three components:

1. The terminal behavior statement

2. The standards of performance

3. The conditions of performance

We will now discuss three specific types of training objectives. These three types form a hierarchy, and each type has the components of terminal behavior, standards, and conditions.

Concluding Objectives

The training program as a whole has objectives that are known as *concluding* objectives. These concluding objectives are the first in a hierarchy of objectives and are the result of a training needs analysis (covered in Chapter 6). They should describe the terminal behavior for the trainees and the standards they should achieve at the end of the training program, as well as the conditions under which the trainees are expected to perform.

Enabling Objectives

Next in the hierarchy come the *enabling* objectives. These split the concluding objectives into manageable parts. They are sometimes referred to as *achieving* objectives because they make it possible to achieve the final program objectives. These enabling objectives also have three components—behavior, standards, and conditions.

Session Objectives

Third in the hierarchy are *session* objectives, which split the enabling objectives into the sessions that will ultimately make up the program. Session objectives define the goal of each session. You may wish to refer back to Chapter 7 for examples of session objectives.

Sometimes session objectives come directly from the concluding objective if the subject matter is specific enough to make enabling objectives unnecessary.

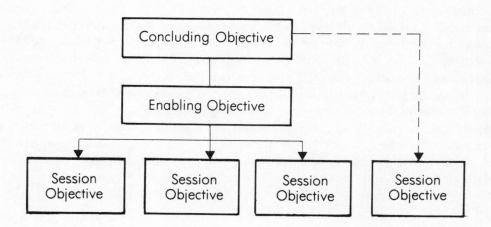

Then in a modular fashion, you can add units to extend the program.

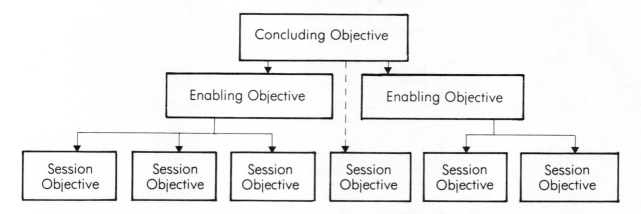

Let's look at an example of the hierarchy of objectives for a one-week training program. The concluding objective for the program might be:

In a private room with one table and two chairs, conduct a 20-minute performance appraisal interview according to standards established during the program.

That's quite a mouthful, so let's simplify it a little.

Conduct a 20' performance appraisal interview.

To achieve this concluding objective, we will need the following enabling objectives. (These have been reduced to the behavior statement for convenience during this discussion. Normally they would contain statements of standards and conditions.)

1. Explain the assessing methods of using an absolute standard and using a comparison.

2. Demonstrate the interviewing skills of questioning, non-verbal feedback, and verbal feedback.

3. Demonstrate the tell and sell, tell and listen, and problem-solving types of performance appraisal interview.

Each of these enabling objectives can be subdivided into session objectives. For example:

Explain the assessing methods of using an absolute standard and using a comparison.

becomes

1. Assess a fellow trainee by using the absolute standard method.

2. Assess a fellow trainee by using the comparison method.

In diagrammatic form, these concluding, enabling, and session objectives can be shown as at the top of the next page.

There is some other information that the trainees will need in order to achieve the concluding objective. This information is:

1. Explain the four steps in appraising performance.

2. Conduct a job analysis.

3. Explain the structure of an interview.

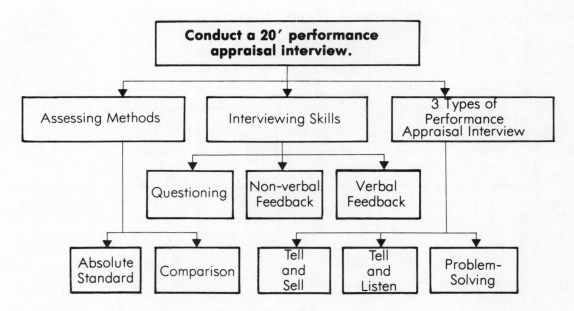

These do not have any enabling objectives and therefore become session objectives.

The hierarchy of objectives for the one-week program appears on the following page.

PROGRAM STRUCTURE: DETAILS

Although it is not possible to say that a training program must follow any definite model (training situations are too diversified and the variables too complex), the theory-session model provides a useful basic structure. It utilizes many of the principles of learning. A program design that is based on it will facilitate learning because of built-in advantages (quite apart from the content and techniques you use). Let's review the structure of the theory-session model:

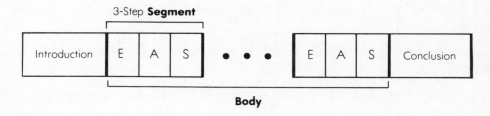

Just as the theory-session structure has an introduction, a body, and a conclusion, so too will the program structure have an introduction, a body, and a conclusion.

1. Introduction

When the trainees first arrive, they will feel strange and probably a little insecure. Your introduction to the program must orient them and point the way ahead. If that sounds familiar, it should! The introduction to a training program is essentially the same as the introduction to a theory session. It should

1. Gain interest.

2. Check current knowledge.

3. Orient.

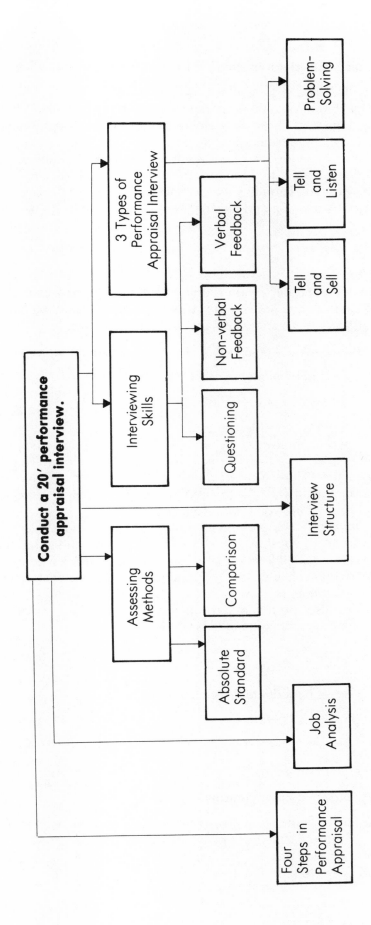

325

4. Motivate.

5. Preview what is ahead (for example, by referring to the concluding objectives).

However, you will also have some other considerations.

Program opening. To reinforce the importance of the program, ask a VIP to open the course and indicate why management chose the trainees to attend. This VIP can be the manager of the training function or, preferably, a senior line manager.

Introductions. Since many of the trainees will not know each other or you, time should be allowed for introductions. From 2 to 5 minutes per trainee is usually sufficient.

Administrivia. Any organization has its red tape, rules, and regulations. Set aside some time to speak on such items as opening and closing times, where lunch can be taken, and where the bathrooms are.

2. Body

Just as the body of the theory session is divided into three-step segments of explanation, activity, and summary, similarly the body of the training program should be divided into three-step segments of explanation, activity, and summary. In a training program:

- The explanation step could be a theory session, a lecture, or a discussion.

- The activity step could be practice, role play, or a skill session.

- The summary step remains a summary.

There are some additional considerations.

Regular reviews. Two or three reviews are needed during a one-week program to give the trainees an opportunity to go over the information covered to that time. This usually takes about 30 minutes and allows the trainee a short "time out" to assimilate the given information before going on to new information. It can take the form of the trainer doing the reviewing, the trainees doing the reviewing (as in group work), or even a test.

The training techniques. Some preliminary analysis of techniques is advisable at the design stage. The important factor to consider is how much information the trainees have, as identified by the training needs analysis. Little information indicates a trainer-centered method (a conventional theory session), while considerable information indicates a more trainee-centered method (a discussion or modified theory session).

Of course, you can also use a variety of methods to produce a variety of learning experiences and to reduce the possibility of trainee boredom.

3. Conclusion

Again, the theory-session model tells us what to do here (with a few additions):

1. Recapitulation.

2. Use a test.

3. Link to subsequent programs.

4. Use questions to clear up any misunderstandings.

5. Allow time for the trainees to give you feedback on their impressions of the program. This is the measurement of the reaction level as discussed in Designing Measurement Criteria and Tools (Chapter 9) and is also a valuable source of information if you wish to redesign the program.

You may also wish to invite a VIP to close the program and to encourage the trainees to transfer back to the job what they have learned. This transfer of training can be further assisted by follow-up activities (see Chapter 10).

PROGRAM STRUCTURE: EXAMPLE

Using our example of a one-week program on performance appraisal interviewing, the session objectives in the figure on page 325 would become a program structure as follows:

1. **Introduction**

2. **Body**

    a. Explanation—Four steps in performance appraisal (a theory session).

      Activity—Would be included in the theory session. No special activity needed.

      Summary—No special summary needed.

    b. Explanation—Job analysis (a theory session).

      Activity—Practice on analyzing two jobs of trainee's choice.

      Summary—Summarize main points.

    c. Explanation—Assessment using an absolute standard (a theory session).

      Activity—Using job analysis as an absolute standard to assess two other people.

      Summary—Summarize main points.

The structure would continue in this way until the conclusion.

✔ Checkpoint: Designing a Program

Indicate true (T) or false (F), or fill in the blank.

1. The hierarchy of objectives in the program structure includes the concluding objectives, the _____ objectives, and the session objectives.

2. The concluding objectives split the session objectives into manageable parts. _____

3. Session objectives define the goal of the session. _____

4. Session objectives can come straight from the concluding objective. _____

5. The program structure has little similarity to the theory-session structure. _____

6. There is no need to allow time for trainees to introduce themselves at the beginning of the program. _____

7. The introduction segment of the program should:
   Gain interest
   Check current knowledge.
   Orient.
   Motivate.
   _____what is ahead.

8. The body of the program is divided into three-step segments of explanation, activity, and summary. _____

9. Training techniques should be taken into account when designing the body of a program. _____

10. The conclusion segment of the program should:
    Recapitulate.
    Use a test.
    Link to subsequent programs.
    Use _____ to clear up misunderstandings.
    Allow time for the trainees to give feedback.

■ **Checkpoint Answers**

1. enabling   2. F   3. T   4. T   5. F   6. F   7. Preview   8. T   9. T   10. questions

SOME OTHER CONSIDERATIONS

Although there are no hard and fast rules for designing training programs, the theory-session analogy is a good basis on which to start. In addition, you should consider the following points.

Needs/Expectations of Trainees

The trainees will arrive at the program with certain expectations of what they want out of it. These should be identified before designing the program. Generally, try to satisfy the trainees' strongest needs as early as possible, even if it goes against the usual "logical" order.

Must Know, Should Know, Could Know

In a similar fashion to what occurred in the theory session, prioritize the information/skills that could be presented during the program into "must know, should know, could know." Present the should-know and could-know material only if time allows.

Building Blocks

If you look at what is to be covered during the program, it will become obvious that some skills or knowledge will have to be covered before other skills or knowledge can be presented and understood. These primary skills and knowledge are referred to as "building blocks." These building blocks have to be identified and then sequenced so that the rest of the program can be built upon them.

In our example of a performance appraisal interview program, we have a session on assessing by the absolute standard method. The absolute standard that is used in performance appraisal is the person specification, and this comes from a job analysis. Therefore, as you will see in our example of a program structure, the session on job analysis comes before the session on assessing using an absolute standard.

On-the-Job Sequence

When designing a program, refer continually to the on-the-job situation. The best advice we have heard on designing a training program is that the trainer should "do or observe the trainee's job and see what information and/or materials the trainee gets, how they arrive, and the sequence of operations that the trainee performs on them."

Activities

We have discussed earlier the importance of activities in designing a training program, and we would like to reinforce it here.

If you have given the trainees some theory—Test it!
If you have given them a skill—Practice it!

Principles of Learning

These should be evident throughout the entire design.

The Interaction

There will be at least four major variables in a training program. Look at the figure below.

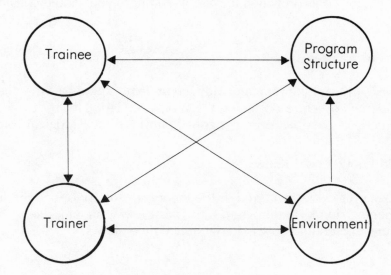

These variables interact with each other. For example, a lack of equipment or a lack of certain trainee skills may necessitate program modifications. Poor program design may demotivate the trainer. A skillful trainer may succeed in creating an environment that is highly supportive of training and trainees. It is difficult to allow for all the situations that may arise from this interaction, and so you can expect some interesting challenges when you actually run the program.

Some problems can, however, be anticipated. Two of these (both related to the environment variable) are:

The first-day syndrome. We have found that the trainees remember little of the early sessions presented to them, particularly during the first half of the first day. They are too busy taking in their new environment. Therefore, try to schedule a fair bit of activity during this time, preferably on should-know rather than must-know material. At the same time, be careful to avoid giving the impression that these sessions are throwaways or that the remainder of the program is a waste of time.

The after-lunch session. Another problem time is the first period after lunch. The trainees tend to be rather sleepy. Again, try to program activities or dynamic speakers. At all costs, avoid films in this time slot.

THE FINAL PRODUCT

The final observable product of all this work is the written training schedule. It should contain:

1. The *concluding objectives* listed clearly on the first page.

2. The *day-by-day schedule*. At the minimum, this should cover

   The time each session commences.

   The title of each session.

   The name of the trainer/guest speaker who will conduct the session.

In addition, the schedule is a valuable place for a brief content statement of each session. You can see an example of this kind of schedule on the next page.

Monday

9:30 a.m. PROGRAM OPENING (Mr. D. E. Leonard, General Manager)

9:45 a.m. PERSONAL INTRODUCTIONS
Interview a fellow program member; then introduce him/her to the group.

10:30 a.m. COFFEE BREAK

10:45 a.m. PROGRAM OBJECTIVES (Program Leader)
Arrangements and Administration

11:15 a.m. PERSONAL OBJECTIVES
What do you want out of this course?

11:45 a.m. REASONS FOR PERFORMANCE APPRAISAL
(Mr. F. Lonsdale, Personnel Manager)
Why the Company sees performance appraisal as important.

12:30 p.m. LUNCH

1:30 p.m. FOUR STEPS IN PERFORMANCE APPRAISAL (Program Leader)
Any performance appraisal system has four steps:
• a person specification
• observation
• comparison
• feedback

3:00 p.m. COFFEE BREAK

3:15 p.m. JOB ANALYSIS (Dr. L. Edwards, University Lecturer)
How to analyze a job and come up with a person specification.

5:00 p.m. ANALYZE A JOB
Select three jobs that you know quite well, and produce a person specification for each.

5:30 p.m. DINNER

6:30 p.m.
to   ANALYZE A JOB (Continued)
8:00 p.m.

3. *The matrix schedule.* It would also be worth your while to include what is known as a *matrix schedule.* The day-by-day written schedule usually extends over several pages, and it is difficult to see the flow of the training program and what interacts with what. With a matrix schedule, the entire program can be seen at one glance. A sample matrix schedule is on the next page.

Performance Appraisal Interview Program

	8:00	9:00	10:00	11:00	12:00	1:00	2:00	3:00	4:00	5:00	6:00	7:00	8:00
Mon.		Progs. Intro-Open. Actions	Coffee	Progs. Pers. Obst.: Ost.	Reasons for Perf. Appraisal	L	Four Steps in Perf. Appraisal	Coffee	Job Analysis	Analyze a Job	D	Analyze a Job (cont.)	
Tues.		Assessing — An Overview	Coffee	Absolute Standard Method / Comparison Method	Practice —Assessing	U	Practice — Assessing (cont.)	Coffee	Structure of an Interview	Practice Struct. Int.	I	Review Film	
Wed.		Questioning	Coffee	Practice —Questioning	Non-Verbal Feedback	N	Practice Verbal — Non-Verbal Feedback	Coffee	Practice Verbal Feedback	Practice —Verbal Feedback (cont.)	N	Social Evening	
Thur.		Types of Perf. Appraisal Interviewing	Coffee	Practice —Types of Appraisal Interviewing		C	Preparation for 20-minute Interviews				E	Review Film	
Fri.		20-Minute Interviews				H	20-Minute Interviews (cont.)	Coffee	Program Review		R		

Comment

In conclusion, designing a training program remains as much an art as a science. A program design used successfully in one situation is often less than successful on another occasion. Individual preferences of trainers and trainees are but two of the significant factors that can vary the situation. You must remain flexible, learn from experience, and carefully assess your training environment before designing programs.

✓ Checkpoint: Some other Considerations and the Final Product

Indicate true (T) or false (F), or fill in the blank.

1. The needs and expectations of the trainees do not need to be taken into account. _____

2. The primary skills and knowledge that need to be covered before other skills and knowledge can be presented and understood are called _____.

3. When designing a program, continually refer to the on-the-job situation. _____

4. If you have given the trainees some theory, _____ it!
   If you have given them a skill, _____ it!

5. The principles of learning should be evident throughout the entire design. _____

6. The four major variables in a training program are the trainee, the trainer, the program, and the _____.

7. During the first half of the first day, the trainees remember little of the sessions presented to them. This is called the _____ syndrome.

8. The after-lunch session is a good time to show a film. _____

9. In the written training schedule, the _____ objectives should be listed clearly on the first page.

10. In the _____ schedule, the entire program can be seen at one glance.

■ **Checkpoint Answers**

1. F   2. building blocks   3. T   4. test, practice   5. T   6. environment   7. first-day
8. F   9. concluding   10. matrix

Checklist: Designing a Training Program

Did I

- [ ] Develop a hierarchy of objectives for the program?
- [ ] Structure an introduction and a conclusion into the program?
- [ ] Use three-step EAS segments for the body?
- [ ] Diagnose, and appropriately build into the program, necessary building blocks?
- [ ] Utilize an on-the-job sequence of events?
- [ ] Schedule activities wherever possible?
- [ ] Appropriately utilize all principles of learning?
- [ ] Produce written day-by-day and matrix schedules?
- [ ] Try to take into account trainee expectations and needs?

SUMMARY

The training needs analysis identifies the concluding objectives of the program. This starts the hierarchy of objectives—the concluding objectives, the enabling objectives, and the session objectives. Using these, you can structure the program. The program structure is similar to the theory-session structure in that it has an introduction, a body, and a conclusion. The body is divided into three-step segments of explanation, activity, and summary.

Chapter 22 Doublecheck

1. What is meant by the hierarchy of objectives?

   _____

   _____

   _____

   _____

   _____

2. What should you do in the introduction to a program? Are there any special considerations?

   _____

   _____

   _____

   _____

   _____

3. How can the body of the program be structured? Are there any additional considerations?

   _____

   _____

   _____

   _____

4. What should be done in the conclusion of the program?

   _____

   _____

   _____

   _____

5. Although the theory-session analogy is a good base for the structure of a program, what other points should be taken into consideration?

_____

_____

_____

_____

_____

■ Doublecheck Answers

1. The hierarchy of objectives is: *concluding* objectives, *enabling* objectives, and *session* objectives.

    The concluding objectives are the objectives for the whole training program. They are the first in the hierarchy and are the result of a training needs analysis.

    The enabling objectives split the concluding objectives into manageable parts. They are sometimes referred to as achieving objectives because they enable these final program objectives to be achieved.

    Session objectives split the enabling objectives into the sessions that will ultimately make up the program. Session objectives specify the goal of each session. Sometimes session objectives come directly from the concluding objectives.

2. You should do the following in the introduction to a program: Gain interest. Check current knowledge. Orient. Motivate. Preview what is ahead.

    Special considerations are: Ask a VIP to open the course and to indicate to the trainees why management chose them. Allow time for the trainees to introduce themselves. Set aside some time to talk about administrivia.

3. The body of the program can be divided into three-step segments of explanation, activity, and summary where the explanation could be a theory session, lecture, or discussion; the activity could be practice, role plays, or a skill session, and the summary step remains a summary.

    Some additional considerations are: Reviews to give trainees "time out" to assimilate the given information before going on to new information. Some preliminary analysis at the design stage on the training techniques to use.

4. In the conclusion, the following should be carried out: Recapitulate. Use a test. Link to subsequent programs. Use questions to clear up any misunderstandings. Allow time for the trainees to give feedback on their impression of the program.

    You may also wish to invite a VIP to close the program and to encourage the trainees to transfer back to the job what they have learned.

5. The trainees will arrive at the program with certain expectations of what they want out of it. These should be identified before designing the program. Generally, try to satisfy the trainee's strongest needs as early as possible.

    Prioritize the information/skills into must know, should know, could know. Only present should-know and could-know material if time allows.

    Some skills or knowledge (building blocks) will have to be covered before other skills or knowledge can be presented and understood.

    Continually refer to the on-the-job situation to see what information and/or materials are received, how they arrive, and the sequence of operations that are performed on them.

    Activities: If you have given them some theory, test it! If you have given them a skill, practice it!

    Ensure that the principles of learning are evident throughout the entire design.

    Take account of the interaction of the four variables: the trainee, the trainer, the program structure, and the environment. In particular, pay attention to the first-day syndrome and the after-lunch session.

23
MARKETING OF TRAINING

Key Concepts

- *Core Concept.* This identifies the use the purchaser will make of the product.
- *Tangible Element.* Describes the physical components of the product.
- *Intangible Element.* The additional and often unrecognized benefits that come with the product.
- *Client decision behavior.* The customer goes through the buying stages of awareness of need, search for means, assessment behavior, and post-action behavior.
- *Buyer roles.* There are five buying roles—initiator, influencer, decider, purchaser, and user.

Learning Objectives

After you have completed this chapter, you should be able to

- Describe the difference between selling and marketing.
- List and describe the three elements of a product.
- Analyze client decision-making behavior.
- List and describe the five buying roles.

SELLING AND MARKETING

"Well, I did everything right and ended up with an A-1 quality program. How come nobody turned up?" This can be the outcome when a competent trainer produces a well-designed program but fails to market it. In fact, the trainer even failed to sell the program.

There is a significant difference between selling and marketing. Selling has its emphasis on making a product, then looking around to find someone to buy it. Marketing, on the other hand, first identifies the customer need, then manufactures the product to fulfill that need.

We consider that training must be viewed from the marketing mode. In this chapter, we will first examine the elements that make up a product (the training program) before looking at the decision steps a potential client goes through when buying a product. Finally, we have to be aware that there are a number of buyer roles and that more than one person may take on these various roles.

ELEMENTS OF A PRODUCT

A training course is a product whose continued existence depends on its ability to satisfy a need. A product has three elements: the core concept, the tangible element, and the intangible element.

Core Concept

The core concept answers the question "what is the purchaser really buying?" When we buy a television set, we are not buying wood, electrical circuits, and plastic but a means of pleasantly passing our spare time. For the line manager who is sending staff to the training program, the core concept may be security for the future or the ability of his or her department to take advantage of an opportunity. For the staff members who are to be trained, the core concept may be the satisfaction of being able to do a job completely or enhanced promotional opportunities.

The Tangible Element

The tangible element of the product is the physical object we see and is sometimes referred to as the formal product. A training course is usually recognized as a formal product by its title, the program, the trainer who is to conduct the course, and the training room in which the course is to be held. For the trainer, the tangible element is the primary focus of attention. However, for the client the tangible element is merely a means to achieve the all important core concept. To illustrate this, let us consider a training course on computer keyboard skills. To the line manager whose staff are attending the course, the tangible element is only a means to an end. The line manager is really interested in ensuring that his staff members enter data into the computers with a minimum of errors.

This differentiation between the core concept and tangible element of a training course is vital when we consider both training needs analysis and evaluation. The core concept usually provides us with the standards of the training objectives. These standards then provide us with the measurements which show the value of the course in the evaluation step.

The Intangible Element

These are the additional and often unrecognized benefits that come with the product. They enhance the acceptability of the product to the customer. These additional but intangible benefits may be part and parcel of the product. If you purchase a well-known local brand of electrical equipment, having any future repairs carried out is that much easier. Sometimes, these benefits are deliberately added to a product or service to encourage sales. For example, the local store will often give free deliveries.

With training, the user often looks for such intangible benefits as:

- Minimization of effort—the staff members are trained without any additional effort being expended by management

- Minimization of post-training risk—the trained staff are assimilated back into the workforce with the minimum of fuss.

- Ease of access—the training is carried out reasonably close to the workplace.

MARKETING THE TOTAL PRODUCT

As trainers, we often concentrate first on the tangible element. We are good at producing programs, glossy folders, and well laid out training rooms. While this is essential for the professional presentation of a training course, we also need to be aware of and emphasize the core concept and the intangible element. We can do this by

- Concentrating on the core concept when carrying out the training needs analysis so that the client's real needs can be identified.

- Ensuring that the core concept is included in the title of the program. Rather than a program called "The Selection Process," for example, use a title such as "Selecting the Right People."

- When advertising the course, include the core concept and the intangible benefits in the description.

- The training needs analysis can be broadened a little to identify the intangible benefits that could be included.

- The core concept can be emphasized in the introduction stage of relevant sessions throughout the course.

- As trainers, we can provide immediate and personalized service whenever a manager indicates that our help would be appreciated. This does not mean that the trainer jumps at every whim of every manager. It does mean that the trainer (with the manager's assistance) makes genuine attempts to establish the needs, offers sound advice, and, if appropriate, customizes training program to meet the needs.

- When evaluating the training program, ensure that the core concept has been satisfied.

✔ Checkpoint: Elements of a Product

Indicate true (T) or false (F), or fill in the blank.

1. The three elements of a product are the _____, the tangible, element, and the intangible element.

2. The core concept answers the question "what is the purchaser really buying?" _____

3. The tangible element is the _____ we see.

4. For the client, the tangible element is merely a means to achieve the all important core concept. _____

5. The intangible element includes the unrecognized deficiencies of a product. _____

6. The trainer should ensure that the core concept is included in the title of the program. _____

7. When evaluating the training program ensure that the _____ has been satisfied.

■ **Checkpoint Answers**

1. core concept   2. T   3. physical object   4. T   5. F   6. T   7. core concept

CLIENT DECISION BEHAVIOR

We have seen that the training product our client purchases is not the simple physical object that makes up the tangible element. There are the added considerations of the core concept and the intangible element. We now need to examine the four decision steps that are involved in the purchase of a product.

1. Awareness of Need

The first step is where the client manager becomes aware of a need. As far as training is concerned, this awareness can come from three areas:

- The manager has a vision of what should be occurring or should happen in the future. It may be a transition to computer-based technology or a change in the organizational climate.

- The control systems or a change in the environment may force the manager to recognize the need for training. So, for example, the quality control system on a production line may show an unacceptable rise in the unsatisfactory connections of an electrical component. Subsequent investigations may show that three new employees do not know how to use the soldering equipment.

- A third party may identify the needs. A common example is a trainer conducting a training needs analysis, which is the standard method of beginning the marketing of training.

The intensity of these needs will also have an effect. The greater the need, the more likely the manager is to go onto the next step.

2. Search for Means

Once a need has been identified and the individual is motivated to satisfy that need, the next step is to search for the means to satisfy that need.

Quite often the client will use past experience. If this need has been experienced before, then the individual will often follow the same path that satisfied the need in the past. If we, as trainers, have helped the manager before and our credibility is good, then the manager is more likely to turn to us for assistance again.

Advertising is the usual approach to assisting a client in the search for a means of satisfying the need. As trainers we can advertise in at least two ways.

- Ensure that managers are aware of the courses we are putting on in the future. Advise them of course dates, title, and a brief description.

- Always advertise your services of training needs analysis.

3. Assessment Behavior

This is where the individual examines the various options discovered in the previous step. Although this step is largely the prerogative of the decision maker, there are at least two actions the trainer can take.

- Ensure that the decision maker is aware of the costs and benefits of each option available.

- Once the decision is made, make sure that the decision maker can contact you easily. Many an opportunity has been lost because the client becomes frustrated over the inability to make contact.

4. Post-action Behavior

As trainers we consider the product, the training course, the most important stage. However, when analyzing the client decision behavior, the actual purchase decision (i.e., the training course) does not require comment. It is the before and after steps of that decision that are important. The final stage to examine, then, is the post-action behavior.

Post-action behavior is important for two reasons:

- It will dictate the future relationship we will have with the client.

- "Word-of-mouth" advertising is the best form of promotion. We should do all in our power to ensure that such advertising is all positive.

After the training program, the client will experience some level of satisfaction or dissatisfaction. To identify this level, the *expectation* of what the program was supposed to achieve is compared with the *perceived actual outcome*. If there is a significant overlap, the client is satisfied. If there is a gap, the client is dissatisfied.

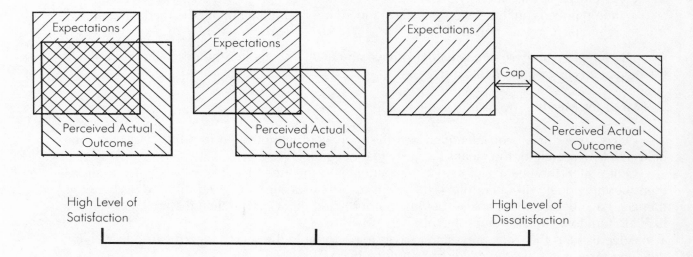

As trainers, we can ensure that there is a higher level of satisfaction by

- Carrying out complete training needs analysis so that the intangible elements as well as the core concepts of the product are identified.

- Ensuring that the program design is flexible enough to meet any changing needs.

- Using the learning principle of meaningful material throughout the course design.

- Having follow-up activities that encourage transfer of training.

- Always evaluating training on all of the four levels of reaction, learning, behavior, and results.

- Providing "after-sales service" support for the client. It is always a good habit to telephone or visit the client after the training course.

✔ Checkpoint: Client Decision Behavior

Indicate true (T) or false (F), or fill in the blank.

1. The awareness of a need can come from the manager having a vision of what should be occurring or should happen in the future. _____

2. The intensity of the need tends to have little effect in the "awareness-of-need" stage. _____

3. In searching for a means to satisfy a need, the client will often use past experience. _____

4. The stages in client decision behavior are awareness of need, search for means, _____, and post-action behavior.

5. The trainer should ensure that the client decision maker is aware of the costs and benefits of each option available. _____

6. Post-action behavior has little effect on the future relationship the trainer has with the client. _____

7. If there is a gap between the client's expectation of what the program was supposed to achieve and his or her perceived actual outcome, the client will be satisfied. _____

■ **Checkpoint Answers**

1. T   2. F   3. T   4. assessment behavior   5. T   6. F   7. F

BUYER ROLES

As trainers, we often assume that the client is one person who makes all the buying decisions as well as enjoying the benefits of the product. The marketing concept of *buyer roles* indicates that this may not be correct. We will examine each of these roles.

Initiator

This is the person who realizes that there is a need for training. It could be someone inside (e.g., a staff member) or outside (e.g., a customer) the organization.

Influencer

The person who recognizes the need may not have sufficient power to have anything done about the need. There are five bases of power:

1. Expert power. A person has significant and specialized knowledge so that others defer to his or her judgment in that area of speciality.

2. Legitimate power. This power is given to individuals simply because of their position in the hierarchy of an organization.

3. Reward power. An individual has the power to reward others.

4. Coercive power. The opposite of reward power—an individual can punish others.

5. Referent power. Some people naturally attract others who will do their bidding.

As far as training is concerned, the influencer usually has expert or legitimate power or some combination of both. Trainers, because of their specialized knowledge, usually have expert power. A manager with line control has legitimate power and, sometimes, expert power as well. Other people who may occupy the influencing role are peers and skilled subordinates.

Decider

As the name suggests, this is the person who makes the decision on whether there will be any training. In most organizations, this person usually holds some budgetary or expenditure control. As such, this is one of the most significant buyer roles.

Purchaser

This role involves the actual exchange of money or, at least, the authority to sign a contract. There is a very fine line between the deciding and purchasing role and in most organizations they are occupied by the same person.

User

The one who uses, or benefits from the use of, the product. In training, the trainees in the course would be considered to be the users.

Implications of Buyer Roles for Training

In training, it is important to recognize that we can be marketing a product to five different sets of people. Although we may be contacted by the initiator, our first priority may be to deal with the influencer. Without this individual's approval, the training will not get off the ground. The person who makes the decision is, of course, the key role. It is always well worth the effort to identify this person because whoever occupies this role is one of our two primary clients. Our other primary client is, of course, the trainee or user. The need to satisfy two primary clients is one of the critical features of the marketing of training.

SUMMARY

As trainers we need to widen our perspective to ensure that we are marketing our product, not just selling it. We need to adjust our focus to emphasize the importance of the core concept of the product and to use the attractions of the intangible elements of the product. We need to recognize which decision stage—awareness of need, searching for a means of satisfying a need, assessing choices, or post-action behavior—our client is at so that appropriate strategies can be used. Finally, we need to identify who is occupying which buying role of initiator, influencer, decider, purchaser, and user so that we can provide each person with appropriate information and assistance.

Chapter 23 Doublecheck

1. What is the difference between marketing and selling?

   _____

   _____

   _____

   _____

2. Describe the core concept of a product.

   _____

   _____

   _____

   _____

3. As trainers, how can we market the total product?

   _____

   _____

   _____

   _____

4. What are the four decision steps involved in the purchase of a product?

   _____

   _____

   _____

   _____

5. How can we gauge the level of satisfaction a buyer experiences during post-action behavior?

_____

_____

_____

_____

_____

6. What is the role of the initiator in the buying decision?

_____

_____

_____

_____

_____

7. What is the difference between the deciding and purchasing roles?

_____

_____

_____

_____

_____

8. Why is it important to recognize the five different buying roles?

_____

_____

_____

_____

_____

■ Doublecheck Answers

1. Marketing first identifies the customer need, then manufactures the product to fulfill that need; selling emphasizes making the product, then looking around for a customer.

2. The core concept answers the question "what is the purchaser really buying?" It describes how the customer will use the product.

3. By emphasizing the core concept and promoting the advantages of the intangible elements. So, for example, we should ensure that the core concept is included in the title of the program, and should include the intangible elements in advertising.

4. Awareness of need; search for means; assessment behavior; post-action behavior.

5. By comparing the client's expectation of what the program was supposed to achieve with the perceived actual outcome.

6. The initiator realizes that there is a need for training.

7. In reality, there is often little difference. The decider is the person who makes the final decision on the purchase of the product while the purchaser is the one who hands over the money or has the delegated right to sign the contract. In most organizations, one person performs both roles.

8. When we are marketing a training course, we may have to interact with five different people, each of whom will need different information.

24
THE TRAINING ROOM

Key Concepts

- *Environment affects learning.* An uninviting or poorly arranged training room can hinder learning.

- *Flexibility.* The trainer must learn how to adjust layouts to suit the physical environment or the demands of the topics.

Learning Objectives

After you have completed this chapter, you will be able to

- Set up an effective training room

- List the advantages of an ideal training room.

- List and describe at least three situations that would require an adjustment in the layout of an ideal training room.

THE TRAINING ROOM LAYOUT

A well-designed training room is like a wallet full of money—you only miss it when it is not there! Although the training room and its equipment are not the most vital determinants of training outcomes, have no doubt that an uninviting or poorly arranged training room can hinder learning. A little time invested in setting up the training room gives the final polish to a thorough and professional presentation. You can also enjoy a sense of security from knowing that you can put your hands on a training aid or piece of equipment at a moment's notice.

Let's look first at an ideal training room layout and its advantages. As trainers are often not fortunate enough to have an ideal room, we will then examine some less-desirable layout variations and discuss how best to overcome the disadvantages of these variations.

We think the layout in the diagram on the next page is generally the most satisfactory from the point of view of the trainer as well as the trainees. In this layout, we are assuming a small group of trainees and no major machinery or workshop requirements.

Here are some advantages of this layout:

1. It uses the full "visual area" of the front wall.

2. You can use the overhead projector at the same time as you use the board.

3. You can use charts either to supplement the overhead projector and the board or to keep a dominant message in front of the trainees.

4. The U-shaped layout of desks avoids the suggestion of a regimented "schoolroom atmosphere."

5. You can easily supervise the work of the trainees.

6. You can easily get to the overhead projector (especially if you are right-handed).

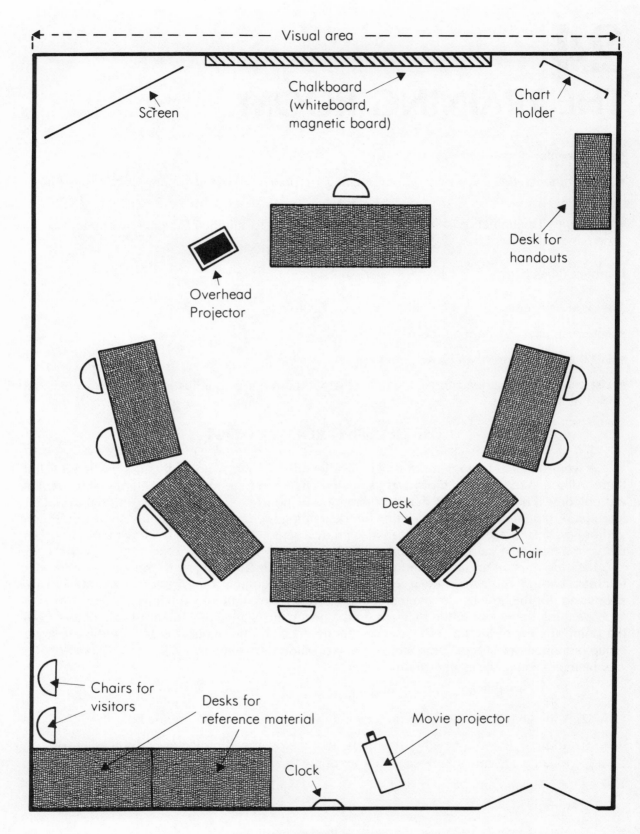

An Ideal Layout

7. You can set up and focus the movie projector for immediate use.

8. The door at the back of the room reduces the disturbance created by people entering and exiting.

9. You can easily read the clock at the back of the room (where it is not a distraction to the trainees).

Variations on the Ideal Layout

Of course, a number of factors can affect the layout of a training room. These factors often create a less than ideal training layout. Generally, we can group these factors under three headings:

1. Availability of physical resources: the shape of the room; the location of electrical outlets, windows, doors; the likelihood of outside distractions such as noise.

2. The training technique: for example, you may need different layouts with group work or for individualized learning.

3. The trainees: the number and preferences of trainees.

If we cannot allow for these factors by moving to a more suitable location, then we make the best arrangement possible and live with it.

Availability of Physical Resources

The shape of the room. Perhaps the worst is a long, narrow room. The only real solution in this case is to use one of the narrow sides as the "visual area." But the side may be too narrow for a board and an overhead projector at the same time. In this situation, we usually opt for the overhead projector and a chart stand with several blank pieces of paper. This paper can then be used instead of a board.

Using the long wall as the "visual area" creates visibility problems for the trainees. The ones in the middle front are too close, and those at the sides cannot see the far end of the "visual area."

Location of electrical outlets, windows, doors. You can overcome the problem of unsuitably located outlets by using extension cords. (Be sure to observe safety practices: For example, tape cords to walls or the floor, or cover them with a mat; and do not overload electrical circuits.) Always have several extension cords and adaptors handy. You can cover windows that have a glare. We have even used brown paper! (The headlines of newspapers can distract the trainees.)

There is not much that you can do about doors. If you have two doors to the room, lock the one that could prove the most bothersome (or barricade it both outside and inside). On the outside, use several chairs or plants and put up a sign indicating the alternative entrance. On the inside, put the charts or even the projector screen in front of the door.

If you have only one door and it is awkwardly placed beside the board, place the charts or the projector screen several feet in front of the door. This cuts down the trainees' view of anyone at the door and quickly indicates to the intruder that he or she is in the wrong room. Of course, you will have to remove the charts or screen at the end of each session, in order to allow the trainees and any guest speakers easy access. Also, be aware of the fire hazard, as blocking an exit in times of fire can cause confusion and panic. For the same reason, be sure you really need to lock unwanted doors before you do it.

As a more permanent solution to these problems, try to equip every door to every training room with both a wide-angle eyepiece viewer (to allow anyone outside the room to see what is happening inside) and a large sign fixed permanently to the outside of the door.

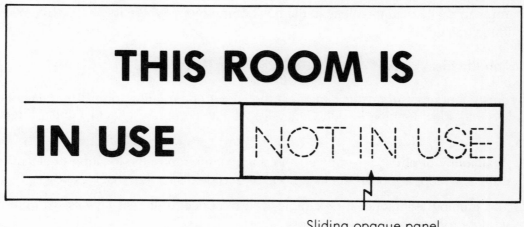

Sliding opaque panel

The Training Technique

The training technique may require its own training room layout. The ideal layout is most suitable for the theory session and for *some* skill sessions. In skill sessions, the type of equipment needed in the task often dictates the layout.

The lecture aims at giving a great deal of information to a large number of people. Quite often you want only chairs, so that the room can accommodate as many people as possible. In this situation, be sure that the ventilation is sufficient (that windows and air-conditioning vents can be opened). If the listeners need to take notes, tables or some other writing surface will have to be provided.

There are most probably as many variations of layouts for the discussion technique as there are trainers using the method. Generally, trainers seem to prefer chairs in a circle (or semicircle). Chairs set in a circle with a single low table in the middle promote a more relaxed, open atmosphere. As the minimum requirement, be sure that all the participants can see each other.

The Trainees

Based on your knowledge of the trainees, arrange the room to suit their preferences (unless, of course, this arrangement interferes with effective learning). You might also give the trainees the opportunity to change the layout (within reason) as it suits them.

General Tips

Finally, here are a few tips when setting up a training room.

1. If you intend to use the overhead projector extensively (and it is usually a good idea to do so), concentrate first on the placement of the projector. Set it up so that it throws a full, well-focused picture. Then set up your desk to facilitate the use of the overhead projector. You can arrange the trainees' desks accordingly.

2. Create a space of about 10 feet (3 meters) between the board and the front of your desk.

3. When you have set up the room, sit in *every* trainee's seat to ensure that all visual aids are visible.

4. Check to ensure that all electrically powered aids (such as overhead and movie projectors) are operational.

✔ Checkpoint: The Ideal and Not-So-Ideal Layout

1. What's wrong here? _____

   a. The door is poorly located.

   b. Not all the trainees can see the screen.

   c. The screen is incorrectly placed.

   d. Nothing.

2. What's wrong here? _____

   a. The door is poorly located.

   b. Not all the trainees can see the screen.

   c. Suggestions of a "regimented school-room" atmosphere.

   d. Nothing.

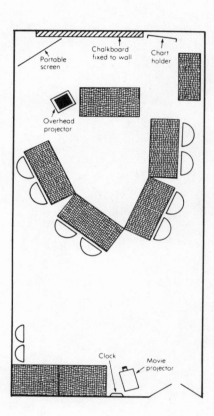

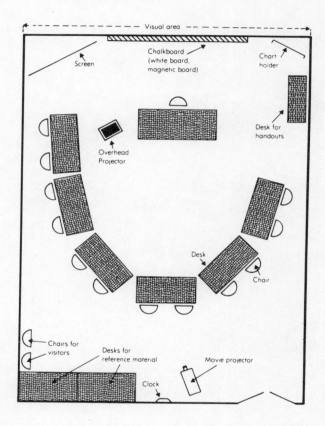

3. What's wrong here? _____

   a. The door is poorly located.

   b. Not all the trainees can see the screen.

   c. Suggestion of a "regimented school-room" atmosphere.

   d. Nothing.

4. What's wrong here? _____

   a. The screen is incorrectly placed.

   b. Not all the trainees can see the screen.

   c. Suggestion of a "regimented school-room" atmosphere.

   d. Nothing.

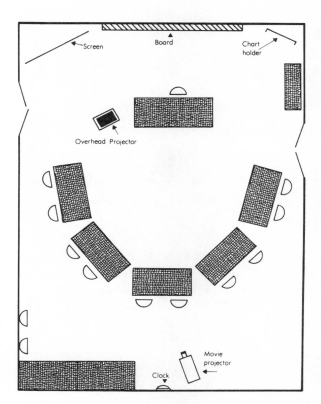

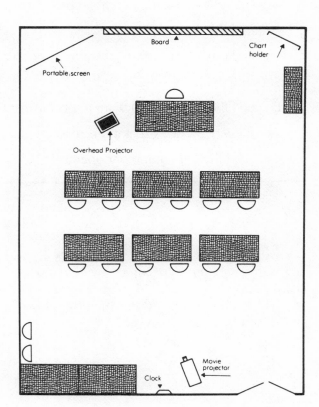

■ **Checkpoint Answers**

1. c. It is difficult to have an ideal layout with a long, narrow room. The worst problem with this layout is that the screen covers part of the board. The best solution would be to swap the chart holder and the screen. This may mean that the desks need changing slightly so that all the trainees can see the screen in its new position.

2. b. The two trainees at the desk near the overhead projector would have difficulty in seeing the screen. To fit in two additional trainees, the U shape should be made deeper and the additional desk placed on the opposite side, near the desk for handouts.

3. a. There are two doors near the front of the room. The best solution would be to barricade the one near the screen. The other could be kept closed when the room is in use with an "occupied" sign hung on the outside of the door.

4. c. The seating is regimented. The seating should be arranged to suit the topic, the training technique, and the needs of the trainee. For a theory session, for example, the U-shaped arrangement is probably best.

Checklist: The Training Room

Have I

☐ Selected the training technique?

☐ Inspected the layout of the training room?

☐ Assessed the number of trainees it needs to accommodate?

☐ Set up and located the overhead projector?

☐ Located my desk?

☐ Located other visual aids I want to position at the front of the room?

☐ Set up the trainees' desks and chairs?

☐ Located the visual aids I want to position at the back of the room?

☐ Sat in *every* trainee's seat to ensure that *all* visual aids are visible?

☐ Checked that all equipment operates?

SUMMARY

Although the training room and its equipment are not the most vital determinants of training outcomes, they are important because an uninviting or poorly arranged room can hinder learning. A well-organized room imparts order to the training atmosphere and encourages a responsible attitude toward the training. However, the trainer must be flexible and willing to adjust to spatial disadvantages.

Chapter 24 Doublecheck

1. List the advantages of an ideal training room.

_____

_____

_____

_____

2. List three factors that can affect the layout of a training room.

_____

_____

_____

_____

3. How can you compensate for the disadvantages of a long, narrow room?

_____

_____

_____

_____

4. What can you do to adjust the room to poorly placed doors and windows?

_____

_____

_____

_____

5. How could you arrange the seating for the following training techniques?

    The theory session. _____

    _____

    _____

    The lecture. _____

    _____

    _____

    The discussion. _____

    _____

    _____

6. What do you do if the trainees prefer a seating arrangement contrary to your layout?

    _____

    _____

    _____

    _____

    _____

■ Doublecheck Answers

1. Use full "visual area" of front wall.

   Use overhead projector as well as a board.

   Use charts to supplement or keep dominant message in front of trainees.

   U-shaped layout avoids suggestion of "schoolroom atmosphere."

   Can easily supervise trainees.

   Can easily get to overhead projector.

   Can set up and focus movie projector for immediate use.

   Door at the back of the room reduces disturbance.

   You can easily read clock at the back of the room, but it is not a distraction to the trainees.

2. Availability of physical resources. The training method. The number of trainees and their preferences.

3. Generally, use one of the narrow sides as the "visual area" because the use of the long wall often creates visibility problems. If the side is too narrow for a board and overhead projector, opt for an overhead projector and a chart stand with several pieces of paper.

4. Poorly placed doors basically have to be put up with. A sign such as "This room is in use" may be helpful. If there are two doors, you may be able to lock or barricade one. Be sure you do not create a fire hazard. (Poorly placed windows can be covered to prevent glare.)

5. The U-shaped layout is probably best for the theory session, as this allows you close contact with all trainees, especialy during the A (activity) steps.

   Quite often you want only chairs for a lecture so that the room can accommodate as many people as possible.(Be sure that ventilation is sufficient.) If note taking is required, provide some writing surface (such as desks).

   There are a number of layout variations for the discussion technique. Generally, there seems to be a preference for chairs in a circle or semicircle with, perhaps, a single low table in the middle.

6. You must balance the motivational effects of accepting the preferences of trainees against the educational desirability of their preference.

25
COORDINATING A PROGRAM

Key Concepts

- *Visibility of coordination.* Although often unaware of many of the fundamental aspects of the training function, trainees are immediately affected by the details of coordination and form judgments based upon their impressions of those details.

- *Before activities.* Coordinating communications and setting the stage for the training activities.

- *During activities.* Coordinating the details that sustain the training action.

- *After activities.* Closing down the program and establishing the basis for follow-up and evaluation.

- *The role of the guest speaker.* Guest speakers can help the trainer to coordinate the program.

Learning Objectives

After you have completed this chapter, you should be able to

- Explain the importance of coordination.

- List in correct sequence the *before, during*, and *after* coordinating activities.

- List in correct sequence the steps that a guest speaker can take to help to coordinate a training program.

INTRODUCTION

Agreed! Coordinating a training program is just one administrative aspect of the total training function. To most trainees, however, the only parts of the training function that are visible are the programs themselves and how the trainer presents and coordinates them. Most trainees are happily unaware of or indifferent to the many other aspects of the training function, such as training needs analysis, designing training programs, choosing training techniques, choosing the training location, selecting the trainees, and evaluating the programs. However, the trainees *are* aware of the effectiveness with which these elements come together in the training experience. They form an opinion based on how the trainer coordinates all the details that affect them. Because of this visibility, you must be able to coordinate a training program in an effective, professional manner.

Coordinating the program starts after the program has been designed and written. We can divide coordinating activities into three stages: *before, during*, and *after* the program.

1. BEFORE: SET THE STAGE

Learning by the trainees can occur before the training program starts. This is one of the reasons why the *before* activities are so important. In addition, training programs are in the center of change, and change is often strongly resisted. To fear the unknown is natural, and so you should use the *before* activities to lower trainees' anxiety by making the program part of the "known" environment and thus bring about the change process in the least traumatic manner possible. Most of the *before* activities are related to establishing good communication and preparing the logistical support for the program.

Communication With Trainees

Although the amount of communication will vary according to the type of program, here are some usual requirements:

1. A "joining" letter. Use a straightforward tone. Be friendly and informative. Tell the trainee what, why, when, where, and how. Give

   Name of program.

   Why trainee has been selected.

   Date and time program commences.

   Duration of program.

   Location of program.

   List of what the trainees will be required to bring: for example, lunch, tools, calculator.

   Clear description of preprogram work the trainees will be required to do.

   Name of person and phone number the trainees can call with any queries.

2. An outline of the full program. This will help to orient the trainee: for example, starting and finishing times, names of trainers and speakers and their topics, and duration of lunch breaks.

3. Any books/manuals/notes for preprogram reading or preprogram work.

Arrange Guest Speakers

Contact all guest speakers (by telephone, if possible, to allow two-way communication) to confirm their availability. If you can, personally visit the speaker in order to discuss the program and the session.

Send each guest speaker an information letter. Use a friendly but businesslike tone. You can relax the tone a little if you have visited the speaker and personally conveyed this information already. Give the following:

Date, time, and duration of the session.

Location of training program.

Session objective(s).

General outline of the session.

A contact name and telephone number.

Guest speakers also appreciate a copy of the program. If you can, offer to assist in preparing visual aids and handouts.

Arrange Handouts, Equipment, Raw Materials

Have all written materials typed and copied. You can provide printed content summaries for theory sessions; equipment diagrams, workflow diagrams, and task breakdowns for skill sessions; and magazine or newspaper articles as starting points for discussions.

Reserve the room(s) and equipment needed. Equipment can include a locomotive, a lathe, sets of tools, safety equipment, computer terminals, audio-visual equipment, and audio-visual programs. If your organization does not own the needed equipment, arrange to borrow or hire it. Check that your equipment works properly and that you have any extras needed for your training environment (for example, portable screens and electrical extension leads).

Ensure that any materials that the trainees will use are available, such as bricks and mortar for a brick-laying program, welding rods and gases for a welding program, computer paper for a computing program, and standard forms for a clerical program.

Advise Trainees' Supervisors

Since trainees are normally selected after consulting their supervisor, this advice is usually for confirmation purposes. Briefly state where the trainees will be on what dates, and give the name and objective(s) of the program. Also outline any follow-up requirements that are part of the program.

We recommend that you formally advise the supervisor because

1. It is good manners to advise the supervisor where his or her subordinate will be.

2. The support and commitment of the supervisor is vital toward overcoming potential training problems (such as encapsulation).

Obtain Nameplates

Have desk-top nameplates made for all trainees, trainers, and guest speakers. The printing on these should be at least 25 mm (1 inch) high. If trainees will not be using desks or tables, use *large* pin-on nametags that you should encourage trainees to wear for at least the first three days of a program.

Set Up the Training Room

The day before the training program is to commence, arrange the furniture of the room and set up all visual aids required (see Chapter 21). Place nameplates on all tables, and be sure that all handouts and materials are stored close to or in the training room.

2. DURING: SUSTAIN THE ACTION

If this is your first program, your feelings will be similar to those experienced when conducting your first session. If this is your first program *and* your first session, we empathize with you! However, you must remember that although your feelings are important, the *trainees* are now your most significant consideration for the rest of the program.

If your *before* activities were intended to set the stage, your *during* activities are intended to sustain and smooth the action. Here are some suggestions in the order in which they are usually done.

The First Day

On the first day, arrive early and check all lights and electrically powered visual aids, open the windows or turn on air conditioning, and so on. Plan to complete these tasks at least 15 minutes before the scheduled starting time.

The First Hour

This is probably the most awkward period of time in the program. It is also very important, because this is when the trainees form their first impressions of the program. Here's a standard scenario.

1. Introduce yourself to each trainee as he or she arrives.

2. Try to have a key person in the organization open your program. (A short five- or ten-minute introduction would be ideal.)

3. Cover the basic administrative information, including starting and finishing times, break times, location of cafeteria and bathrooms, and the standard operating procedures of the program.

4. Allow approximately five minutes for each trainee to be introduced to the group. You can do this in two ways:

   Have each trainee introduce him/herself. This method can cause embarrassment among trainees who aren't sure how much to say about themselves.

   Have each trainee interview his or her neighbor. Each trainee then introduces his or her neighbor to the entire group. The introduction should cover the name, where he or she works, a brief work history, and personal interests or hobbies. (If the trainees are talkative, this can take up more than five minutes, and you may have to allow more time per trainee.)

While some trainees feel the latter introduction exercise is mildly stressful, mild stress in a supportive environment will often promote commitment to the program. The introduce-your-partner technique tends to lower the stress level by having trainees talk about another person rather than talking about themselves.

Of course, you will also have to be introduced. You can either do this yourself or have the opening speaker do it for you.

Personal Objectives

As we have previously noted, each trainee will have his or her own needs and expectations of the program. To allow the trainees to identify these, allot time for the trainees to jot down personal objectives for the program. This can be used as a personal record for the trainees or be the basis of a group discussion and psychological contract-setting exercise.

Guest Speakers Again

1. Each morning, check to be sure that the guest speaker(s) for that day is available.

2. During the session, make sure the guest speaker's nameplate is easily visible at the front of the room.

3. Introduce the guest speaker personally, giving name, title, workplace or department, title of the session, and the reason why you chose the guest speaker for this session.

4. Don't use the guest speaker as an excuse to get away from the training room. He or she may need some help with the projectors, handouts, and so on. More importantly, once the guest speaker has left, the trainees regard the trainer as the reference point on that topic, so your attendance is almost mandatory.

5. Be sure that the guest speaker's handouts are easy to get and that he or she knows where they are before the session starts.

Reviews and Tests of Learning

Organize regular reviews and tests so that you can evaluate the training at a later time.

Closing the Program

1. Go over the objectives of the program and ask the trainees to assess whether or not they have been achieved. Have the trainees also achieved personal objectives?

2. Briefly review each major session of the program (or even better, have the trainees review the sessions).

3. Ask the trainees to complete a Program Evaluation Sheet (as in Chapter 9). When completed, you can collect them immediately or discuss them first with the trainees.

4. Ensure that the trainees have your telephone number. Encourage them to call you, especially if they need help in applying their learning to the job.

5. Thank the trainees for their attendance and interest.

3. AFTER: TIE UP LOOSE ENDS

Administration

You have undoubtedly heard of the saying "The job's not finished until the paperwork is done." Once you have finished the program, you need to tie up the loose ends. Here's a list.

1. Clean up the room and return all equipment, films, and other aids.

2. Store all handouts and materials.

3. Complete all administrative forms (trainee history cards, etc.)

4. Pay all bills (for films, guest speakers, etc.).

5. Write letters to all guest speakers thanking them for their participation and giving trainees' assessment of their sessions, if available.

6. Note and file suggestions for improving the program.

Evaluation

Collate the information you have about the trainees' reactions to the program and what they learned from the program. Set up a procedure to evaluate the trainees' behavior on the job and to measure changes to the organization's results. When these data are available, assess the effectiveness of the program.

Using these assessment data, review the program and design improvements.

✔ Checkpoint: Before, During, and After

Indicate true (T) or false (F), or fill in the blank.

1. Most trainees form an opinion of a training experience based on how the trainer coordinates the details that most directly affect them. _____

2. You can use the *before* coordination to ease the trainees into an atmosphere of change. _____

3. A joining letter should not explain to a trainee why he or she has been selected. _____

4. *Before* activities concentrate on developing and coordinating _____.

5. If you have called a guest speaker to confirm an engagement, you can dispense with a letter. _____

6. Try to involve a trainee's supervisor in the information flow. _____

7. Mutual introductions are a useful activity on the first day of a program. _____

8. *During* activities concentrate on helping guest speakers. _____

9. Use a guest speaker as an opportunity to attend to coordinating activities outside the training room. _____

10. When administration is finalized, *after* activities concentrate on _____ the program.

■ **Checkpoint Answers**

1. T   2. T   3. F   4. communications   5. F   6. T   7. T   8. F   9. F   10. evaluating

Checklist: Before and After

BEFORE

Have I

☐ Composed and sent a joining letter to each trainee?

☐ Included a copy of the program?

☐ Called each guest speaker?

☐ Visited each guest speaker?

☐ Composed and sent an information letter to each guest speaker?

☐ Arranged for handouts, equipment, raw materials?

☐ Involved each trainee's supervisor?

☐ Obtained desk-top nameplates?

☐ Set up the training room?

AFTER

Have I

☐ Cleaned the training room?

☐ Stored all handouts and materials?

☐ Completed all administrative forms?

☐ Paid all bills?

☐ Composed and sent thank-you letters?

☐ Assessed the effectiveness of the program?

☐ Reviewed the program for improvements?

THE ROLE OF THE GUEST SPEAKER

Frequently, managers are involved in training programs on a session basis. If you are called in to present a session because of your expertise in a particular area of knowledge or skill, here are some things you can do to assist the trainer who is coordinating the program.

1. Question the trainer closely about the objectives of the program and session, the expected content of the session, how the session relates to other parts of the program, and who the trainers are.

2. Ask why the trainer chose you. Are the reasons valid?

3. Ask for a few days to prepare an outline of the session.

4. Check with the trainer that the session (as outlined or as modified by mutual agreement) meets his or her needs.

5. Check on proposed payment, if any.

6. Give a definite agreement to run the session.

7. Tell the trainer what equipment and materials you will need.

8. Seek from the trainer the following information in writing:
   Name of program.
   Outline of program.
   Name of session.
   Objective(s) of session.
   Date and time(s) of session.
   Duration of session.
   Location of session.
   Details of what you will be expected to bring to the session.
   Details of what will be supplied.
   Description of the trainees—age, work background, attitudes to training, likely participation level.
   Trainer's name and phone number.

9. Give the trainer the following information in writing:
   Your name.
   Your qualifications (if relevant).
   Your workplace or department, and position (title) therein.
   Brief outline of what you plan to do in the session (including training technique).
   Statement of what equipment and materials you will provide.
   Details of what equipment and materials the trainer should provide.

10. Check with the trainer a day or two before your session to be sure that everything is in order.

11. Be sure to arrive at least ten minutes before your session is scheduled to start.

12. Check with the trainer for last-minute suggestions.

13. After the session, ask the trainer to send you the results of the evaluation of the session.

14. Based on your experience in the session, give the trainer any suggestions you have for improving the session.

SUMMARY

Coordinating is a very visible aspect of the training function. It is part of the overall management of training.

We can divide the coordinating activities into *before*, *during*, and *after* activities. *Before* sets the stage, *during* sustains the action, and *after* involves completing the paperwork and forming the basis for follow-up and evaluation. By following a procedure, guest speakers can assist in coordinating a training program.

Chapter 25 Doublecheck

1. Why is coordination important to a training program?

_____

_____

_____

_____

_____

2. Describe the major function of each of the following coordination activities.

Before. _____

_____

During. _____

_____

After. _____

_____

_____

3. Compare the two common ways of getting every trainee introduced to the group.

_____

_____

_____

_____

4. What do you include when you introduce a guest speaker?

_____

_____

_____

■ Application Exercise

The following is a phone conversation between Phyllis Thompson, Chief Trainer of Nationwide Distributors, and Dick Robson, Systems Sales Manager at Digital Data. Twelve months ago, when Dick was a systems analyst, he installed a Digital Data computer system in Nationwide's major distribution center. The day is Friday, 1:30 p.m.

Phyl: Hello, Dick. Phyl Thompson here. Long time no see!

Dick: Yeah! How have you been?

Phyl: Terrific! You?

Dick: Fair to muddling, Phyl. What can I do for you?

Phyl: Well, I've got a problem and I thought I'd come to the expert. You remember how we trained all the order clerks to operate the computer when you installed it? Well, we've got a new batch of clerks, and I'm running a two-day program for them starting Monday morning. I sure would appreciate it if you would come and talk to them on Monday afternoon. You know, tell them what a computer is and isn't, all those things that seem to worry people about computers.

Dick: Yeah, I expect I could do that, Phyl. I sure owe you one from last time, eh? I've still got the set of overheads that I had made to sell the system to your board. I'll bring them along and talk about them. You know me, never short a word.

Phyl: That will be tremendous, Dick. I'll leave the details to you because you know the system inside out. What do you say we meet for lunch at 12:30 Monday and go on to the session from there?

Dick: Sorry, no lunch, I'm afraid. I'm booked up. I'll just go straight to the session from here. I'll squeeze the time with a bit of luck. See you then, Phyl.

Phyl: OK, Dick. See you then.

How could this briefing of a guest speaker for a session be improved?

_____

_____

_____

_____

_____

_____

_____

■ Doublecheck Answers

1. Coordination is one of the few aspects of training that is highly visible to trainees. Poor coordination can reduce the effectiveness of the program by creating negative attitudes among trainees.

2. Before—Setting the stage. Establishing good communication and preparing the logistical support for the program.

   During—Sustaining the action. Doing the administrative activities that keep the program running smoothly.

   After—Tying up the loose ends. Completing the paperwork and evaluating the effectiveness of the program.

3. *Self-introduction* may cause embarrassment because it is sometimes difficult for trainees to know how much to say about themselves. *Introducing another trainee* will cause less stress but take more time. Because an interview precedes the introduction, this approach ensures that each trainee knows one other trainee at some depth from the beginning of the program.

4. Name, title, workplace or department, title of session, and why you chose this person as guest for this session.

■ Application Exercise Notes

1. Phyl waited too long to arrange a guest speaker for Monday.

2. There was no clear statement of the objectives of the course or session. Phyl may be assuming that Dick remembers them from a year ago. Phyl should ensure that Dick is clear on the objectives.

3. Dick did not check that the computer system was still the same, or that the trainees this time are similar to the trainees last time.

4. Dick's motivation for agreeing to do the session is somewhat suspect. "I owe you one" doesn't necessarily motivate top performance.

5. Dick immediately starts developing a session around available material (overheads) rather than the needs of the trainees. Phyl should have picked this up.

6. A session based on overheads prepared for members of the board may not be suited to order clerks. Phyl should have checked on this.

7. The fact that Dick knows the system inside out does not guarantee a suitable presentation. It may be more complicated or technical than new order clerks require. So Phyl should not have left it completely to Dick. She should have obtained a brief proposed outline of the session.

8. The exact starting time and place of the session were not specified. Presumably Dick is assuming that the time (of the after-lunch session) and the place are the same as last year. Perhaps Phyl is assuming that Dick is assuming this. There are too many assumptions.

26
EVALUATING A PROGRAM

Key Concepts

- *Need to evaluate*. Evaluating allows the trainer to measure outcomes. The training function must demonstrate its value to the organization in terms of beneficial outcomes (benefits).

- *Benefits*. Desirable results: ultimately, improved performance and increased productivity.

- *Costs and benefits*. The trainer must be able to demonstrate the value of training in terms of benefits received for costs incurred.

Learning Objectives

After you have completed this chapter, you should be able to

- Explain the importance of evaluation for the organization and for the training function.

- Explain ways to collect and categorize costs.

- Explain how to identify organizational benefits.

WHY EVALUATE?

SURVIVAL! At root, that is the reason for evaluating training. Unless you can show that money invested by the organization in training has produced tangible results, then the training service and its personnel may be dispensed with. Positive reactions by trainees and evidence that trainees have learned are just not sufficient contribution in the context of total organization performance. The training effort must demonstrably assist the organization to achieve its goals. Only then will training be accepted as an integral organization function, with the trainer having influence and credibility throughout the organization.

In this chapter, we will examine the evaluation of training at the organizational (or *macro*) level. This kind of evaluation involves the process of assessing the net contribution made by training to the results of the organization. The stages are

1. Collecting and categorizing costs.

2. Identifying organizational benefits.

3. Making cost-benefit comparisons.

HOW TO COLLECT AND CATEGORIZE COSTS

Any training activity costs money. These expenses start with the training needs analysis and only finish with the cost of evaluating the training effort. From the organization's point of view, these costs are an investment just as much as an investment in new machinery or in securities. And the investment is expected to produce a return in some future period. That management should expect a return in some future period is not unreasonable, and management will compare training costs against training benefits to ensure that the benefits are higher than the costs.

For you, one of the major concerns in identifying costs is to establish a *cutoff* point, or *include/exclude* point. For example, when you are conducting a training needs analysis, you know that you must include the costs of your time. But what is the cost in terms of the people you will interview? You are taking up their time also; so strictly speaking you should include their costs. In fact, you should include the costs of the telephone calls that you make while doing the training needs analysis as well as the cost of the paper on which you make notes. The list can go on and on, until you find yourself spending more time identifying training costs than you spend on training itself!

A useful rule for establishing a cutoff point is to use your training budget as a guide. Include those costs that are debited against the training budget, and allow those costs that are not included in the budget to remain unidentified. For example, most organizations do not charge rent for the training room or a fee for in-house printing services against the training budget. Using the training budget as a guide may not itemize all costs, but it gives you a practical working rule for identifying (and not identifying) costs.

You can categorize costs into the various activities composing the training process.

1. Conducting the Training Needs Analysis

Hours
Trainer (hours) × hourly rate.
Others (hours) × hourly rate.

Materials
Actual costs (for example, cassette tape for recorder).

Incidentals
Travel fees.

2. Designing the Training Strategy

Hours
Trainer (hours) × hourly rate.
Others (hours) × hourly rate.
External consultant (hours) × hourly rate, or agreed contract price.

Materials
Actual costs.

Incidentals
Travel fees.
Hiring expenses to preview films, etc.
Promotion costs (for example, posters or brochures).

We have adapted the following guidelines for calculating the number of hours needed to produce each hour of presentation from Laird's *Approaches to Training and Development*.

If the format is...	Then budget this many *hours of production* for each hour of presentation:
Technical formal courses	5 to 15
Self-contained for handoff to other instructors	50 to 100
Conventional management development	20 to 30
Programmed instruction	80 to 120
Technical on-site	1 to 3
Computer-assisted instruction	Up to 350

If the methods are…	Then for each class hour, budget this many *preparation hours*:
A tell-and-show by instructor	2 to 10
Mediated tell-and-show	1 (to preview the program)
Group discussion	2 to 6
Action or experiential	1.5 (The instructor should do the role plays, games, etc., and then analyze the probable dynamics.)

3. Conducting Sessions

Hours
Trainer (hours) × hourly rate.
Guest speakers (hours) × hourly rate, or agreed contract price.
Trainee (hours) × hourly rate. (When using the trainees' hourly rate, you might like to use an average or median rate to simplify the calculation.)
Trainee replacements (hours) × hourly rate. (Only if these are actual additional costs.)
Others (hours) × hourly rate. (When calculating the number of hours of the trainer and others, don't forget the time included to set up the training room and to clean up afterwards.)

Materials
Consumable materials; use actual costs.

Non-consumable materials: $\dfrac{\text{Actual costs}}{\text{Expected no. of times they will be used.}}$

(Depreciation is allowed for equipment.)

Incidentals
Rental of equipment and aids (e.g., films).
Rental of training room (if debited against training budget).
Travel fees (trainers, guest speakers, trainees).
Any fringe benefit allowances to trainer or trainees (e.g., travel allowance).

4. Evaluating the Program

Hours
Trainer (hours) × hourly rate.
Others (hours) × hourly rate (includes those from whom you gather information).
Interviewers (hours) × hourly rate, or agreed contract price.
(For simplicity, divide the hours into the time needed to design the evaluation and the time needed to carry out the evaluation.)

Materials
Actual costs.

Incidentals
Printing of report.
Mailing questionnaires, etc.
Travel expenses.

✔ Checkpoint: Strategies and Costs

Indicate true (T) or false (F), or fill in the blank(s).

1. The fact that trainees learn is sufficient justification for training. _____

2. Training is an investment. _____

3. When identifying costs, you must establish an _____/_____ point.

4. The training budget is a practical guide to identifying the costs you should take into account. _____

5. It is useful to categorize costs as hours, materials, and _____.

6. Computer-assisted instruction requires up to _____ hours of production for each hour of presentation.

7. A group discussion requires _____ to _____ hours of preparation for each hour of presentation.

■ **Checkpoint Answers**

1. F   2. T   3. include/exclude   4. T   5. incidentals   6. 350   7. 2 to 6

HOW TO IDENTIFY ORGANIZATIONAL BENEFITS

Kirkpatrick, in *A Practical Guide to Supervisory Training and Development*, identifies four areas (reaction, learning, behavior, results) in which training outcomes can be measured. When outcomes are desirable from management's point of view, we call them benefits. As we have noted in Chapter 10, measures of trainee reaction and learning are of comparatively little importance in assessing organizational benefits. While the learning of new material may be a prerequisite for improved behavior on the job, there is no guarantee that new learning will result in improved behavior. Similarly, positive reactions to learning may increase the likelihood that learned material will be transferred to the job, but they do not guarantee that the transfer will occur. For these reasons, your evaluation of the contribution of training to the achievement of organizational goals must concentrate on changes in the areas of job behavior and organizational results.

Evaluation Design

To evaluate the effect of training on job behavior and organizational results, continue to monitor the organizational indexes that you examined during the training needs analysis. Some of the more common indexes are listed on page 69. You must then answer two questions:

1. Have changes in behavior or organizational results occurred?

2. If so, are the changes an outcome of training?

What must we do to be able to say that changes have occurred? We must take our measurements *at least* twice, using the first measurement as a base or standard figure against which we can compare all later measures so that changes in behavior or results can be clearly seen. If we take measurements on more than two occasions, we have a time series that we can use in assessing the effectiveness of different parts of the training course or in measuring how long material is remembered after the course. Basically, however, we can give a definite answer to the first question if we have an initial measure and a final measure to compare it against.

Assume for a moment that we have taken initial and final measures and that we have found a difference between them. How can we be sure that this difference is an outcome of training (second question)? The answer lies in using experimental and control groups. These groups will be equivalent to each other in all respects except that the experimental group will take the training program, while the control group does not. Because they are equivalent in all respects except for the training program, any change in outcome that occurs in the experimental group but does not occur in the control group must, logically, be an outcome of the training program.

An example may clarify these points. Let's say that we are going to run an advanced skills course for assemblers of carburetors. The number of trainees is limited to 12. First, we take an initial measure (pretest) of about 30 carburetor assemblers. We can use a written test, a special production time trial, or an examination of individual production records. On the basis of this test, we select two groups each of 12 carburetor assemblers so that the groups are *equal* on initial performance. One group of 12 then receives training (the experimental group), while the other group continues assembling (the control group). In all other respects, the groups are treated equally. At the conclusion of training, the experimental group returns to normal work duties. After a period, we again measure the performance of the two groups of assemblers (posttest). By comparing pretest and posttest results within groups, we can determine if a change in performance has occurred in a group. By comparing posttest results between the experimental and control groups, we can say whether or not any change is the outcome of the training provided.

Review the design of evaluation investigations on the following page. Note that this design assumes that there will be no difference between the pretest and posttest results in the control

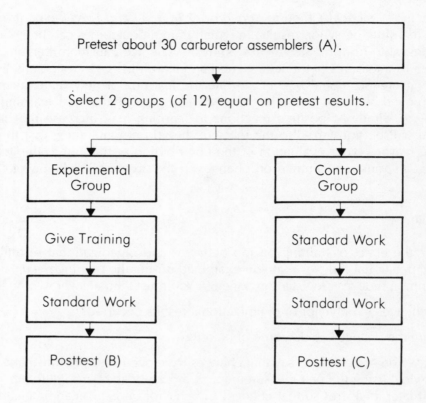

1. Has a change occured?
   Compare pretest results (A) and posttest results (B).

2. Is the change an outcome of training?
   Compare posttest results (B) and posttest results (c).

group. If no difference occurs here, well and good. However, changes in factors over which you have no control can sometimes create a change in performance within the control group. When this happens, you can allow for the change through advanced methods of statistical analysis (which are beyond the scope of this discussion). We advise you to consult a practical statistics book or to talk to someone knowledgeable in statistics if this situation arises. Note also that you can extend and modify the basic design to suit different situations. More advanced designs are outlined in Goldstein's *Training: Program Development and Evaluation*.

We must also acknowledge the problems that may arise in selecting experimental and control groups. For example, a union might object if it thought that the individuals assigned to the control group would be disadvantaged by missing out on training. This problem would have to be overcome through consultation with the unions.

If it is impossible to use a matched control group, an alternative is to use a *pseudo control group*. By a careful investigation of the indexes of organizational performance, you may be able to isolate a segment of the organization that, over a period, shows performance trends similar to the segment of the organization that is about to undergo training. This other segment may then be used as a substitute control group, providing it is subject to more or less the same influences as the experimental group (except for training, of course). For example, if carburetor assemblers in factory A show performance trends similar to carburetor assemblers in factory B, you may be able to provide training for all the factory A assemblers and use factory B assemblers (or rather, measures of their performance) as a pseudo control group.

Utilizing pretesting and posttesting as well as experimental and control groups allows us to give definite answers to these questions:

1. Have changes in behavior or organizational results occurred?

2. If so, are the changes an outcome of training?

In this way, we have a procedure that can help us to establish what benefits the organization derives from training.

The Time Frame of Benefits

Benefits from training occur within a time frame. This creates two problems. First, a training program conducted now, and incurring all its costs now, may create benefits in this year, and next year, and the year after. In such cases, a net present-value analysis will have to be conducted. For these situations, we suggest that you refer to a text on cost-benefit analysis or consult an accountant in your organization.

The second problem concerns how long after the program the benefits may become evident. If the training program is designed to improve immediate performance to meet preset standards, then the benefits (or lack of them) will be observable fairly quickly. However, if the training objective is to prepare potential managers to meet the organization's predicted future needs for managers, it may be years before a trainee is promoted to the managerial level and is given the chance to display the benefits of his or her training. Evaluation of this type of future-oriented training is very complex and bedeviled with uncertainty to the extent that its benefits must be accepted largely on trust. This is one area in which a high level of trainer credibility is essential.

COST-BENEFIT COMPARISON

Having learned how to collect and analyze the costs and benefits of training, we can begin to describe the value of training as a financial investment. Is the training effort producing returns (benefits expressed in financial terms) that are greater than the costs involved? This, ultimately, is what management must know.

SUMMARY

Evaluating allows the trainer to measure outcomes. Trainers must measure programs in order to demonstrate to management the value of the training function. For management, training represents an investment in the conventional sense. Thus its value must be expressed in cost-benefit terms.

Chapter 26 Doublecheck

1. Why evaluate organizational outcomes of training?

_____

_____

_____

_____

2. What are the two basic questions you must answer when identifying benefits?

_____

_____

3. Insert the missing words.

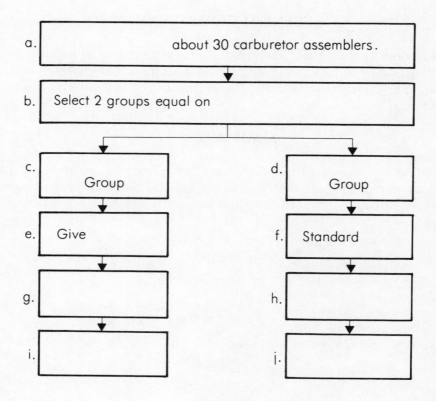

4. Using the diagram in Question 3, what do we compare to see if changes have occurred?

_____

What do we compare to see if changes are an outcome of training?

_____

5. What is a pseudo control group?

_____

_____

_____

_____

6. Describe two time-related problems in the measurement of benefits.

_____

_____

_____

_____

_____

■ Doublecheck Answers

1. To provide feedback to the training department. To demonstrate that training is helping to achieve organizational goals, is producing increased credibility and influence for training, and is enhancing its chances of survival. To measure the effectiveness of the investment in training.

2. Have changes in behavior or results occurred? If so, are the changes an outcome of training?

3. a. Pretest   b. pretest results   c. Experimental   d. Control   e. training   f. work   g. Standard work   h. Standard work   i. Posttest   j. Posttest

4. Pretest to posttest. Posttest of experimental and control groups.

5. A segment of an organization showing performance trends similar to the segment undergoing training. You can use the pseudo control group as a control group, providing it is subject to more or less the same influences as the experimental group.

6. When the benefits are spread over several financial periods, a net present-value analysis may be necessary. When future-oriented training programs result in no chance of benefits being observable for several years, a high level of trainer credibility is essential.

CAREER DEVELOPMENT REVIEW

Let's close this book by pointing the way ahead.

Those memories of your first experience in front of a group, with its excitement, tensions, satisfaction, or even despair, may be recent or ancient history. No matter how far you have come since that memorable occasion, there are always newfound methods to try, new skills to learn, new concepts to explore, and new experiences to analyze and utilize. To adapt to these changes, you have to engage in continual review and self-development. This applies whether you take only an occasional session in a program or consider yourself a career trainer.

So now is a good time to assess your present skills, determine what additional skills you need, and decide how you should close the gap between the two. In short, do a training needs analysis on yourself!

WHAT CAN YOU DO NOW?

We hope that having worked with this book, you are aware of what a training needs analysis is (and why it is a prerequisite for training). We also hope that you can design a training program, can select appropriate training techniques, can coordinate the training program after setting up the training venue and considering the requirements of the learner in the training process, can carry out the evaluation to see if the investment in training was worthwhile, and, finally, can conduct any follow-up training that is necessary.

However, you are your own best judge. Refer to the training model in Chapter 1. Use it as a "checklist" to decide where your competencies lie and which areas need improvement. You can also refer to the learning objectives at the start of each chapter and rate your abilities in relation to the skills required. We suggest using a rating scale and an action plan as follows:

TOPIC: _____

1	2	3	4	5
Poor	**Barely** Acceptable	Satisfactory	Good	Excellent

WHAT NEEDS IMPROVEMENT _____

_____

_____

Action Plan—*What* _____

By Whom _____

By When _____

Do this for each of the skills presented. As an alternative, or just as a check on your opinion, you can ask another trainer to rate you.

Whatever method you use, identify your current skills and weaknesses. Unless you are aware of these, you have no firm base from which to look forward.

WHAT CAPABILITIES DO YOU NEED?

What you need to be able to do, of course, depends largely on you and the organization in which you work. Ideally, you will be looking for a match between your abilities, needs, and aspirations and the needs and goals of the organization.

The range of a trainer's activities is very wide and, perhaps, a little confusing. However, a number of research efforts have pinpointed areas in which a trainer may require competence. Some of these publications include:

American Society for Training and Development, "A Self-Development Process for Training and Development Professionals," *Training and Development Journal*, May, 1979, pages 6–12.

Chalofsky, N., and Lincoln, C. I., *Up the HRD Ladder: A Guide for Professional Growth*, Addison-Wesley, 1983.

Nadler, L., *Developing Human Resources* (2nd ed.), Learning Concepts, 1979.

Ontario Society of Training and Development, *Core Competencies of a Trainer*. A report published in October, 1976.

Pinto, P. R., and Walker, J. W., *A Study of Professional Training and Development Roles and Competencies*, American Society for Training and Development (ASTD), 1978.

Spaid, O. A., *The Consumate Trainer*, Prentice-Hall, 1986.

Based on this research and our own experience, we suggest that you consider self-development in the following areas.

1. Human Resource Planning

An organization should plan its human resources in the same way that it plans its financial and material resources. This includes not only numbers of employees but also skills, future organizational goals, and future technological and social changes.

References

Bennison, M., and Casson, J., *The Manpower Planning Handbook*, McGraw-Hill, 1984.
Lynch, J. J., *A Manpower Development System*, Pan, 1971.
McGehee, W., and Thayer, P. W., *Training in Business and Industry*, Wiley, 1961.
Pettman, B. D., and Tavernier, G., *Manpower Planning Workbook*, Gower, 1976.
Walker, J., *Human Resource Planning*, McGraw-Hill, 1981.

2. Advanced Training Needs Analysis

In this book we have discussed TNA at an introductory level only. The techniques used to gather and analyze the information could be a focus of your self-development.

References

Turrell, M., *Training Analysis*, Macdonald and Evans, 1980.
Ulschak, F. L., *Human Resource Development*, Reston, 1983.
Zemke, R., and Kramlinger, T., *Figuring Things Out—A Trainer's Guide to Needs and Task Analysis*, Addison-Wesley, 1982.

3. Advanced Evaluation

Complex Experimental Design. In some circumstances, the design outlined in Chapter 26 may allow the possibility of error. More advanced designs are used to combat this problem.

References

Goldstein, I. L., *Training: Program Development and Evaluation*, Brooks/Cole, 1974. Chapters 4 and 5 are a concise introduction to advanced experimental design.
Kirkpatrick, D. L. (ed.), *Evaluating Training Programs*, American Society for Training and Development, 1975.

Statistics. In a similar fashion, statistical methods can be used to minimize the effects of measurement error.

References

Any comprehensive statistical text, preferably oriented toward the behavioral sciences, will do. Two useful books are:

Runyon, R. P., and Haber, A., *Fundamentals of Behavioral Statistics*, Addison-Wesley, 1967.
Siegel, S., *Nonparametric Statistics for the Behavioral Sciences*, McGraw-Hill, 1956.

Cost-Benefit. The concept of cost-benefit analysis is developing rapidly and is assuming considerable importance in training.

References

Gramlich, E. M., *Benefit-Cost Analysis of Government Programs*, Prentice-Hall, 1981, (Chapter 9).
Kearsley, G., *Costs, Benefits, and Productivity in Training Systems*, Addison-Wesley, 1982.

4. Learning Theory

In Chapter 2, we discussed the concept that some people have different learning styles from others. Specific approaches are discussed in:

Honey, P., and Mumford, A., *The Manual of Learning Styles*, 1982.
Howe, M. J. A. (ed.), *Adult Learning—Psychological Research and Concepts*, Wiley, 1977.
Knowles, M. S., *The Adult Learner: A Neglected Species*, Gulf, 1978.
Knowles, M., et al, *Andragogy in Action*, Jossey-Bass, 1984.
McLagan, P. A., *Helping Others Learn: Designing Programs for Adults*, Addison-Wesley, 1978.
Rogers, J., *Adult Learning*, Penguin, 1971.

5. Advanced Training Techniques

In addition to advanced techniques discussed briefly in Chapters 17 and 18, we suggest you examine simulations (action maze, in-basket, games), individualized learning, and social skills training. To overview the wide range of techniques available, the best reference is Huczynski, A., *Encyclopedia of Management Development Methods*, Gower, 1983. Other references follow.

References

Craig, R. L. (ed.), *Training and Development Handbook* (2nd ed.), McGraw-Hill, 1976.
Dean, C., and Whitlock, Q., *A Handbook of Computer Based Training*, Kogan Page, 1984.

Elgood, C., *Handbook of Management Games*, Gower, 1984.

Engel, H. M., *Handbook of Creative Learning Exercises*, Gulf, 1973.

Johnson, R. B., and Johnson, S. R., *Toward Individualized Learning*, Addison-Wesley, 1975.

Kearsley, G., *Authoring: A guide to the design of instructional software*, Addison-Wesley, 1986.

Kearsley, G., *Training for Tomorrow*, Addison-Wesley, 1985.

Laird, D., *Approaches to Training and Development*, (2nd ed.), Addison-Wesley, 1985.

Lakin, M., *Interpersonal Encounter: Theory and Practice in Sensitivity Training*, McGraw-Hill, 1972.

Otto, C. P., and Glaser, R. O., *The Management of Training*, Addison-Wesley, 1970.

Pfeiffer, J. W., and Jones, F. E., *Structured Experiences for Human Relations Training*, University Associates, 1972.

Quick, J., and Wolff, H., *Small Studio Video Tape Production* (2nd ed.), Addison-Wesley, 1976.

Rackham, N., Honey, P., and Colbert, M., *Developing Interactive Skills*, Wellens Publishing, 1971.

Suessmuth, P., *Ideas for Training Managers and Supervisors*, University Associates, 1978.

Utz, P., *Video User's Handbook*, Prentice-Hall, 1980.

Watson, C. E., *Management Development Through Training*, Addison-Wesley, 1979.

Zoll, A. A., III, *Dynamic Management Education* (2nd ed.), Addison-Wesley, 1969.

6. Organizational Development (OD)

The term *organizational development* (OD) has been used to cover a large range of strategies. We define an OD intervention as any activity that attempts to solve problems, in an organized manner, by using the energies and skills of the people affected by the problem.

References

Dunphy, D. C., and Dick, B., *Organizational Change by Choice*, McGraw-Hill, 1983.

Dyer, W. G., *Team Building—Issues and Alternatives*, Addison-Wesley, 1977.

Fordyce, J. K., and Weil, R., *Managing with People* (2nd ed.), Addison-Wesley, 1979.

French, W. L., and Bell, C. H., *Organization Development* (2nd ed.), Prentice-Hall, 1978.

Harvey, D. F., and Brown, D. R., *An Experiential Approach to Organization Development*, Prentice-Hall, 1976.

Huse, E. F., *Organization Development and Change*, West Publishing, 1975.

Margulies, N., and Raia, A. P., *Conceptual Foundations of Organizational Development*, McGraw-Hill, 1978.

Merry, V., and Allerhand, M. E., *Developing Teams and Organizations*, Addison-Wesley, 1977.

7. Group Dynamics

The following books provide an understanding of the processes that go on within a group.

References

Bion, W. R., *Experiences in Groups*, Ballantine, 1975.

Johnson, D. W., and Johnson, F. P., *Joining Together* (2nd ed.), Prentice-Hall, 1982.

Jones, J. E., and Pfeiffer, J. W., *The 1973 Annual Handbook for Group Facilitators*, University Associates, 1973, pages 127–129.

Reid, C. H., "The Authority Cycle in Small Group Development," *Adult Leadership*, April, 1965, pages 141–146.

8. Management Development

This includes succession planning, career path planning, and the development of management skills and attitudes that will enhance the future viability of the organization.

References

Certo, S. C., *Principles of Modern Management*, Wm. C. Brown, 1985.
Cooper, C. L. (ed.), *Developing Social Skills in Managers*, Macmillan, 1976.
Farnsworth, T., *Developing Executive Talent*, McGraw-Hill, 1975.
Fox, J. M., *Executive Qualities*, Addison-Wesley, 1976.
Francis, D., and Woodcock, M., *50 Activities for Self-Development*, Gower, 1982.
Hague, H., *Executive Self-Development*, Macmillan, 1974.
Koontz, H., and O'Donnell, C., *Management: A Book of Readings*, McGraw-Hill, 1972.
McLarney, W. J., and Berliner, W. M., *Management Training*, Irwin, 1970.
Newport, M. G., *The Tools of Managing*, Addison-Wesley, 1972.
Newstrom, J. W., Reif, W. E., and Moncza, R. M., *A Contingency Approach to Management: Readings*, McGraw-Hill, 1975.
Scanlan, B., and Keys, J. B., *Management and Organizational Behavior*, Wiley, 1979.
Taylor, B., and Lippitt, G., *Management Development and Training Handbook* (2nd ed.), McGraw-Hill, 1983.
Torrington, D. P., and Sutton, D. F. (eds.), *Handbook of Management Development*, Gower, 1973.
Warr, P., Bird, M., and Rackman, N., *Evaluation of Management Training*, Gower, 1978.
Watson, C. E., *Management Development Through Training*, Addison-Wesley, 1979.

9. Personal Development and Counseling

Personal development and counseling will help to encourage individuals to develop their self-acceptance, recognize their strengths and limitations, and strengthen their self-identity.

References

Alberti, R. E., and Emmons, M. L., *Your Perfect Right* (2nd ed.), Impact, 1977.
Brammer, L. H., *The Helping Relationship—Process and Skills*, Prentice-Hall, 1973.
Dyer, W. W., *Your Erroneous Zones*, Avon, 1977.
Johnson, D. W., *Reaching Out* (2nd ed.), Prentice-Hall, 1981.
Kelley, C., *Assertion Training*, University Associates, 1979.
Narcisso, J., and Burkett, D., *Declare Yourself—Discovering the Me in Relationships*, Prentice-Hall, 1975.
Nelson-Jones, R., *Practical Counseling Skills*, Holt, Rinehart & Winston, 1983.
Shertzer, B., and Stone, S. E., *Fundamentals of Counseling*, Houghton Mifflin, 1974.

10. Managing the Training Function

You manage training by planning, organizing, and controlling the training effort within the organization.

References

Craig, R. L., (ed.), *Training and Development Handbook*, McGraw-Hill, 1976.

Hamblin, A. C., *Evaluation and Control of Training*, McGraw-Hill, 1974.
Pepper, A. D., *Managing the Training and Development Function*, Gower, 1984.
Tavernier, G., *Industrial Training Systems and Records*, Gower, 1971.
Tracey, W. R., *Managing Training and Development Systems*, Amacom, 1974.

HOW DO YOU PROMOTE YOUR DEVELOPMENT?

You promote your development by your own efforts. Advanced trainer development is mainly self-development. Quite a lot of assistance is available, but it will not come to you. You must seek it out and use it.

We suggest that you investigate the following sources:

1. Other trainers at your workplace. Keep in close contact with them, be aware of what they are doing, and test your ideas against their pooled experience.

2. The wider body of trainers, particularly those operating in an environment similar to your own. Probably the best way to contact these people is through joining a professional association of trainers. Become actively involved in the association's program, and help others learn while you develop yourself.

3. Government departments and/or agencies. No matter what their political persuasion, all governments support and attempt to foster training activities. Make inquiries and then use the services, facilities, and support available in your area.

4. Reading. Because of the quantity of material available, you must be selective in choosing what to read, especially if you are not a full-time trainer. To be selective, you must be aware of what is available. With this awareness as a goal, get yourself on the mailing lists of bookstores and consulting organizations that specialize in training. Most major cities have at least one such source.

   Another way of keeping up with the literature is through regular attention to selected journals. As a starting point, we suggest that you read the journal published by your professional association of trainers. Equivalent journals in other countries may also be useful. Numerous more specialized journals are also available, and you can select appropriate titles as your interests develop.

   One additional suggestion in relation to reading is useful. If your organization has a library, make use of the fairly highly developed interlibrary loan system to increase the range of resources available to you.

5. Programs. Appropriate programs range from the college level, requiring years of study, down to half-day seminars on specific topics. The bodies most likely to run useful courses are universities, colleges, technical institutes, professional bodies (especially institutes or associations of management, personnel management, human relations, and training), and consultants. Be selective with respect to programs.

6. Resource centers. Education departments and most tertiary education establishments maintain resource centers. When approached, the staffs of these centers are usually willing to advise professional trainers, particularly in relation to equipment and media resources. Advice (sometimes partisan) on these matters is also available from equipment and media suppliers, and you should register with these organizations so that you receive their regular mailings.

7. Finally, yourself. You are the one who should plan a self-development program (if one is not prepared with you by your organization), and you should be the pri-

mary motivator of such a program. In addition, you should approach the problems and opportunities that come your way from a creative, open viewpoint. Every good idea originates with someone, so develop your own ideas, examine them carefully, and try them out. In this way, you learn from your own experiences, both positive and negative, and develop your bank of information and repertoire of skills on a continuing basis.

EPILOGUE

Training is a dynamic activity. It needs a special type of individual, variously described as

"The Self Starter"
"The High Achiever"
"A Relationship Person"
"A Helper"

Whatever the description, the competent trainer needs determination, a sense of purpose, and a sense of humor! There is no doubt that training can be satisfying if you are willing to make a personal commitment, sometimes at the expense of other personal goals. Trainers often use the expression "You will only get out of it what you put into it." This applies especially to training itself. If you are prepared to make a commitment, the rewards are there. We have enjoyed our careers as trainers—especially as trainers of trainers. One result of that enjoyment is this book. And if this book succeeds in assisting and encouraging other trainers, then the rewards we feel will be even greater.

SELECTED READINGS

Chapter 1

General sources on training

Abella, K. T., *Building Successful Training Programs*, Addison-Wesley, 1986.

Blank, W. E., *Handbook for Developing Competency Based Training Programs*, Prentice-Hall, 1984.

Chalofsky, N., and Lincoln, C. I., *Up the HRD Ladder*, Addison-Wesley, 1983.

Friedman, P. G., and Yarbrough, E. A., *Training Strategies from Start to Finish*, Prentice-Hall, 1985.

Laird, D., *Approaches to Training and Development* (2nd ed.), Addison-Wesley, 1985.

Rae, L., *The Skills of Training*, Gower, 1983.

Chapter 2

Boud, D. (ed.), *Developing Student Autonomy in Learning*, Kogan Page, 1981.

Gagne, R. M., *The Conditions of Learning* (2nd ed.), Holt, Rinehart & Winston, 1970.

Goldstein, I. L., *Training: Program Development and Evaluation*, Brooks/Cole, 1974.

Howe, M. J. A. (ed.), *Adult Learning — Psychological Research and Applications*, Wiley, 1977.

Knowles, M., *The Adult Learner — A Neglected Species* (2nd ed.), Gulf, 1978.

Knowles, M., et al, *Andragogy in Action*, Jossey-Bass, 1984.

Kolasa, B. J., *Introduction to Behavioral Science for Business*, Wiley, 1969.

Pedler, M. (ed.), *Adult Learning in Practice*, Gower, 1983.

Any textbooks on educational psychology are also appropriate reading.

Chapter 4

Cratty, B. J., *Teaching Motor Skills*, Prentice-Hall, 1973.

Davies, I. K., *The Management of Learning*, McGraw-Hill, 1971. Chapter 13 analyzes the teaching of psychomotor skills.

Gane, C., *Managing the Training Function*, George Allen & Unwin, 1972.

Gardner, J. E., *Helping Employees Develop Job Skill*, B.N.A., 1976.

Rae, L., *The Skills of Human Relations Training*, Gower, 1985.

Chapter 5

Argyle, M., *The Psychology of Interpersonal Behavior*, Pelican, 1978.

Cartwright, D., and Zander, A. (eds.), *Group Dynamics*, Tavistock, 1968. A classic source on groups.

Gibb, C. A. (ed.), *Leadership*, Penguin, 1969.

Johnson, D. W., and Johnson, F. P., *Joining Together* (2nd ed.), Prentice-Hall, 1982.

Johnson, D. W., *Reaching Out* (2nd ed.), Prentice-Hall, 1981.

Laird, D., *Approaches to Training and Development*, Addison-Wesley, 1978. Contains some suggestions.

Sprott, W. J. H., *Human Groups*, Pelican, 1978.

Suessmuth, P., *Ideas for Training Managers and Supervisors*, University Associates, 1978. Chapters 11, 12, 13, 14, 49, and 50 are useful.

Sydney, E., Brown, M., and Argyle, M., *Skills with People*, Hutchinson, 1973.

Tracey, W. R., *Designing Training and Development Systems*, American Management Assoc., 1971. Has a chapter on selecting trainees.

Chapter 6

Useful sources specifically on TNA

Boydell, T. H., *A Guide to the Identification of Training Needs*, BACIE, 1975.

Moore, M. L., and Dutton, P., "Training Needs Analysis: Review and Critique," *Academy of Management Review*, July, 1978, pp. 532–545.

Newstrom, J. W., and Lilyquist, J. M., "Selecting Needs Analysis Methods," *Training and Development Journal*, October, 1979, pp. 52–56.

Turrell, M., *Training Analysis*, Macdonald and Evans, 1980.

Ulschak, F. L., *Human Resource Development*, Reston, 1983.

Zemke, R., *Computer-Literacy Needs Assessment*, Addison-Wesley, 1985.

Zemke, R., and Kramlinger, T., *Figuring Things Out — A Trainer's Guide to Needs and Task Analysis*, Addison-Wesley, 1982.

General training books emphasizing TNA

Goldstein, I. L., *Training-Program Development and Evaluation*, Brooks/Cole, 1974.

McGehee, W., and Thayer, P. W., *Training in Business and Industry*, Wiley, 1961.

Other useful sources

Bennison, M., and Casson, J., *A Manpower Planning Handbook*, McGraw-Hill, 1984.

Boydell, T. H., *A Guide to Job Analysis,* BACIE, 1970.

Gael, S., *Job Analysis*, Jossey-Bass, 1983.

Oppenheim, A. N., *Questionnaire Design and Attitude Measurement*, Heinemann, 1966.

Siegel, L., *Industrial Psychology*, Irwin, 1969. Has chapter at introductory level on job analysis, interviewing, performance rating, psychological testing, and worker efficiency in a physical environment.

Stewart, C. J., and Cash, W. B., *Interviewing — Principles & Practices*, (3rd ed.), Wm. C. Brown, 1982.

Chapter 7

Gronlund, N. E., *Stating Behavioral Objectives for Classroom Instruction*, Macmillan, 1970. A basic explanatory text.

Mager, R. F., *Preparing Instructional Objectives* (2nd ed.), Fearon, 1975. A classic programmed learning guide to writing objectives.

Chapter 8

Gagne, R. M., and Briggs, L. J., *Principles of Instructional Design*, Holt, Rinehart & Winston, 1974. Chapters 6 and 8.

Otto, C. P., & Glaser, R. O., *The Management of Training*, Addison-Wesley, 1970. Chapter 9.

Tracey, W. R., *Designing Training and Development Systems*, Amacom, 1971.

Chapter 9

Deming, B. S., *Evaluating Job-Related Training*, ASTD and Prentice-Hall, 1982.

Denova, C. C., *Test Construction for Training Evaluation*, ASTD/Van Nostrand Reinhold, 1979.

Easterby-Smith, M., *Evaluating Management Training and Development*, Gower, 1983.

Hamblin, A. C., *Evaluation and Control of Training*, McGraw-Hill, 1974.

Kirkpatrick, D. L., *A Practical Guide to Supervisory Training and Development*, Addison-Wesley, 1971. Chapter 9 examines levels of training outcomes. Numerous articles by Kirkpatrick and others in the *Training and Development Journal* over the last ten years also contain this basic information.

Kirkpatrick, D. L. (ed.), *Evaluating Training Programs*, ASTD, 1975.

Otto, C. P., and Glaser, R. O., *The Management of Training*, Addison-Wesley, 1970. Examines types of questions and how to write them.

Stewart, C. J., and Cash, W. B., *Interviewing — Principles & Practices*, (3rd ed.), Wm. C. Brown, 1974. A useful reference on the skills needed in oral testing.

Theobald, J., *Classroom Testing: Principles and Practice*, Longman (Hawthorn, Aust.), 1974.

Tuckman, B. W., *Measuring Educational Outcomes*, Harcourt Brace Jovanovich, 1975.

Chapter 10

Deegan, A. X., *Coaching*, Addison-Wesley, 1979.

Tracey, W. R., *Designing Training and Development Systems*, AMA, 1971.

Chapter 11

Saunders, N., *Classroom Questions: What Kinds?* Harper & Row, 1966.

Any book on interviewing skills.

Chapter 13

Abercrombie, M. L. J., *Aims and Techniques of Group Teaching* (3rd ed.), London, Society for Research into Higher Education, 1974.

Brilhart, J. K., *Effective Group Discussion*, Wm. C. Brown, 1974.

Debenham, A. I. S., *The Training Officer's Guide to Discussion Leading*, London, BACIE Training Manual No. 5, 1968.

Hyman, R. T., *Improving Discussion Leadership*, Teachers College Press, 1980.

Otter, D., and Anderson, M. P., *Discussion in Small Groups: A Guide to Effective Practice*, Wadsworth, 1976.

Chapter 14

Bligh, D. A., *What's the Use of Lectures?* Penguin, 1972.

Goldstein, I. L., *Training: Program Development and Evaluation*, Brooks-Cole, 1974.

Mumford, A., *The Manager and Training*, Pitman, 1971.

Otto, C. P., and Glaser, R. O., *The Management of Training*, Addison-Wesley, 1970.

Chapter 15

The Case Study

Craig, R. L. (ed.), *Training and Development Handbook* (2nd ed.), McGraw-Hill, 1976.

Engel, H. M., *Handbook of Creative Learning Experiences*, Gulf, 1973.

Otto, C. P., and Glaser, R. O., *The Management of Training*, Addison-Wesley, 1970.

Zoll, A. A., III, *Dynamic Management Education* (2nd ed.), Addison-Wesley, 1969.

The Role Play

Craig, R. L. (ed.), *Training and Development Handbook* (2nd ed.), McGraw-Hill, 1976.

Engel, H. M., *Handbook of Creative Learning Exercises*, Gulf, 1973.

Maier, N. R. F., Salem, A. R., and Maier, A. A., *The Role Play Technique*, University Associates, 1975.

Pfeiffer, J. W., and Jones, F. E., *Structured Experiences for Human Relations Training*, University Associates, 1972.

Shaw, M. E., et al., *Role Playing*, University Associates, 1980.

Zoll, A. A., III, *Dynamic Management Education* (2nd ed.), Addison-Wesley, 1969.

Chapter 16

Dean, C., and Whitlock, Q., *A Handbook of Computer Based Training*, Kogan Page, 1983.

Hickey, A. E., "Computer-assisted and Computer-managed Instruction," In Craig, R. L., *Training and Development Handbook* (2nd ed.), McGraw-Hill, 1976.

Hofmeister, A., and Maggs, A., *Microcomputer Applications in Education and Training*, Holt, Rinehart & Winston, 1984.

Kearsley, G., *Authoring: A guide to the design of instructional software*, Addison-Wesley, 1986.

Kearsley, G., *Training for Tomorrow*, Addison-Wesley, 1985.

Kearsley, G., *Computer-Based Training*, Addison-Wesley, 1983.

Zemke, R., *Computer-Literacy Needs Assessment*, Addison-Wesley, 1985.

Chapter 17

Action Learning

Boddy, D., "Putting Action Learning into Action," *Journal of European Industrial Training*, Vol. 5, No. 5, 1981.

Mumford, A., "A Review of Action Learning," *Management Bibliographies and Reviews*, 1985, vol. II, no. 2.

Pedler, M., *Action Learning in Practice*, Gower, 1983.

Revans, R. W., *The ABC of Action Learning*, Chartwell Bratt, 1983.

Mentoring

Deegan, A. X., *Coaching*, Addison-Wesley, 1979.

Diaries

Boud, D., et al. (eds.), *Reflection: Turning experience into learning*, Kogan Page/Nicholls, 1985.

Holly, M. I., *Keeping a Personal-Professional Journal*, Deakin University, 1984.

Progoff, I., *At a Journal Workshop*, Dialogue House, 1975

Chapter 18

Overview of advanced techniques

Huczynski, A., *Encyclopedia of Management Development Methods*, Gower, 1983.

The Algorithm

Gane, C., *Managing the Training Function*, George Allen and Unwin, 1972.

Horabin, I., and Lewis, B., *Algorithms*, Educational Technology Publications, 1978.

Joinson, D., *Algorithms*, Instructa (Sydney), 1976. An audio-tutorial course on constructing algorithms.

Wheatley, E. M., and Unwin, A. W., *The Algorithm Writers' Guide*, Longman, 1972.

Programmed Instruction

Bullock, D. H., *Programmed Instruction*, Educational Technology Publications, 1978.

Craig, R. L. (ed.), *Training and Development Handbook* (1st and 2nd ed.), McGraw-Hill, 1967 and 1974.

Goldstein, I. L., *Training — Program Development and Evaluation*, Brooks/Cole, 1974.

The film *Programmed Learning*, Stewart Films Ltd., 1970 (made for the Royal Navy).

Thiagarajan, S., *The Programming Process: A Practical Guide*, Charles A. Jones, 1971.

Behavior Modeling

Rosenbaum, B. L., "Back to Behavior Modeling," *Training and Development Journal*, 1984, November, pp. 88–89.

Wehrenberg, S., and Kuhnle, R., "How Training Through Behavior Modeling Works," *Personnel Journal*, 1980, July, pp. 576–581.

Contract Learning

Bergquist, W. H., and Phillips, S. R., *A Handbook for Faculty Development*, vol. 3, Council of Independent Colleges, 1981.

Knowles, M. S., "The Magic of Contract Learning," *Training and Development Journal*, 1980, June, pp. 76–78.

Knowles, M. S., *The Adult Learner: A neglected species*, Gulf, 1973.

STAG

Joinson, D., *STAGS*, Instructa (Sydney), 1978.

Growth Groups

Argyle, M. (ed.), *Social Skills and Work*, Methuen, 1981.

Pfeiffer, J. W., and Jones, J. E., *A Handbook of Structured Experiences for Human Relations Training*, University Associates, 1973 onwards.

Smith, H. C., *Sensitivity Training*, McGraw-Hill, 1973.

Smith, P. B. (ed.), *Small Groups and Personal Change*, Methuen, 1980.

Distance Learning

Council for Educational Technology (CET), *How to Write a Distance Learning Course*, vols. 1–11, CET, London, 1980.

Kearsley, G., *Training for Tomorrow*, Addison-Wesley, 1985.

Lee, A. M., "Management Training by Distance Learning," *Training Officer*, 1984, September, pp. 276–278.

National Home Study Council, *Home Study: Course Development Handbook*, National Home Study Council, Washington, D.C., 1980.

Other sources on individualized learning are:

Craig, R. L. (ed.), *Training and Development Handbook* (2nd ed.), McGraw-Hill, 1976.

Johnson, R. B., and Johnson, S. R., *Towards Individualized Learning*, Addison-Wesley, 1975.

Knowles, M., *The Adult Learner—A Neglected Species* (2nd ed.), Gulf, 1978.

McLagan, P. A., *Helping Others Learn: Designing Programs for Adults*, Addison-Wesley, 1978.

Chapter 19

Brown, J. W., and Davis, R. B. (eds.), *A.V. Instructional Technology Manual* (5th ed.), McGraw-Hill, 1977.

Bullard, J. W., and Mether, C. E., *Audio Visual Fundamentals*, Wm. C. Brown, 1974.

Goudket, M., *An Audio Visual Primer* (rev. ed.), Teachers College Press, 1974.

Kemp, J. E., *Planning and Producing Audio Visual Materials*, Harper & Row, 1980.

Wiman, R. V., *Instructional Materials*, Charles A. Jones, 1972.

Chapter 20

Brown, J. W., and Davis, R. B. (eds.), *A.V. Instructional Technology Manual* (5th ed.), McGraw-Hill, 1977.

Bullard, J. W., and Mether, C. E., *Audio Visual Fundamentals*, Wm. C. Brown, 1974.

Goudket, M., *An Audio Visual Primer* (rev. ed.), Teachers College Press, 1974.

Kemp, J. E., *Planning and Producing Audio Visual Materials*, Harper & ROW, 1980.

Wiman, R. V., *Instructional Materials*, Charles A. Jones, 1972.

Chapter 21

Anderson, R. H., *Selecting and Developing Media for Instruction*, Van Nostrand Reinhold, 1976. A useful guide to selecting the audio-visual technique most suited to a specific objective.

Bensinger, C., *The Home Video Handbook*, Video-Info Publications, 1978.

Bensinger, C., *The Video Guide*, Video-Info Publications, 1977.

Elliot, G., *Video Production in Education and Training*, Croom Helm, 1984.

Gayeski, D. M., *Corporate and Instructional Video*, Prentice-Hall, 1984.

Iuppa, N. V., *Practical Guide to Interactive Program Design*, Knowledge Industries, 1984.

Kemp, J. E., *Planning and Producing Audiovisual Materials*, Harper & Row, 1980. A good general source.

Millerson, G., *Effective TV Production*, Focal Press, 1976.

Utz, P., *Video Users Guide*, Prentice-Hall, 1980. An excellent introduction to video.

Finally, any instruction manuals supplied with audio-visual equipment are good reading for trainers.

Chapter 22

Blank, W. E., *Handbook for Developing Competency Based Training Programs*, Prentice-Hall, 1984.

Nadler, L., *Designing Training Programs: The Critical Events Model*, Addison-Wesley, 1982.

Otto, C. P., and Glaser, R. O., *The Management of Training*, Addison-Wesley, 1970. Chapter 9 examines the hierarchial breakdown of training material.

Tracey, W. R., *Designing Training & Development Systems*, American Management Assoc., 1971. Chapter 7 deals with selecting and sequencing course content.

Watson, C. F., *Management Development through Training*, Addison-Wesley, 1979. Chapter 4 looks at planning programs.

Chapter 23

Bagozzi, R. P., *Principles of Marketing Management*, SRA, 1986.

Kotler, P., *Marketing Management: Analysis, Planning, and Control* (4th ed.), Prentice-Hall, 1984.

McCarthy, E. J., and Perreault, W. D., *Basic Marketing: A Management Approach*, Irwin, 1984.

Chapter 24

Lord, K. W., *The Design of the Industrial Classroom*, Addison-Wesley, 1977. Examines construction requirements in detail.

Chapter 25

Pepper, A. D., *Managing the Training and Development Function*, Gower, 1984.

Watson, C. F., *Management Development through Training*, Addison-Wesley, 1979. Chapter 6 examines the role of the program coordinator.

Chapter 26

Cost-benefit analysis

Dewhurst, R. F. J., *Business Cost Benefit Analysis*, McGraw-Hill, 1972.

Johnson, R. W., *Capital Budgeting*, Wadsworth, 1970.

Kearsley, A., *Costs, Benefits, and Productivity in Training Systems*, Addison-Wesley, 1982.

Roid, G. H., "Issues in Judging the Cost Effectiveness of Self Instructional Programs: A case study," in Programmed Dental Instruction, *Improving Human Performance*, Vol 3:2, 1974, pp. 49–63.

Design of measuring schemes

Goldstein, I. L., *Training: Program Development and Evaluation*, Brooks/Cole, 1974.

Statistics

Bruning, J. L., and Kintz, B. L., *Computational Handbook of Statistics*, Scott, Foresman, 1968.

Roscoe, J. T., *Fundamental Research Statistics for the Behavioral Sciences*, Holt, Rinehart & Winston, 1975.

General

Hamblin, A. C., *Evaluation and Control of Training*, McGraw-Hill, 1974.

Kane, J. S., "The Evaluation of Organizational Training Programmes," *Journal of European Training*, 1976, 5, 6, pp. 291–335.

Laird, D., *Approaches to Training and Development*, Addison-Wesley, 1978.

Tracey, W. R., *Managing Training and Development Systems*, Amacom, 1974.

INDEX

NOTES

NOTES